To Joe,
 In commemoration
or celebration! of completing
this project !!
 And, more seriously,
with warm affection.

Jack

May 27, 1987

PRESS AND POLITICS IN PRE-REVOLUTIONARY FRANCE

PRESS AND POLITICS IN PRE-REVOLUTIONARY FRANCE

EDITED BY
JACK R. CENSER
AND
JEREMY D. POPKIN

UNIVERSITY OF CALIFORNIA PRESS
BERKELEY   LOS ANGELES   LONDON

University of California Press
Berkeley and Los Angeles, California

University of California Press, Ltd.
London, England

© 1987 by The Regents of the University of California

Library of Congress Cataloging-in-Publication Data

Press and politics in pre-revolutionary France.

Contents: Historians and the press/by Jack R. Censer and
Jeremy D. Popkin — The Journal des dames and its female edi-
tors/by Nina Rattner Gelbart—The Gazette de Leyde and
French politics under Louis XVI/by Jeremy D. Popkin — [etc.]
    1. Press and politics — France — History — 18th century —
Addresses, essays, lectures. 2. France — Politics and govern-
ment — 18th century — Addresses, essays, lectures. I. Censer,
Jack Richard. II. Popkin, Jeremy D., 1948 –.
PN5184.P6P68 1987   070'.944   85-23220
ISBN 0-520-05672-8 (alk. paper)

Printed in the United States of America
        1 2 3 4 5 6 7 8 9

Contents

Preface

Historians of the French press, like historians concerned with so many other aspects of French life, have always assumed that the French Revolution marked a major break in their subject's history. Indeed, in few other areas of French life does the evidence of change from the Old Regime to the revolutionary era seem so sharp. Until the Estates General convened in May 1789, the newspapers and periodicals published in France were all officially licensed, their editors carefully screened by the government, and their contents rigorously censored; by the end of 1789, however, France was swarming with publications that were independent of all authority, their editors self-proclaimed representatives of the people's will, their contents totally unfettered. The pre-revolutionary French press seemed to meet all the criteria of the "authoritarian" model of the press outlined in Frederick Siebert's contribution to *Four Theories of the Press*, a standard work for American journalism students, and it stood in total contrast to the "libertarian" model of press freedom that was supposedly developing in En-

The contributors to this volume would like to thank Jonathan Dewald, Lynn Hunt, Joseph Klaits, and Sarah Maza for their critical comments on the project as a whole. Joan Hinde Stewart offered helpful comments on the introductory essay. Sheila Levine of the University of California Press has been both helpful and supportive. Jane Turner Censer worked valiantly to bring editorial and stylistic consistency to the work of five determined individualists. George Mason University's Word Processing Center provided valuable support services in the preparation of the manuscript, and that same university funded a leave for Jack R. Censer during which he accomplished much of his contribution to this book.

gland and America during the eighteenth century; with the coming of
the Revolution, France, too, joined the "libertarian" ranks.[1]

Certainly the French Revolution opened the way to a new kind of
political press in France and a new mode of representation for that
nebulous concept, public opinion. But the last five essays in this volume will show that this change was far less radical and sudden than
the simple contrast between absolutist and libertarian principles
would suggest. French press laws up to 1789 did indeed conform to an
authoritarian model, but French practice long before 1789 had broken
away from their prescriptions. Long before 1789 there were periodicals
circulating regularly in France that had largely escaped the elaborate
system of privileges and censorship written into the law, and these
periodicals had a legitimate claim to represent the views of their public
of readers rather than the views of the king and his ministers. The
"press revolution" of 1789, like so many other aspects of the French
Revolution, was the culmination of a long process of development,
not the sudden collapse of old institutions. The purpose of the essays
in this collection is to elucidate that process and analyze its significance through a set of case studies.

The theme of this volume — the role of the periodical press as a
public forum for the discussion of politics in Old Regime France — is
not merely a contribution to a better understanding of political journalism before the French Revolution. The nature of the pre-revolutionary political press is central to a major historiographical debate
about the nature of the French Revolution itself. That debate centers
on the question of how the political culture of the French Revolution
developed and to what extent it had its roots in the political life of the
pre-revolutionary monarchy. The formal institutions of the French
absolute monarchy were in almost every respect opposed to the principles of representative government adopted by the revolutionaries. But
formal institutions in any society seldom reflect the full reality of
political life. The concept of political culture, developed by anthropol-
ogists such as Clifford Geertz to study power relations in societies
without the elaborate institutional arrangements of the modern Western world, offers a helpful framework for the analysis of the way in
which politics actually worked in Old Regime France. A similar notion

1. Frederick S. Siebert, Theodore Peterson, and Wilbur Schramm, *Four Theories of
the Press: The Authoritarian, Libertarian, Social Responsibility, and Soviet Communist
Concepts of What the Press Should Be and Do* (Urbana, Ill., 1956).

has been fruitfully applied to eighteenth-century England in John Brewer's seminal work on ideology and politics.[2] Brewer has shown how informal mechanisms and social rituals, not codified as part of the "legal" constitution, enabled groups ostensibly excluded from politics to influence both the king and Parliament.

This approach has not been thoroughly explored before because of an assumption, deeply embedded in most of the historiography of the French Revolution, that the events of 1789 created a completely new form of politics in France, if not in the world as a whole. The classical tradition of revolutionary history, represented by Alphonse Aulard, Albert Mathiez, Georges Lefebvre, and Albert Soboul, saw the Revolution as the triumph of a new set of values, whether labeled republican or bourgeois; even when these historians conceded the importance of the political conflicts at the end of the Old Regime in provoking the Revolution, they categorized the conflicts as part of a backward-looking aristocratic reaction that left no legacy to the new order. The ideological roots of the Revolution, according to this interpretation, were to be found among political outsiders in pre-revolutionary France, particularly the philosophes, who were consequently portrayed as an intelligentsia locked in mortal combat with a hostile regime until circumstances permitted its overthrow. Even historians who reject many features of the classical interpretation of the Revolution's origins, such as William Doyle in his recent synthesis of the "revisionist" explanation of 1789, or Lynn Hunt, who has applied the concept of political culture to the decade from 1789 to 1799 in original and provocative ways, have continued to stress the originality of revolutionary politics and its separation from the world of the Old Regime.[3]

Against this emphasis on the novelty of revolutionary politics there has, of course, been an alternative historiographical tradition putting more emphasis on continuities between the Old Regime and its successor, a tradition of which Alexis de Tocqueville remains the most distinguished proponent. Inspired to some extent by him and by the revisionist critics of the classical tradition, some historians, such as François Furet and Ran Halévi, have argued that a new political culture developed in such informal institutions as reading clubs and Masonic lodges, where the ordinary rules of a hierarchical society

2. *Party Ideology and Popular Politics at the Accession of George III* (London, 1976).
3. Doyle, *The Origins of the French Revolution* (New York, 1980); Hunt, *Politics, Culture, and Class in the French Revolution* (Berkeley and Los Angeles, 1984).

were suspended.[4] Other scholars, notably Dale Van Kley in his studies of the political quarrels of the 1750s and 1760s,[5] have located the origin of many key revolutionary ideas and political practices within the formal political institutions of the old monarchy itself.

The contributors to the present collection have, each in his or her own way, helped to strengthen the case for the importance of pre-revolutionary political culture in preparing the Revolution; these studies show, among other things, that the press was a vital link between such formal institutions as the parlements and the new public that participated in reading groups and Masonry and provided the readership of most periodicals as well. In emphasizing the importance of the pre-revolutionary political press, the essays of this book thus encourage a conception of the Revolution that includes continuity as well as change.

The periodicals analyzed in the four contributions by Nina Rattner Gelbart, Jeremy D. Popkin, Carroll Joynes, and Jack R. Censer were not among the officially licensed publications of the Old Regime. They were not like the *Gazette de France,* founded in 1631 as an instrument of Richelieu's state-building policies, nor did they resemble the provincial *affiches* that sprang up in many French cities after 1750 and remained carefully apolitical until the last months before the Estates General. Nor can they be classed with the variety of officially licensed periodicals that appeared, particularly after 1770, as aggressive entrepreneurs like the publisher Charles-Joseph Panckoucke chipped away at the exclusive privileges of existing enterprises without trying to change the legal limits on contents.[6] With the exception of the *Journal des dames* for part of its career, these publications were unauthorized and theoretically should not have been able to circulate in France at all. Indeed, the *Gazette de Leyde,* the subject of Popkin's and Joynes's essays, and the *Courrier d'Avignon,* with which Censer concerns himself, were not even published in the country. But, in contrast to the

4. Furet, *Penser la Révolution française* (Paris, 1978); Halévi, *Les Loges maçonniques dans la France de l'ancien régime: Aux origines de la sociabilité démocratique* (Paris, 1984).

5. *The Jansenists and the Expulsion of the Jesuits from France, 1757–1765* (New Haven, 1975) and *The Damiens Affair and the Unraveling of the Ancien Régime, 1750–1770* (Princeton, 1984).

6. Gilles Feyel, "La Presse provinciale sous l'ancien régime," in *La Presse provinciale au XVIIIe siècle,* ed. Jean Sgard (Grenoble, 1983); Suzanne Tucoo-Chala, *Charles-Joseph Panckoucke et la librairie française* (Pau, 1977).

clandestine *libelles* that exposed the seamier side of French public life in the last decades of the Old Regime, publications such as the *Journal des dames*, the *Gazette de Leyde*, and the *Courrier d'Avignon* solicited subscriptions openly and arrived undisguised via the royal mails. And, in contrast to the manuscript newsletters that kept foreign aristocrats and a few Frenchmen informed about their nation's news, these publications and others like them were available to a general public — a public limited to a small fraction of France's total population, to be sure, but open to members of all three estates, whether or not they held an official position, so long as they had the requisite income to buy the periodicals and the education to read them.

These tolerated periodicals mattered in pre-revolutionary French life because they were open to voices other than the ones broadcast via the official press. Sometimes, the voices belonged to organized opposition groups that controlled positions of power within French society but could not legally address the public at large, such as the Jansenist zealots and parlementaire agitators who used the *Gazette de Leyde* to propagate their claims, as Carroll Joynes shows in his essay. Or they might be the voices of true outsiders, such as the women editors of the *Journal des dames* examined in Gelbart's contribution. At times, the voices heard in such periodicals simply belonged to honest chroniclers who recognized, as a revolutionary writer later put it, that "a people that wants to educate itself is not satisfied with the *Gazette de France*,"[7] and who responded to what they perceived as the public's wishes by giving it a reasonably truthful picture of France's political affairs and the world beyond. In any case, the voices did not belong to an omniscient higher authority telling readers what they were to think, as the authoritarian model of the press suggests. They belonged to private individuals asserting their right to comment on issues of public interest; they spoke to an anonymous readership quite different from the closed corporate groups that supposedly enjoyed a monopoly on the right to act in the political arena. Whether or not the tolerated periodicals actually reflected public opinion, they played a crucial role in giving substance to the concept, as Keith Michael Baker argues in the concluding essay in this collection. As Baker shows, by the end of the Old Regime, French politicians had already come to realize that public opinion was the ultimate source of legitimacy in the political system;

7. Pierre Manuel, *La Police de Paris dévoilée* (Paris, 1790), 1:201.

although it might be manipulated, it could not be ignored. This recognition implied a de facto legitimation of the unofficial press: without it, the rulers of the country had no satisfactory means of communication with their subjects. It took the Revolution to give the periodical press in France legal freedom, but uncensored periodicals were a de facto part of the French political system long before 1789.

The evidence presented in this collection of essays thus contributes to a revision of our understanding of the Old Regime. It suggests that the development of the French press fits a pattern now familiar from other studies of French life, in which long-standing developments under the old monarchy provide the basis for the actions of the revolutionary legislators. The pattern, which also shows that the contrast between France and England was by no means as sharp as works like Siebert's *Four Theories of the Press* suggest, has clear implications for the understanding of the conditions under which democratic institutions can emerge.

To document these assertions about the eighteenth-century press in France, the contributors to this volume have undertaken a detailed examination of several periodicals. The titles they have chosen are not entirely unknown to specialists in the history of the period, but their content has never been closely studied. The approach of these scholars has been different from the recent collaborative efforts of French scholars surveying the full range of the French press at certain specific dates — 1734, 1757, 1768, 1778. Each contributor has looked at a single periodical over a relatively long span of time, with an eye toward understanding how it came to have its distinctive journalistic personality and how it interacted with the political forces in France at a particular period. The periodicals included in these studies were not chosen systematically, and they do not represent a carefully balanced sample of the eighteenth-century press. They do, however, range widely in time and place of publication. By focusing on the newly emerging feminism of the *Journal des dames*, the long-term independence of the *Gazette de Leyde*, and the unsettling notions available in the *Courrier d'Avignon*'s foreign reports, these essays suggest how widespread troublesome writings had become. But more important, the authors chose their periodicals because they had become convinced that they were dealing with publications that had made important statements and exercised a significant influence on the age in which they appeared. When these studies, individually conceived and executed, were brought together, it became clear that they added up to more than the sum of their parts: collectively, they demonstrate truths about the eighteenth-century press and its role in French life that none of them could prove in isolation. The concluding essay by Keith Michael Baker, written after reading the other contributions, provides both an overview of the subject's significance and a theoretical framework for the rest of the collection. By analyzing the evolution of a unique French understanding of the concept of public opinion, Baker indicates the nature of the public forum in which the periodicals studied here operated and underlines the degree to which their existence marked the abandonment of absolutist politics in France.

Although the contents of this volume provide new perspectives on eighteenth-century French press and politics, they all draw in various ways on a long historiographical tradition. In the opening essay, Jack R. Censer and Jeremy D. Popkin survey the existing literature on the eighteenth-century French press from Eugène Hatin's pioneering efforts over a century ago to the latest contributions by members of the *Annales* school, Robert Darnton, and the French *équipes*. The contributors to *Press and Politics in Pre-Revolutionary France* are well aware that there is still much to be said about the French press of the eighteenth century; like the journalists of that era whom they have studied, they hope above all to have contributed to an ongoing process of learning and discussion.

Jack R. Censer and Jeremy D. Popkin

Chapter One

Historians and the Press

JACK R. CENSER AND JEREMY D. POPKIN

The study of the press is rapidly becoming central to an understanding of the French public mind in the Age of Enlightenment, to an analysis of the roots of the French Revolution, and to a better understanding of how the media of communications have affected French society. In 1969, when the first volume of the Presses universitaires de France's *Histoire générale de la presse française* appeared, it could have been realistically described as the twentieth century's equivalent to Eugène Hatin's pioneering *Histoire politique et littéraire de la presse en France*. But although Hatin's monumental work dominated the field for over a century, the *Histoire générale*'s treatment of the French press in the eighteenth century is already ripe for replacement. The first volume of this survey of periodical publications, the most thorough yet undertaken for any major country, included a major contribution by Louis Trenard entitled "La Presse française des origines à 1788," which summed up a century of scholarly investigation. In light of the succeeding fifteen years of research, Trenard's essay is already obsolete.

Although much has been written about the French press, periodicals have never been as important in general French history or the history of French literature as they have, for example, in British studies, where Joseph Addison's *Spectator*, the literary quarterlies of the early nineteenth century, and the *Times* regularly receive respectful treatment. For the period up to the French Revolution in particular, the

1

press has often been dismissed as uninteresting because of the presumption, fostered by the revolutionaries and accepted ever after, that, stifled by censorship, it reflected only an officially approved view of the world. Hence the first serious student of the eighteenth-century press was not a historian or a literary scholar, but a librarian and bibliographer. Eugène Hatin's *Histoire politique et littéraire* and his three other major works on the press reflected a lifetime spent identifying and classifying periodical publications in connection with his post at the Bibliothèque impériale, which gave him access to the largest extant collection of such materials.[1]

The extent of Hatin's work is staggering. But admirable as his book is, even by modern standards, it was limited by his background and interests as well as by the sheer volume of the material he set out to study. Much of his work was descriptive, and his descriptions were necessarily hasty. Often he based the thumbnail sketches that make up the bulk of his work on publishers' prospectuses rather than on a thorough reading of the journals in question, although the advertising puffery produced to launch a new publication rarely reflected its actual content. Hatin was well aware that a study of the periodical press required background information about the journalists who produced it, but he relied uncritically on the printed memoirs available at the time, often excerpting long passages directly into his own text. Finally, he assessed the interest of most periodicals according to the individuality of their political content. A shrewd judge of the merit of the numerous political newspapers of the revolutionary period, he obviously missed in the eighteenth-century press the free-swinging vigor he found in the pages of Marat, Hébert, or the counterrevolutionary *Actes des apôtres.*

Instead of stimulating further scholarship on the periodical press, Hatin's multi-volume survey seemed to satisfy students of French history and literature well into the twentieth century. Subsequent histories of the French press drew heavily on Hatin and added little new information; his bibliography, although it is known to contain only about one-third of the periodicals that appeared in the eighteenth century, has yet to be replaced. Hatin had considered the eighteenth-

1. *Histoire politique et littéraire de la presse en France,* 8 vols. (Paris, 1859 – 61), *Bibliographie historique et critique de la presse périodique française* (Paris, 1866), *Manuel historique et critique de la liberté de la presse* (Paris, 1869), *Les Gazettes de Hollande et la presse clandestine aux XVIIᵉ et XVIIIᵉ siècles* (Paris, 1865).

century press important in its own right, but the general assumption among professional historians was that censorship must have prevented the pre-revolutionary press from publishing anything of interest. Scholars studying the literature of the period focused on well-known texts by famous authors, rather than ephemeral journalistic productions. Scholars interested in the Bourbon monarchy tended to equate politics with legislative debates, treating domestic politics as inconsequential and ignoring the publications that discussed the subject.

The historiography of the eighteenth-century press thus grew slowly, and no new syntheses comparable to Hatin's were produced until recently. Work in other fields of eighteenth-century studies did point to questions for which periodicals were obviously important sources, but few scholars undertook the massive research efforts necessary to produce reliable answers. Daniel Mornet's classic *Les Origines intellectuelles de la Révolution française* not only formulated the case for a social approach to the history of ideas but remains one of the major analyses of French thought in the eighteenth century.[2] Mornet concluded that it was not enough to study the great minds of the Enlightenment to determine that movement's impact and its relationship to the Revolution: the ideas that actually shaped people's actions had been transmitted by an army of secondary writers through piles of forgotten volumes. Obviously, most journalists fell into this category of secondary writers, but Mornet, a literary scholar, did not single them out for special study. Indeed, he focused his own attention more on books, however monotonous or extravagant, than on newspapers or magazines or, for that matter, political pamphlets. Mornet's pioneering attempt to measure the diffusion of texts by analyzing library holdings statistically also undervalued the importance of periodicals, since they rarely appeared in the inventories he used as sources.

Mornet's work still stands as one of the most important contributions to the social history of French ideas. As many recent scholars in the field have noted, however, it had little immediate impact on the historiography of the period. Mornet, a literary scholar by origin, was

2. *Les Origines intellectuelles de la Révolution française* (Paris, 1933). Other early works that attempted to trace the evolution of pre-revolutionary public opinion paid primary attention to manuscript journals and newsletters rather than periodicals. See Charles Aubertin, *L'Esprit public au XVIIIᵉ siècle: Etude sur les mémoires et les correspondances politiques des contemporains, 1715 à 1789* (Paris, 1889); and Frantz Funck-Brentano, *Figaro et ses devanciers* (Paris, 1909).

not linked to the *Annales* school, and his exclusive focus on the *mentalité* of the literate distanced him from the efforts by Marc Bloch, Lucien Febvre, and others to recover the mental world of the lower classes who did not read, or at least did not read the works Mornet covered. The study of the French Revolution's origins was dominated by Georges Lefebvre and his followers, who stressed its social roots and downplayed the significance of ideology. The early forays against this social interpretation of the Revolution in the works of Alfred Cobban, G. V. Taylor, and others focused on different issues; both sides in the "revisionist" debate accepted Mornet's conclusions but saw the central questions in understanding the Revolution as lying elsewhere.[3]

As a result, when Louis Trenard was writing his essay for the first volume of the collective *Histoire générale de la presse française* he could draw on a number of specialized monographs written over the decades since Hatin, but the history of the eighteenth-century press had not benefited from any major shift in perspective since Hatin's day. Trenard dealt with some classes of periodicals Hatin had neglected, such as the provincial *affiches*, and he corrected many of his predecessor's factual errors. On the other hand, he lacked the wealth of firsthand information that Hatin had accumulated, as well as the visible enthusiasm for the subject that still makes the older historian more fun to read.[4]

The new historiography on the eighteenth-century press was not directly inspired, then, by Mornet's classic work or by challenges raised in the *Histoire générale de la presse française;* it grew out of new work in other areas of French history in the 1960s. One stimulus was a revived interest in the history of book publishing in the eighteenth century. Much of this came from historians of the *Annales* school, who brought their approach to bear on questions that had traditionally been left to literary scholars and to specialists in the development of printing techniques. Lucien Febvre and Henri-Jean Martin's *L'Avènement du livre*, published in Paris in 1958, offered a new model of the social history of the printed word that was considerably more comprehensive than Mornet's concentration on the study of content and

---

3. For a thorough review of the recent historiography of the French Revolution's origins and a statement of the "revisionist" thesis, see William Doyle, *The Origins of the French Revolution* (New York, 1980).

4. "La Presse française des origines à 1788," in *Histoire générale de la presse française,* vol. 1, *Des origines à 1814,* ed. Claude Bellanger et al. (Paris, 1969), 27–402.

diffusion. Febvre and Martin insisted on the importance of the economic underpinnings of publishing and on a global analysis of the printed products of the past rather than a more traditional focus on the diffusion of particular ideas destined for a glorious future. Martin's own massive monograph on the seventeenth-century Paris book trade offered an ambitious example of this approach applied to a particular time and place.[5]

The two collective volumes authored by François Furet and others in 1965 and 1970 under the title *Livre et société* marked the integration of the study of printed materials into the mainstream of the *Annaliste* tradition.[6] This approach applied quantitative methods to the content of published works and relied heavily on archival sources, particularly the registers of privileges and *permissions tacites,* rather than on just the content of the books themselves. Works such as Geneviève Bollème's study of almanacs and Robert Mandrou's analysis of the *Bibliothèque bleue* demonstrated that the study of printed materials could help to reconstruct popular ways of thinking about the world and so linked this body of scholarship to the *Annales* school's traditional interest in the common people.[7] The ambition in the *livre-et-société* school's volumes to produce a social and economic history of the printed word has stimulated an immense amount of fresh research and has established the study of literacy rates, book distribution networks, and library inventories as an essential part of any general social history that attempts to go beyond data on demography and socioeconomic stratification to reconstruct an *histoire des mentalités.* It has culminated on the one hand in specialized monographs, of which Jean Quéniart's study of reading patterns in western France during the eighteenth century is perhaps the outstanding example, and on the other hand in a vast collaborative summa, the *Histoire de l'édition française,* which brings together contributions from scholars all over the world, many of them not directly associated with the *livre-et-société* school, and offers an overview of the current state of research.[8]

5. *Livre, pouvoirs, et société à Paris au XVIIIᵉ siècle,* 2 vols. (Geneva, 1969).
6. Geneviève Bollème et al., *Livre et société dans la France du XVIIIᵉ siècle* (Paris, 1965); M. T. Boussy et al., *Livre et société dans la France du XVIIIᵉ siècle* (Paris, 1970).
7. Bollème, *Les Almanachs populaires aux XVIIᵉ et XVIIIᵉ siècles* (Paris, 1969); Mandrou, *De la culture populaire aux XVIIᵉ et XVIIIᵉ siècles* (Paris, 1964).
8. Quéniart, *Culture et société urbaine dans la France de l'ouest au XVIIIᵉ siècle* (Paris, 1978); Henri-Jean Martin and Roger Chartier, eds., *Histoire de l'édition française,* 2 vols. to date (Paris, 1983 –).

Quéniart's monograph demonstrates how much can be achieved by using the quantitative techniques that the *livre-et-société* school has taken over from the social and economic historians of the *Annales* tradition. Applying sophisticated methods to marriage registers, which are the best guides to literacy, and to the inventories of estates, which provide clues to book ownership, Quéniart carefully distinguishes the types of reading material that found their way to different social groups and shows the wide variations in patterns from one city or region to another. In another work, Daniel Roche provides a similar analysis of reading in eighteenth-century Paris.[9] Studies like these have pushed the social history of the book as far as the sources permit; they indicate both the wide variation in reading habits in the French population during the eighteenth century and the limits of the method: these quantitative sources tell us who owned what sorts of books but leave us to speculate about why the owners acquired them and how they reacted to them. Frustration at this impasse has now turned the attention of many of the book-history scholars to a new subject, the history of reading, involving a search for new types of sources and a move away from the methods of quantitative social history. Recent essays by Daniel Roche and Roger Chartier point in this direction.[10]

The volume of the *Histoire de l'édition française* covering the period from 1680 to 1830 also admirably displays the achievements of the scholars inspired by Febvre and Martin. The international team of collaborators summarizes recent research on all aspects of book history, from paper-making techniques to the evolution of genres. Although the overall results are impressive, the place accorded to the press exemplifies its treatment during the thirty years of the social history of the book. In a seven-page contribution titled "La Multiplication des périodiques," the press historian Jean Sgard combatively

9. *Le Peuple de Paris* (Paris, 1981), 204–41.
10. Roche, "Urban Reading Habits During the French Enlightenment," *British Journal for Eighteenth-Century Studies* 2 (1979): 138–49, 221–31. See also Roche's comments in Pierre Goubert and Daniel Roche, *Les Français et l'ancien régime* (Paris, 1984), 2:233–37. For an example of Chartier's work, see "Du livre au lire," in *Pratiques de la lecture* (Marseilles, 1985), 62–88. The German scholar Rolf Engelsing presents a provocative general thesis on the shift in reading habits during the eighteenth century in *Der Bürger als Leser* (Stuttgart, 1974). Engelsing's distinction between the intensive rereading of a small number of texts, usually religious, and the extensive reading of a wide variety of ever-changing texts explains many distinctive characteristics of eighteenth-century publishing, and his hypothesis deserves serious testing against the data available for France.

asserts the significance of the genre, concluding, "The journal did not absorb the book, but, although long considered as the book's poor relation, it actually opened the path to fortune." [11] Sgard's contention that periodicals were in some senses more central to the Enlightenment and to the eighteenth-century market for reading material than books echoes the judgments of some observers at the time, such as the author of the preface to the Physiocrats' periodical, *Les Ephémérides du citoyen*, who saw periodical literature as the appropriate form of publication in a society where knowledge was no longer confined to a narrow elite of professional specialists. [12] But it flies in the face of conventional assumptions that have dominated the field of book history, and Sgard's fellow contributors virtually ignore the subject.

Sometimes this neglect of periodicals is due to the nature of the sources; thus Quéniart, in his monograph, acknowledges that one of his fundamental conclusions — that book buying tended to stagnate toward the end of the Old Regime — might have to be revised if readers had actually been shifting from books to periodicals, which were rarely included in the death inventories on which he relied. But, in general, the subject simply has not interested the social historians of the book working in France. Relevant sources do exist: students of the social history of reading in Germany, where there is no central archive of publications, have turned instead to reading-room catalogues and other sources. Here the importance of eighteenth-century periodicals has been inflated to the point of obscuring the role of books, rather than the other way around. [13] Reading rooms also existed in eighteenth-century France, but they have received little study, although recent research has demonstrated their importance in providing an audience for periodicals in the decades after 1800. [14]

While French scholars inspired by Febvre and Martin were mounting their massive statistical offensive on eighteenth-century ques-

11. Martin and Chartier, *Histoire de l'édition française*, 2:198–205; the quotation appears on p. 205.

12. "Des feuilles périodiques," preface to first issue of *Les Ephémérides du citoyen, ou Chronique de l'esprit national*, 4 Nov. 1765.

13. Irene Jentsch, "Zur Geschichte des Zeitungslesens in Deutschland am Ende des 18. Jahrhunderts" (Diss., Leipzig University, 1937); Marlies Prüsener, "Lesegesellschaften im 18. Jahrhundert: Ein Beitrag zur Lesergeschichte," *Archiv für Geschichte des Buchwesens* 13 (1972): 369–594.

14. Jeremy D. Popkin, "The Book Trades in Western Europe During the Revolutionary Era," *Papers of the Bibliographical Society of America* 78 (1984): 403–45; Françoise Parent-Lardeur, *Lire à Paris au temps de Balzac* (Paris, 1981).

tions, American researchers were beginning to make their own contributions to the field. Although David Pottinger's *The French Book Trade in the Ancien Régime*, published in the same year as *L'Avènement du livre*, represented an older style of book history, based on printed sources alone and inclined to mistake legal prescriptions for historical reality, Raymond Birn's work on Pierre Rousseau pointed in a new direction.[15] Drawing heavily on archival materials, Birn highlighted the importance of extraterritorial publication in the French Enlightenment; at the same time, he showed that the over-the-border publishers enjoyed a certain degree of toleration from the French regime and that the publishers of the Enlightenment could not be portrayed simply as heroic figures struggling against a resolutely obscurantist existing order. His focus on periodicals that popularized the ideas of the philosophes for a broad audience, rather than on the great texts of the period, enhances the originality of the study.

Birn's pioneering study and his subsequent articles established him as one of the leading American scholars in French book history. Another American who made major contributions in this field is Robert Darnton, whose studies on eighteenth-century publishing began to appear in the late 1960s. In a variety of articles appearing from the late 1960s to the present, of which the most important were recently collected in *The Literary Underground of the Old Regime*,[16] Darnton has used publishers' records, primarily those of the now-celebrated Société typographique de Neuchâtel (STN), to illuminate the manner in which books, particularly ones that could not hope to obtain a privilege, were actually produced. Darnton's colorful prose made the history of the book come alive; in his hands the obscure and apparently unpromising topic of the publishing of the third edition of the *Encyclopédie* became the subject of a scholarly hit.[17] His seminal article, "The High Enlightenment and the Low Life of Literature," broke new ground by drawing attention to the importance of the social position of the authors of ephemeral literature in shaping their work. Critical of the statistical approach that dominated the *Livre et société* volumes,

15. Pottinger, *The French Book Trade in the Ancien Régime* (Cambridge, Mass., 1958); Birn, *Pierre Rousseau and the Philosophes of Bouillon* (Geneva, 1964).
16. *The Literary Underground of the Old Regime* (Cambridge, Mass., 1982). One particularly important piece omitted from this volume is "The World of the Underground Booksellers in the Old Regime," in *Vom Ancien Régime zur Französischen Revolution*, ed. Ernst Hinrichs, Eberhard Schmitt, and Rudolf Vierhaus (Göttingen, 1978), 439–78.
17. *The Business of Enlightenment* (Cambridge, Mass., 1979).

Darnton preferred to highlight particular cases drawn from the voluminous STN archives in order to answer the questions raised by the French scholars. Darnton used the marketing strategies of publishers and authors as direct evidence of what the French desired to read. Since he found that both scurrilous pamphlets and high Enlightenment works like the *Encyclopédie* sold primarily to an elite audience, he concluded that the ideas of the Enlightenment and the desacralizing attacks on the leaders of the *ancien régime* had thoroughly penetrated France's upper classes before the Revolution. In his most recent work, Darnton has tried to analyze how readers understood the books they consumed. These investigations, based on STN records, closely parallel his studies of publishing strategies, for his goal is once again to attack the notion that the inventories of produced and purchased works could explain the beliefs of book-owners. Although at this writing Darnton's findings remain preliminary, he has shown, among other things, how heartfelt the response was to Rousseau's *Emile* and, on a more general level, how readers took texts as guides to living.[18]

Although the French book-history school came to share some of Darnton's conclusions and included him among the contributors to the *Histoire de l'édition française*, Darnton himself had earlier been quite critical of the dominant, *Annales*-inspired approach in France. He strongly attacked studies based on the registers of books published with French government permission or toleration for their omission of the unmeasured mass of clandestine and foreign-printed books circulating in France, and he pointed to contradictory conclusions resulting from different studies of similar subjects included in the *Livre et société* volumes.[19] Darnton's critiques have helped to clarify many significant problems. They have led, for example, to a clearer distinction between books that were contraband because they purveyed forbidden content and those that were illegal because they were unauthorized editions of otherwise tolerated works; nevertheless, a clear evaluation of the statistical weight of illegal publication in the eighteenth-century French

18. "Readers Respond to Rousseau: The Fabrication of Romantic Sensitivity," in *The Great Cat Massacre and Other Episodes in French Cultural History* (New York, 1984), 215–56, and "First Steps Toward a History of Reading" (Paper presented to the George Rudé Seminar held at Monash University, Melbourne, Australia, in August 1984).

19. "In Search of the Enlightenment: Recent Attempts to Create a Social History of Ideas," *Journal of Modern History* 43 (1971): 113–32. For a somewhat less critical view of the French work, see Raymond Birn, "*Livre et société* After Ten Years: Formation of a Discipline," *Studies on Voltaire and the Eighteenth Century* 151 (1976): 287–312.

book market remains a frustrating task. Darnton has also challenged the thesis, which was formulated by Henri-Jean Martin and supported in much of the subsequent French work, that eighteenth-century book-publishing patterns on the whole reflect a greater persistence of traditional patterns of thought and belief than classical approaches to the study of the Enlightenment had indicated.

Darnton's objections to the French school's work have often been firmly grounded, but his own work also raises questions. His argument that the people and incidents highlighted in his case studies were typical remains open to challenge, since it is not yet clear how his special cases are related to the mass of material in the Neuchâtel archives, nor is it certain that the STN fairly represents French-language publishing as a whole. In short, despite Darnton's often relevant criticism of the body of data used in many of the French quantitative studies, his own conclusions rest on an implicitly statistical assumption about the representative nature of the STN records, but the data to demonstrate this have not yet been published. Darnton's work also rests implicitly on some very traditional views of the questions to be answered through the study of eighteenth-century publishing. He has looked for traces of the Enlightenment in some unusual places, such as the pornographic *libelles* characteristic of the period; although he has not provided any clear definition of "Enlightenment," he assumes that the spread of that movement's ideas is the key problem in any social approach to the history of ideas. He further tends to assume, in traditional fashion, that the spread of the Enlightenment is the underlying ideological cause of the French Revolution. Finally, although Darnton has greatly expanded the range of printed works to be taken into account in the history of the book by including everything from the *Gazetier cuirassé* to the *Encyclopédie méthodique*, he has so far completely excluded periodicals from his focus. This omission is unfortunate inasmuch as the periodical press has much to offer for the understanding of many of Darnton's key questions. Thus, Nina Rattner Gelbart's contribution to this volume and her other recent work, as well as Jack R. Censer's ongoing research, indicate the extent to which the nonacademic hacks about whom Darnton has written used periodicals as means of expression and tools for making a living.[20] And even the picture of the eighteenth-century printshop that

20. Gelbart, "'Frondeur' Journalism in the 1770s: Theatre Criticism and Radical Politics in the Pre-revolutionary French Press," *Eighteenth-Century Studies* 17 (1984): 493–514; Censer, "Eighteenth-Century Journalism in France and Its Recruits: A Selec-

Darnton and the Swiss scholar Jacques Rychner have drawn from the STN materials needs a reexamination in light of the production methods necessary to print a periodical like the *Gazette de Leyde;* the exigencies of biweekly publication indicate that it could not have emerged from the chaotic, undisciplined workplace they have described.[21]

The current interest in the eighteenth-century periodical press, both newspapers and journals, reflects an interest in new questions about this period, such as the ones raised by the *livre-et-société* approach and by Darnton's work, as well as an attempt to study old questions in a new way. Whereas traditional intellectual history looked primarily to great works and great thinkers, regardless of their immediate impact on the world around them — indeed, sometimes, as in the case of Diderot, finding its richest sources in unpublished works and papers that were unknown to contemporaries — the social history of ideas focuses on the intellectual commonplaces of an age and the works that were most widely received. Inevitably, this orientation has led to an interest in periodicals. Not only were journals often more widely read than the famous texts of the French philosophes, but the continuous relationship between subscribers and periodicals suggests that they can often be taken as a more reliable index of their readers' tastes and outlook. Similarly, the recent interest in the economic history of publishing in eighteenth-century France, also exemplified by Darnton's work, requires a study of the market for periodical literature.

In addition to these new areas of exploration, recent reformulations of old historiographical questions have led scholars to the periodical. Three of the contributors to this collection, for instance, deal with the classic problem of the ideological origins of the French Revolution. In their work, Jeremy D. Popkin, Carroll Joynes, and Jack R. Censer deal with issues that have been raised by recent work in this field. Scholars such as François Furet, Keith Michael Baker, and Dale Van Kley have challenged the long-standing emphasis on social change as the fundamental key to understanding 1789. They have encouraged a closer

tive Survey," in *Consortium on Revolutionary Europe: Proceedings 1984*, ed. Harold T. Parker, Sally Parker, and William Reddy (Athens, Ga., 1986), 165–79.

21. Darnton, *Business*, 177–245; Jacques Rychner, "A l'ombre des lumières: Coup d'oeil sur la main-d'oeuvre de quelques imprimeries du XVIIIᵉ siècle," *Studies on Voltaire* 155 (1976): 1925–55; I. H. Van Eeghen, "De Amsterdamsche Courant in de achttiende Eeuw," *Jaarboek Amstelodamum* 44 (1950): 31–58.

study of political and ideological developments in the last decades of the *ancien régime* and of the role of the governing elites before the Revolution in spreading the subversive ideas and forms of organization that made the overthrow of the monarchy possible.[22] A recognition of the full range of political news and ideological content carried in the gazettes that circulated in France during the last decades of the Old Regime adds powerful support to this renewed interest in the political and ideological dimensions of the revolutionary process.

Developments in the history of literature have also raised interest in the periodical. Anxious to go beyond reexamining the most illustrious authors, scholars have turned to books and then periodicals that, although famous in their day, have since been neglected, largely because they were assumed to be deficient as works of art. In addition, as investigators focused less on the literary quality of a piece and more on the structure of thought embedded in it, prosaic literature such as periodicals became a promising subject for study. Such trends (which parallel efforts undertaken by historians of the book) explain the number of students of literature, particularly in the French collaborative volumes discussed below, now exploring the Old Regime periodical.

The new range of questions that historians have tried to answer in studying the press has called forth new methodologies as well. Both the sheer bulk of the source material and its relatively regular form have encouraged the application of quantitative techniques. Computerized content analysis has encountered many difficulties, but there is no doubt that this approach will shape future efforts to use periodicals as a measure of broad social attitudes. Other scholars have imported into the study of these humble texts the most sophisticated techniques of literary interpretation, drawing attention not only to the overt content, which earlier historians generally analyzed, but also to the nuances and silences of discourse. At the same time, another group of

---

22. Furet, *Penser la Révolution française* (Paris, 1978), drew attention especially to the work of Augustin Cochin on reading societies as a seedbed of revolutionary ideas and forms of discussion. In *The Jansenists and the Expulsion of the Jesuits from France, 1757–1765* (New Haven, 1975) and *The Damiens Affair and the Unraveling of the Ancien Régime, 1750–1770* (Princeton, 1984), Van Kley examined the significance of the political controversies at the end of the Old Regime and especially the role of the Jansenist *parti* in formulating key concepts in the revolutionary ideological arsenal. Baker pursued the development of revolutionary ideology in French political writing of the eighteenth century in "French Political Thought at the Accession of Louis XVI," *Journal of Modern History* 50 (1978): 279–303, and "On the Problem of the Ideological Origins of the French Revolution," in *Modern European Intellectual History: Reappraisals and New Perspectives,* ed. Dominick LaCapra and Steven Kaplan (Ithaca, N.Y., 1982), 197–219.

scholars has made important findings by searching with renewed diligence for archival sources — notarial records, police reports, and the like — that make it possible to understand more clearly the motives behind periodicals.

The most recent French work on press history has often been collaborative, as in the important volumes appearing under the separate or joint editorship of Jean Sgard of Grenoble and Pierre Rétat of Lyons; other collaborators have furnished major articles to several of these collections and, in some cases, are now beginning to publish independent monographs as well. Some of their work has taken up challenges posed by the new work in the book-history field; some has gone back to older traditions in the history of the periodical press itself; some has offered fundamentally new perspectives.

Under Jean Sgard's direction, a large team of scholars is pursuing the task Hatin undertook single-handedly a century ago: the identification of journals and journalists. They have produced the *Dictionnaire des journalistes*,[23] bringing together information about journalists who published in French, whether or not they resided inside the kingdom, and they are currently compiling a checklist of French periodicals, both magazines and newspapers, for the eighteenth century. When both these projects are completed, scholarship in this field will finally be able to proceed from a solid bibliographical and prosopographical base that has heretofore been lacking.

Other collective efforts, dominated by French scholars with some contributions from researchers in neighboring countries, began to appear in 1972 with the publication of *L'Etude des périodiques anciens*, a collection of papers suggesting profitable paths for future research, and in the following year with the first of three volumes of *Etudes sur la presse au XVIIIe siècle*.[24] Subsequent collections include one coedited by Sgard and Rétat, two edited by Rétat, and two produced by teams under the direction of Paule Jansen.[25] All these volumes share a desire

23. *Dictionnaire des journalistes, 1600–1789* (Grenoble, 1976). Four supplements have appeared, the last in 1985.
24. Marianne Constance Couperus, ed., *L'Etude des périodiques anciens: Colloque d'Utrecht* (Paris, 1972); *Etudes sur la presse au XVIIIe siècle* (Lyons: 1973; vols. 2 and 3 appeared in 1975 and 1978).
25. Jean Sgard and Pierre Rétat, eds., *Presse et histoire au XVIIIe siècle: L'Année 1734* (Paris, 1978); Pierre Rétat, ed., *L'Attentat de Damiens: Discours sur l'événement au XVIIIe siècle* (Paris, 1979); Pierre Rétat, ed., *Le Journalisme d'ancien régime* (Lyons, 1982); Jean Varloot and Paule Jansen, eds., *L'Année 1768 à travers la presse traitée par ordinateur* (Paris, 1981); and Paule Jansen et al., eds., *L'Année 1778 à travers la presse traitée par ordinateur* (Paris, 1982).

to discover new paths in the study of periodical literature and, in particular, to escape from the traditional concentration on the careers of individual journalists and the content of individual publications. Collaborative authorship allows the undertaking of projects that are beyond the range of a single researcher, in particular the ambitious attempts to compare the content of a full range of periodicals appearing in a single year—the year 1734, the year following Damiens's attempted assassination of Louis XV in 1757, the year 1768 — and the efforts to analyze comprehensively the content, methods, and impact of the periodical press from a multidisciplinary perspective.

Two of these collections, *L'Année 1768* and *L'Année 1778*, were specifically designed to test the value of the computer in studying periodicals' contents. Periodicals make an attractive target for computerized content analysis: they tend to be fairly homogeneous over time, making sampling possible; they facilitate comparative research using standardized protocols for classifying content so that projects are not dependent on the idiosyncrasies of a single researcher. The contributors to the Varloot and Jansen volumes encountered formidable difficulties in achieving the necessary level of standardization, however, and it is not entirely clear that these difficulties can be overcome. Their essays do demonstrate the range of content in the periodicals published during their chosen sample years, but the most successful contributions are the ones that combine computer-generated data with a thorough use of traditional sources like the archival material François Moureau unearthed to explain the political content of the *Courier du Bas-Rhin*.[26]

Of these collective volumes, the study of the assassination attempt on Louis XV is certainly the most coherent and successful, thanks to its clear focus. The authors carefully classify according to genre the periodicals that treated the event. They pay attention to the degree of government control over each class of publication, distinguishing among the reactions of the official, the tolerated, and the genuinely underground press. In addition to studying press content, they seek to determine the sources feeding the different genres of publication and the impact of printed reports and engravings. Many of the contributors, including Rétat himself, came to the project from disciplines outside history, and the most important methodological contribution

---

26. "Les *Mémoires secrets* de Bachaumont, le *Courier du Bas-Rhin*, et les 'bulletinistes' parisiens," in *L'Année 1768*, ed. Varloot and Jansen, 58–79.

of the work is its application of the methods of literary analysis to texts that have usually been read simply in terms of their overt content. By drawing attention to the mechanisms by which eighteenth-century journalists decided what to emphasize and what to omit, the contributors to this volume reveal more fully than any other recent scholars of the press the complexity that lies behind the seemingly simple texts found in eighteenth-century newspapers and magazines.

In general, however, most of these collective volumes suffer from a lack of focus. In the case of the Couperus collection and *Le Journalisme d'ancien régime*, this is the almost inevitable result of publishing all the papers delivered at a broadly defined conference. The contributions to both collections range from narrow monographs to extremely general overviews, and few pieces stand out. The third volume of the *Etudes sur la presse* suffers from similar problems. The first two volumes do concentrate on a single periodical, the *Journal de Trevoux*. Nevertheless, even these studies are not sharply focused on a common theme and do not add up to a coherent whole. Such works are most useful as surveys of the variety of problems and approaches presently employed in the field. Sgard and Rétat's study of the press in 1734 is important, for example, for its attempt to produce a typology of eighteenth-century periodicals: the issue of classification is important for comparative purposes and as a clue to the nature of intended audiences.

The collective works just discussed have undoubtedly made the greatest contribution to the development of new methods for the study of the press; almost all of them have concentrated on questions that were virtually absent from Trenard's synthesis in the *Histoire générale*. But individual scholars using more traditional methodologies have also made major contributions to the field since Trenard. Several leading journalists of the period have been the subjects of major interpretive biographies — notably the philosophes' bitter opponent Fréron, Linguet, and Mallet du Pan.[27] All these studies demonstrate

27. Jean Balcou, *Fréron contre les philosophes* (Geneva and Paris, 1975); Darline Gay Levy, *The Ideas and Careers of Simon-Nicolas-Henri Linguet: A Study in Eighteenth-Century French Politics* (Urbana, Ill., 1980); Ginevra Conti Odorisio, *S. N. H. Linguet dall'ancien regime alla Rivoluzione* (Rome, 1976); Frances Acomb, *Mallet du Pan (1749–1800): A Career in Political Journalism* (Durham, N.C., 1973). In addition to Birn's *Pierre Rousseau and the Philosophes*, other recent monographs concentrating on important journalists and their publications include Marianne Constance Couperus, *Un Périodique français en Hollande: Le Glaneur historique (1731–1733)* (The Hague and Paris, 1971), which treats not only a journal but its author, Jean-Baptiste le Vilain de la Varenne; and Jacques Wagner, *Marmontel journaliste et le Mercure de France (1725–1761)* (Grenoble, 1975).

the vitality of political journalism under the Old Regime, in spite of the panoply of censorship restrictions. Both Fréron and Linguet emerge as far more important figures in French cultural and political history than had been previously realized; their work clearly foreshadows the journalism of the revolutionary period, and both personally influenced many later writers.

Another major biography with considerable importance for the understanding of French journalism in the late eighteenth century is Suzanne Tucoo-Chala's study of Charles-Joseph Panckoucke.[28] Panckoucke, the most important Parisian publisher in the last decades of the Old Regime and the founder of the revolutionary *Moniteur,* plays a central role in Darnton's study of the publishing of the *Encyclopédie.* But he was also one of the first great French press barons, accumulating privileges for periodicals and dreaming of creating truly modern political and literary journals that would give him a virtual monopoly on the market. Tucoo-Chala's study describes the role of economic forces in the periodical market, where their influence was at least as great as in the book-publishing field. It also demonstrates that the multiplication of new periodicals, a striking feature of the second half of the century, was accompanied by a process of concentration, pointing toward the creation of a few great national periodicals — a development sharply reversed with the coming of the Revolution.

The economic and institutional pressures on journals are also documented in an excellent study by René Moulinas of publishing and bookselling in the papal enclave of Avignon.[29] Although Avignon was entirely surrounded by French territory, it was not affected by French regulations on printing and censorship. The city thereby was able to become a major exporter of clandestine and counterfeit works. The most important product of Avignon's presses, however, was a major French-language newspaper, the *Courrier d'Avignon,* published from the 1730s into the Revolution. Moulinas's chapters on the *Courrier* are the best study to date of the functioning of any of the extraterritorial newssheets that circulated regularly in France during the eighteenth century and played an important part in the country's political life.

The latest monograph to stress the economic and institutional aspects of eighteenth-century journalism is Gilles Feyel's study of the

---

28. *Charles-Joseph Panckoucke et la librairie française* (Pau, 1977).
29. *L'Imprimerie, la librairie, et la presse à Avignon au XVIIIe siècle* (Grenoble, 1974).

provincial editions of the *Gazette de France*.[30] The proprietors of the *Gazette*, France's first authorized political newspaper, franchised reprints of that paper in a number of provincial centers during the first half of the century, and these papers, which added local advertising to the articles they reprinted from the Paris edition, constitute a previously unrecognized stage in the growth of the French provincial press.

The major monographs in French press history of the past fifteen years have thus deepened our understanding of a number of its features, especially the development of French political journalism and the influence of considerations of marketing on particular journals. An authoritative study of many features of eighteenth-century French-language journalism must await the completion of the inventories of journalists, publications, and contents currently under way, but a sketch of the picture now emerging can serve to indicate both the conclusions that have been established and the areas where further research is needed. Jean Sgard has made a broad-ranging synthesis of the results of his colleagues' work in a recently published volume of essays in German on the French Enlightenment. His summary covers a good deal more ground than his contribution to the *Histoire de l'édition française* and presents significant statistical data compiled from the *Dictionnaire des journalistes* and the initial version of the checklist for French-language periodicals.[31] Sgard's synthesis leaves no doubt that French periodical journalism in the eighteenth century, although obviously limited by censorship and other forms of political control, was a lively medium for communicating ideas and played a central role in eighteenth-century intellectual life. The mechanisms that allowed the circulation of books that could not qualify for an official privilege worked for periodicals as well, and even a genuinely clandestine periodical like the long-lived Jansenist *Nouvelles ecclésiastiques* circulated despite severe repressive measures. Most major currents in French political, intellectual, and social life were reflected in the press. The periodical press promoted the religious concerns of the

---

30. *La "Gazette" en province à travers ses réimpressions, 1631–1752* (Amsterdam and Maarssen, 1982). See also Feyel, "Réimpressions et diffusion de la Gazette dans les provinces: 1631–1752," in *Journalisme d'ancien régime*, ed. Rétat, 69–86.

31. "Journale und Journalisten im Zeitalter der Aufklärung," in *Sozialgeschichte der Aufklärung in Frankreich*, ed. Hans Ulrich Gumbrecht, Rolf Reichardt, and Thomas Schleich (Munich and Vienna, 1981), 2:3–33. As of this writing, this article has not appeared in a French version.

century's major protest movement, Jansenism; the ideas of the Enlightenment; even, as Nina Rattner Gelbart's contribution to this collection proves, such advanced notions as female equality. A public
realm of debate existed by at least midcentury: if the philosophes had
their organs, so too did their opponents, such as Fréron, whose *Année
littéraire* was the rallying point for a number of minor writers opposed
to the Enlightenment, Jansenism, and challenges to royal authority.
And other journals catered to concerns beyond those of the philosophes and their detractors.

There is no doubt that the number of periodicals increased fairly
steadily throughout the century; Sgard has shown that they tended to
last longer as well. The data that point to a rise in the publication of
books through most of the period also confirm other general characteristics of the European world in the eighteenth century, such as a
growth of the market for secular printed literature and, presumably,
an increase in the number of people reading it. Nevertheless, the
often-cited figure of approximately one thousand periodical titles
published during the century is somewhat misleading. Most journals
were short-lived, and the total number appearing at any one time was
considerably more modest: twenty-two in 1715, fifty-two by 1755, sev-
enty-nine in 1785.[32] Moreover, although French journals demonstrated
impressive growth over the course of the century, they lagged far
behind the journals of other countries. Joachim Kirchner catalogued
well over two thousand titles of magazines alone for eighteenth-century Germany, not counting the several hundred newspapers that also
appeared there.[33] This phenomenon was partly the result of French
political centralization, but it also reflected the generally lower level of
literacy in France, as compared to Protestant northern Germany, and
the absence of the network of universities that provided an institutional base of support for many German periodicals. In comparison

32. *Dictionnaire des journaux (1600–1789): Liste alphabétique des titres* (Grenoble,
1978), 30–32.
33. *Das deutsche Zeitschriftenwesen* (Wiesbaden, 1958), 1:115. Needless to say, the
number of magazines appearing in Germany at any one time was much lower than this
figure would suggest, since most enterprises were short-lived. A critical review of
Kirchner's data shows, for example, that during the decade 1770–80, only eighteen
periodicals surviving more than three years were aimed at a general reading audience
rather than academic specialists (Martin Welke, "Zeitung und Offentlichkeit im 18.
Jahrhundert," in *Presse und Geschichte* [Munich, 1977], 73). Still, there were many more
newspapers in eighteenth-century Germany than in France: at least 92 have been
identified in the five-year period 1745–50 and 151 in the year 1785 alone (Martin Welke,
"Die Legende vom 'unpolitischen Deutschen': Zeitunglesen im 18. Jahrhundert als
Spiegel des politischen Interesses," *Jahrbuch der Wittheit zu Bremen* 25 [1981]: 183).

with England, the limited evidence available about readership suggests a smaller total audience for France and one more heavily weighted toward the upper end of the social scale.

In addition to growing in number, periodicals in eighteenth-century France began to be published in more places. The periodical press had been an invention of Paris in the seventeenth century, and the capital remained the great national center of such publication — indeed, it has continued to do so ever since. But the gradual spread of provincial newspapers and general-interest magazines, especially in the last decade of the Old Regime, shows the development of local markets. These local periodicals reflected definite regional characteristics and were a sign of that growing local self-consciousness that Daniel Roche notes in his massive study of the provincial academies.[34] Other periodicals appeared abroad, although they were intended for a French audience.

A more striking trend was the differentiation in types of journals. Although newspapers remained wedded throughout the century to a fairly narrow definition of political news that emphasized wars, diplomacy, court events, and struggles between the government and major corporate bodies (particularly the parlements), magazines became increasingly diversified and often highly specialized. From the all-purpose *Journal des sçavans* of the late seventeenth century grew a wide variety of learned journals, as different branches of knowledge gradually achieved distinct identities. Specialized titles dealing with medicine, economics, and other disciplines appeared; a recent monograph by Marc Martin examines the creation of the first French journal concerned with military science. Other new periodicals aimed to entertain rather than educate; out of the *Mercure de France* came journals devoted to individual arts, and magazines for fashion and other "frivolous" topics existed by the time of the Revolution. Mimicking the *Spectator*, the English journal published by Richard Steele and Joseph Addison, the French developed a large number of journals that used satire to make social commentary.[35] A better knowledge of the devel-

34. *Le Siècle des lumières en province: Académies et académiciens provinciaux, 1680 – 1789*, 2 vols. (Paris, 1978).

35. Martin, *Les Origines de la presse militaire en France à la fin de l'ancien régime et sous la Révolution (1770 – 1799)* (Château de Vincennes, 1975). For a survey of fashion and women's magazines, see Evelyne Sullerot, *Histoire de la presse en France des origines à 1848* (Paris, 1966); for information on the imitators of the *Spectator*, consult "Le Journaliste masqué: Personnages et formes personnelles," in *Journalisme d'ancien régime*, ed. Rétat, 285 – 313.

opment of specialized journals in France would open the way to some fruitful cross-cultural comparisons, such as an inquiry into the apparent paucity of historical journals in France and their proliferation in Germany.

Scholars only incompletely understand the forces behind this diversification. Economic factors certainly played a role: aggressive entrepreneurs recognized the potential for profits in a successful periodical and searched for unexploited segments of the market. But for the most part, French periodical publishers were relatively unimaginative in their approach; Panckoucke, with his expansive visions, was ahead of his time, and his main intent was to monopolize the existing market, not to expand it. The impetus for the creation of most journals came from authors with a message to communicate or from intellectual institutions, as the journals that Nina Rattner Gelbart discusses in this collection and the numerous journals sponsored by academies, agricultural improvement societies, and other noncommercial groups indicate. The reluctance of French political newspapers to carry commercial advertising in later periods has often been noted, but it was already characteristic of the pre-revolutionary period. Although market considerations were undoubtedly important in determining the success of journals during the eighteenth century, French journalism was probably less commercial than its English and German contemporaries.

A corollary of this situation was the slow development of the journalistic profession during the eighteenth century. Journalism was a career that people turned to when they failed to establish themselves in academic or literary life. It did offer money and some opportunity to continue to participate in literary society, but little prestige. People who went into journalism customarily spent one-half of the rest of their lives employed in their new business, and the career became slightly more professionalized as the century wore on.[36] The fates of the most prominent practitioners, however, did not encourage imitation. Fréron's career was compromised by eventual failure and disgrace, and Linguet's sensational success with his *Annales politiques* was offset by his equally sensational sojourn in the Bastille.[37] Al-

36. Censer, "Journalism"; Sgard, "Journale und Journalisten," 26–31.
37. Actually Fréron was not the first professional journalist of note; he had learned his business from P.-F.-G. Desfontaines, whom contemporaries saw as setting a new standard in literary journalism. Since, however, Fréron was Desfontaines's only imita-

though the development of Parisian journalism has received the most attention, émigré writers and editors, from Bayle and Le Clerc in Holland at the beginning of the century to Théveneau de Morande in London toward its close, also contributed greatly to the field. Truly separated from any other career possibilities, these men turned to journalism as the only way to continue to play a role in French life. The great Huguenot writers have been well studied, but the institutionalization of this journalistic diaspora throughout the eighteenth century requires more elucidation.

The size and composition of the journal-reading audience in eighteenth-century France remains something of an unanswerable question. Without sufficiently detailed postal records or extensive collections of publishers' business records, it is difficult to say anything definite about the subject. The relatively high price of most journals suggests that the periodical press did not reach a genuinely popular audience. Collective reading groups, similar to the German *Lesegesellschaften*, may have overcome this barrier by enabling poorer readers to pool their sous, but no institution emerged in France comparable to the ubiquitous English coffeehouses that provided newspapers for their clients. Little is known about the extent of reading groups in France; it is indicative of the state of research that at a recent symposium on reading societies in Europe, the French contribution dealt with Masonic lodges rather than simple reading groups.[38] A recent comparative study of advertisements in French and British newspapers of the period concludes that the French papers' publicity aimed at a more elite audience than the English papers' did;[39] French readers tended to be more elite than readers of the German press as well. Periodicals explicitly intended for the *peuple* began to appear in England and Germany by the end of the eighteenth century but not in France, which also indicates that the audience for periodicals was essentially drawn from the educated bourgeoisie and the aristocracy. The numerical size of this audience is not at all clear, however. Ray-

---

tor, his efforts might likewise be regarded as a false start. See Thelma Morris, *L'Abbé Desfontaines et son rôle dans la littérature de son temps* (Geneva, 1961).

38. Daniel Roche, "Literarische und geheime Gesellschaftsbildung im vorrevolutionären Frankreich: Akademien und Logen," in *Lesegesellschaften und bürgerliche Emanzipation*, ed. Otto Dann (Munich, 1981), 181–96.

39. Stephen Botein, Jack R. Censer, and Harriet Ritvo, "The Periodical Press in Eighteenth-Century English and French Society: A Cross-Cultural Approach," *Comparative Studies in Society and History* 23 (1981): 464–90.

mond Birn has ventured a figure of thirty to fifty thousand people who read regularly, and periodical subscribers would presumably be drawn primarily from this group;[40] this figure may be reasonable, but as Birn would admit, it is no more than an educated guess. Global estimates of literacy, such as the ones furnished in François Furet and Jacques Ozouf's *Lire et écrire*,[41] have little bearing on the question: subscribing to a periodical required not only the literacy to read it but also the money to pay for it, the leisure to peruse it, and above all the desire to do so. The circulation figures that exist for individual titles are scattered and not always reliable; the highest confirmed figures for any one journal are for the *Mercure de France* in the 1780s, when it reached a level of over twenty thousand copies per issue.[42] This journal, a general literary and cultural review that also carried such entertainment features as the *logogriphe* in each issue, presumably had a broader potential appeal than almost any other periodical of the period.

Finally, recent research makes it possible to begin to assess the impact of periodicals on French life on a somewhat more sophisticated level, instead of simply assuming that articles always achieved their stated purposes. The studies assembled in *L'Attentat de Damiens* are the most successful attempt so far to go beyond this simplistic approach, and they demonstrate the kinds of ambiguities present even in officially sponsored press propaganda: celebrations of Louis XV's recovery from his wounds reinforced the echo of Damiens's assault and kept it fresh in the public's memory; the parallel between Damiens's attack and the assassinations of Henri III and Henri IV revived suspicion of the Jesuits at a critical moment in the struggle between the *parti janséniste* and the Crown.

The studies by Joynes, Popkin, and Censer in this volume focus specifically on how the political newspapers of the eighteenth century affected the workings of the French political system. They leave no doubt that France, at least from the time of the refusal-of-sacraments controversy under Louis XV, had a significant political news press and that all political actions in the country had to be taken in the full knowledge that they would be publicized through a regular system of periodical reporting. It was not only the overt content of these publi-

40. Birn, "*Livre et société* After Ten Years," 294.
41. *Lire et écrire*, 2 vols. (Paris, 1977).
42. Tucoo-Chala, *Panckoucke*, 220.

cations that made them significant — although they were often critical of ministerial policy or, implicitly, of the French political system — it was above all the mere fact of their existence, which implied a public right to know what was being done at Versailles and, ultimately, a public right to judge the government. The studies by Joynes and Popkin point to the key role of the propaganda issued by the Jansenist *parti* and the parlements in the press coverage of French domestic politics after 1750; they thus reinforce the suggestions by Dale Van Kley, Keith Michael Baker, and others that the Jansenist issue and the parlementary struggle against royal authority familiarized the French reading public with such vital political notions as constitutionalism, national sovereignty, and the need for representative institutions. This thesis challenges the previous concentration on the progress of the Enlightenment as an index of the decay of traditional French political values. Although the parlementaires drew to some extent on the writings of the philosophes, their doctrines had other sources as well, including the antihierarchical conciliarist and Richerist strains within Catholic thought that had become intertwined with Jansenism during the eighteenth century. Censer's analysis of the portrayal of English politics in the *Courrier d'Avignon* demonstrates the extent to which potentially subversive notions could circulate through the periodical press because of the French government's relative indifference to what was said about events in other countries.

This historiographical survey suggests that interest both in the circulation and expression of ideas and in the causes of the Revolution has encouraged the study of the press. Had a comprehension of the beliefs, attitudes, and reading material of a broad spectrum of society not become central to these established and dynamic fields of inquiry, the recent flurry of research on the press might not have occurred and the directions these inquiries took well might have been different. Yet the examination of the press has also contributed and will continue to contribute to the older questions. The ubiquity of periodicals among educated people means that this medium can provide a vision of the elite in their various roles as authors, entrepreneurs, readers, and participants in public opinion. Current findings already suggest that no future study of French thought, politics, or social issues in the eighteenth century can afford to neglect the periodical press.

Chapter Two

~

The *Journal des dames* and Its Female Editors: Politics, Censorship, and Feminism in the Old Regime Press

NINA RATTNER GELBART

The monthly paper *Journal des dames* appeared intermittently during the twenty years from 1759 to 1778, a more than respectable lifetime for a periodical in the Old Regime.[1] Its longevity can be attributed to its succession of nine zealous, idiosyncratic editors who, attracted by its title for different reasons, refused to be thwarted when book-trade authorities obstructed their path. For some the title evoked frivolous literary fluff; for others feminist grievances; still others used it as a smoke screen for more general political criticism, hoping such a paper might escape serious scrutiny by the censors. Although the *Journal des*

I would like to thank each of my fellow contributors to this volume for their invaluable advice on this paper, archivists at the Comédie-Française and the Minutier Central in Paris for their assistance over the years, and the National Endowment for the Humanities for a full-year fellowship supporting my work on the *Journal des dames*.

Throughout this article I have intentionally referred to the female editors as Mme and to the men by their family names only, because the women were so determined to call attention to their sex and to the uniqueness of their role as *éditrices*.

1. Jean Sgard's *Inventaire de la presse classique (1600–1789)* (Grenoble, 1978), 30–33, provides charts and tables showing that the vast majority of papers launched after 1750 were ephemeral, only about one in six lasting more than ten years and most perishing after just a few numbers.

dames began and ended in the hands of men, during its middle period it bore the names of three female editors who took decisive control. Originally conceived by its male founder, a staunch royalist, as an innocuous bauble to amuse ladies at their toilette, in its later years under Louis-Sébastien Mercier the paper became blatantly *frondeur,* supporting the parlements against the Crown.[2] In between, from October 1761 to April 1775, the three women were in charge, not merely as the owners of the paper but as the true shapers of its policy and content, and it was their influence that transformed a trivial bagatelle into a serious oppositional publication addressing social issues, preaching reform, and attempting to make its audience think. Their *Journal des dames* had not a single fashion illustration, in contrast to later papers published for women by men. It was designed to nourish the mind and discourage vanity. Assuming their readers could handle it, they served up stern stuff, for they believed in the female public's right — and obligation — to be informed about controversial matters. In lenient periods the paper's oppositional views were expressed quite baldly; in repressive periods they were camouflaged, and elliptical messages had to be extracted from passing remarks and allusions. Twice the censors and book-trade directors suspended the paper; the editors themselves also kept it silent for four years. But the three women relaunched the paper after each suspension; they thus represent an important transitional stage in the evolution of the *Journal des dames,* converting it from a politically conformist *rien délicieux* into a thorn in the government's side and finally turning it over to male revolutionaries. How and why they did so is the subject of this study.

The tumultuous *Journal des dames* attracted the attention of contemporaries. Chroniclers, *nouvellistes,* and rival journalists followed its saga with interest, amazed at its repeated resurrections as it continually changed hands. In his *Mémoires secrets* Louis Petit de Bachaumont marveled each time "the corpse stirred with new life," and other periodicals noted its death-defying persistence, "after so many plummeting falls each of which seemed fatal."[3] Readers too were intrigued

2. What Mercier did with the paper is beyond the scope of this study but is treated in my article "'Frondeur' Journalism in the 1770s: Theatre Criticism and Radical Politics in the Pre-revolutionary French Press," *Eighteenth-Century Studies* 17 (1984): 493–514, and in my book, *Feminine and Opposition Journalism in Old Regime France: "Le Journal des Dames"* (Los Angeles and Berkeley, 1987).

3. *Mémoires secrets pour servir à l'histoire de la république des lettres en France, depuis 1762 jusqu'à nos jours,* 31 vols. (London, 1777–89), 7:159, 10:35, 16:294. See also *Journal*

by the *Journal des dames*'s resilience and subscribed in considerable numbers. At 12 livres a year, it was priced far lower than most of the literary monthlies.[4] Although no subscription lists or *tirage* figures for the paper have been found, it seems to have had a paying audience of well above three hundred if we take one editor's word. Another editor, the last, even counted on one thousand subscribers, an overly sanguine expectation as it turned out but one probably based on some now lost information on the journal's track record.[5] This readership pales in comparison with such hot journalistic sellers as the international *Courrier de l'Europe* or Simon-Henri Linguet's *Annales politiques* with figures from five to seven thousand. But for a paper circulating mostly within France, the *Journal des dames* had a better than average following; the privileged, government-protected *Mercure de France* itself had only around 1,500 during this period.

The social composition of the *Journal des dames*'s growing readership appears to have become broader during its twenty years, if we use advertisements and letters-to-the-editor as "consumer feedback." Although the number of advertisements is insufficient to justify any statistical breakdown and although letters sent to the journal may not all have been genuine, this evidence nevertheless suggests an expanding audience. At first, when a novelty, the *Journal des dames* attracted anonymous society ladies who subscribed as if they were joining some secret club, responding enthusiastically to this new medium that promised to air their views, feature their work, and reduce their sense of isolation.[6] Very soon, however, such rhapsodic letters vanished, yielding to a variety of contributions on many subjects from readers of both sexes. The few advertisements carried in the *Journal des dames*, mostly for services, show it reaching beyond a pampered elite to a

---

(historique) de Verdun, Feb. 1774, 132; *Avant coureur*, 1761, 255; *Observateur littéraire*, 1761, 2:354–57.

4. Only the *Journal de Verdun* was lower, at 8 livres 8 sols a year. The *Feuille nécessaire* and *Annales typographiques* cost the same as the *Journal des dames*. But the *Journal de Trevoux, Censeur hebdomadaire, Journal étranger, Mercure, Année littéraire*, and *Journal encyclopédique* ranged higher, from 15 livres to more than 30 for a subscription. See Jèze, *Etat ou tableau de la ville de Paris* (Paris, 1761), 199–209.

5. Bachaumont, *Mémoires secrets*, 10:32 and 16:294–95.

6. See, for example, the *Journal des dames* (hereafter cited as *JD*), June 1761, 271–77, and Aug. 1761, 180.

more practical-minded readership.[7] By its end, a rival journalist, Jean-François de La Harpe, then editor of the *Journal de politique et de littérature*, quipped scornfully that nobody "well-bred" would look at the *Journal des dames*, for it was written in the "style of the populace."[8] It is unlikely that La Harpe would have bothered to discredit a paper unless its broad appeal threatened his own enterprise.

Female journalists were rare in the eighteenth century. Their courage was extraordinary, for they meant to be career women in an age that had no such thing. They hoped, that is, to exercise a profession independently and with dignity and to be taken seriously by contemporaries of both sexes. Profit was not their motivation. They wished to prove their capability and gain an audience. The few women who had attempted to edit papers earlier — we are not even sure the anonymous *Spectatrice* of the 1720s was female — had frightened fast, and there were no successful role models from which to draw inspiration.[9] Journalism was not for the lily-livered. Yet the three female editors of the *Journal des dames* took on their job with high hopes and higher expectations for their readers. The first one, who blamed men for having kept women in bondage, imagined that she could single-handedly and quickly establish feminine equality. Despite her impassioned pleas, however, women were not galvanized into action. In fact, a major drop in circulation indicates that she scared away most of her subscribers with her aggressive, demanding, bossy, provocative rhetoric. Her two female successors were more realistic. The passivity of their audience convinced them that profound and far-reaching changes would need to take place before women realized they were as much to blame as men for their subordination. As one of their favorite featured authors, Marie Anne Roumier-Robert, put it: "I am always astonished that women have not yet banded together, formed a separate league, with an eye to avenging themselves against male injustices. May I live long enough to see them make such profitable use of their courage! But up until now, they have been too coquettish and

7. For services advertised, see the last pages of *JD* for Oct. and Dec. 1764, Apr. and Oct. 1765, Apr. and Nov. 1766, May 1767; Feb. 1775, 266 – 68; Apr. 1775, 131.

8. *Journal de politique et de littérature*, 1776, 3:260. See also La Harpe's *Correspondance littéraire . . . depuis 1774 jusqu'à 1789*, 5 vols. (Paris, 1801–7), 2:55.

9. On earlier female editors, see Caroline Rimbault, "La Presse féminine de la langue française au XVIIIᵉ siècle: Place de la femme et système de mode" (Thèse de IIIᵉ cycle, Ecole pratique des hautes etudes, Paris, 1981).

dissipated to concern themselves seriously with the interests of their sex."[10]

Seeing that their cause necessitated wide-ranging social and political change, the female editors of the *Journal des dames* accepted the help and supported the efforts of male reformers and even radicals. Their own plight had sensitized them to other forms of social injustice, and they began to see the woman's issue in a broader political context. Enemies of feminine frivolity, they contrasted the solidity of bourgeois family values with the promiscuity and license of *les grands*, much as Jean-Jacques Rousseau did. And, their almost puritanical moralizing, like Rousseau's, went hand in hand with a growing political hostility to the regime.[11] Although forced to work within the old system, courting patrons and protectors, the female journalists aided and abetted men who were busy fomenting its overthrow. In particular, they lent their support to, and won the support of, many *frondeurs*, whose parlementary and Jansenist sympathies propelled them toward political radicalism. These men identified strongly with the Fronde, that "revolution manquée" that despite its frivolous name had raised serious constitutional challenges to French absolutism and had brought together in a fleeting but explosive alliance princes of the blood, magistrates, and city mobs. The *Journal des dames* was associated with such *frondeurs* as the prince de Conti, the magistrate Laverdy, the Jansenist provincial Mathon de la Cour, the underground *nouvelliste* Pidansat de Mairobert, and the notorious forbidden author Mercier. And it was this *frondeur* ideology, far more than the paper's feminist claims, that bothered the authorities.

The *Journal des dames* spanned a stormy period in French history. Only by placing its story in its political context can we hear, as contemporaries did, the resonance of the messages hidden in the copy. When the paper was started in 1759, France was being trounced in the Seven Years' War, and Damiens, in a wild attempt at assassination, had slashed at the king with a knife. What better antidote to the gloom and

10. This quotation is from Roumier-Robert's *Voyage de Milord Ceton dans les sept planètes* (The Hague and Paris, 1765–66), discussed in L. Abensour, *La Femme et le féminisme avant la Révolution* (Paris, 1923), 429. For reviews of Mme Robert's work in *JD*, see, for example, Jan. 1762, 31–35, and Aug./Sept./Oct. 1763, 93–100.

11. Robert Darnton has pointed out this same mix in the most rabidly defamatory political attacks on the regime, which grew out of a puritanical bourgeois ethic. See his "Reading, Writing and Publishing," in *The Literary Underground of the Old Regime* (Cambridge, Mass., 1982), 204–5.

"fermentations" of the times than a light, mindless paper for women? Such a publication would be entirely uncontroversial, and it would calm restless tongues. "If I am not mistaken," the conservative male founding editor wrote to the book-trade director Lamoignon de Malesherbes, "the government should do all it can to encourage authors who propose to entertain, in an age where it is unsafe to teach the people how to think." [12] A *déclaration* issued in 1757 by the police and book trade had threatened to put to death anyone who "attacks religion, stirs up discontent, undermines the government's authority, troubles the established order, or disturbs tranquillity." [13] The *Journal des dames* had obviously been designed to demonstrate perfect compliance with this declaration. Its prospectus promised to serve up only "delicious nothings . . . felicitous wisps of imagination . . . [and] pleasure," leaving to others the "glory of announcing useful discoveries" and trying to change the world.[14]

The first female editor, however, one obscure Mme de Beaumer, who took over the *Journal des dames* in October 1761, did not believe in obsequiously respecting such limits, and she initiated the paper's nonconformist tone. She was an enigma even to her contemporaries. After the abbé de la Porte stated in his *Histoire littéraire des femmes françaises* that Mme de Beaumer lacked fortune, beauty, or grace, he added that he had been able to find no documents on her birth or marriage. He mentioned only that she had strong ties with Holland, traveling there often and dying there miserably in 1766.[15] Almost surely she was a Huguenot. This would explain the absence of records on her civil status; Protestants preferred to baptize their children and marry clandestinely, rather than be branded "illegitimate" by the official Catholic church.[16] It would also explain the intensity of her commitment not only to women but to persecuted minorities in general; her hatred of Richelieu ("destroyer of La Rochelle");[17] the dedication of her *Journal des dames* to the Protestant Condé branch of royal cousins;

12. Bibliothèque nationale, Manuscrits français (henceforth BN ms.fr.) 22134, fol. 164.

13. BN ms.fr. 22093, pièce 124.

14. *Prospectus pour le Journal des dames*, in the Réserve des imprimés of the bibliothèque nationale. It is identical to the "Avant propos" in the issue of Jan. 1759.

15. Joseph de la Porte, *Histoire littéraire des femmes françaises*. . . . (Paris, 1769), 4:525.

16. See C. P. Stewart, "The Huguenots Under Louis XV," *Proceedings of the Huguenot Society of London* 12, no. 1 (1920): 55–65, especially 61.

17. See, for example, JD, Sept. 1762, 268.

her residence in Paris with the Huguenot Jaucourt family for over a
year, during which she shuttled back and forth to Holland; and finally
her choice of a successor, Mme de Maisonneuve, who used the paper
to seek justice in the Calas affair.

Mme de Beaumer's radical sympathies had surfaced before she
took over the *Journal des dames.* She was probably the author of the
cryptonymous *Lettres curieuses, instructives, et amusantes,* an abortive
periodical launched in The Hague in 1759 by a Mme de Beau* and
distributed by precisely the same bookdealers in Leiden, Rotterdam,
Utrecht, Breda, Groningen, and Middelburg who handled the *Journal
des dames* two years later. "In order to publish these letters," the
French author had explained about their appearance in Holland, "I
was forced to resort to a foreign land . . . to that happy country
where truth, supported by her sister freedom, enjoys the inestimable
privilege of making her voice heard, without having to fear those
infamous spies so numerous [in France] . . . that detestable brood of
informers which, to our country's shame, have begun to swarm
lately." [18] This denunciation of royal censors and police suggests that
Mme de Beaumer and the French authorities had already clashed, but
despite her misgivings about publishing in France she decided to do so
in 1760. She went to some efforts to protect herself, however, by
disguising her message in allegory and fable and by paying lip service
to the regime. Some strong oppositional sentiments got by the censors
before they caught on, allowing us to glimpse Mme de Beaumer's
popular, even insurrectionary leanings. She was prime Bastille material. A champion of women's abilities, she also crusaded for the poor
and downtrodden, for social justice, religious toleration, Freemasonry, republican liberty, international peace, and equality before the
law. Far more passionate than logical, she never defined these terms
rigorously but repeated them provocatively in both her public and
private writings. Mme de Beaumer wanted sweeping and speedy
changes in government and society. An ideological firebrand and
something of a desperado on borrowed time, she meant to set the

18. *Lettres curieuses, instructives, et amusantes, ou Correspondance historique, gal-
lante, critique, morale, philosophique, et littéraire entre une dame de Paris et une dame de
Province . . . publiées par Mme de Beau* à La Haye chez Isaac Beauregard (1759),* iv –vii.
JD later attributed these *lettres* to Mme le Prince de Beaumont, but the tone is far more
belligerent than this author's other writings.

process in motion herself. Outrageous as her grandiose claims appear at times, they cannot be dismissed as ridiculous, because for all her eccentricity, Mme de Beaumer profoundly bothered the authorities.

Slipped in between the purplish odes and mythological allegories of her 1760 *Oeuvres mêlées*, for example, was a "Dialogue entre Charles XII, roi de Suède, et Mandrin, contrebandier." Mandrin, a real Robin Hood of a bandit who had just been captured and burned alive after successfully eluding massive deployments of police for years, became the hero of a vast pamphlet literature in the Revolution. Mme de Beaumer was one of his earliest champions. She now depicted Mandrin outwitting corrupt tax-farmers, defending the weak and needy, and winning the admiration of millions through his courage, cleverness, and generous spirit. He had made the world a better place. On the other hand, King Charles, born into a life of luxury, had abused his power through war and conquest. Military historians, wrote the pacifist Mme de Beaumer, "commit a crime by glamorizing battle," for they perpetuate in impressionable readers an appetite for power. King Charles had been dazzled by stories of Alexander the Great. If rulers could instead read the truth about carnage, pillaging, suffering, and their waste of human life, there would be no warring nations.[19] Mme de Beaumer espoused the Masonic ideals of a worldwide spiritual brotherhood, public service, and industry and energy in manual as well as intellectual labor. Her identification with the lower classes next inspired her *Lettres de Magdelon Friquet*, modeled on a heroine of the democratic *genre poissarde* whose name later became a popular revolutionary pseudonym.[20] Because her manuscript was refused and never printed, no trace of it remains, and we cannot know exactly what it contained or whether it was meant to be a single book or a new periodical in disguise, as *lettres* often were. But the censor De la Garde who turned it down was on record for permitting many dubious

19. *Oeuvres mêlées* (Liège, 1760, 1761). The most complete set of fragments is in the Bibliothèque historique de la ville de Paris, 21061, nos. 4 and 5, pp. 1–26. On the significance of Mandrin for the Revolution, see L. S. Gordon, "Le Thème de Mandrin, le 'brigand noble' dans l'histoire des idées en France avant la Révolution," in *Au siècle des lumières* (Paris, 1970), 189–207.

20. In 1789 a "Magdelon Friquet" penned a pamphlet called *Grande et Horrible Conspiration des demoiselles du Palais Royal contre les droits de l'homme*. It was soon followed by *Avis important d'une dame des Halles (Magdelon Friquet) pour la diminution des vivres*. For a discussion of this type of popular heroine, see Alexander P. Moore, *The "Genre poissard" and the French Stage of the Eighteenth Century* (New York, 1935).

works. His outright rejection of Mme de Beaumer's newest project suggests, therefore, that it was explosive; it seems to confirm her penchant for daring fare.[21]

In October 1761, when she took on the *Journal des dames*, the paper had aroused no political suspicion whatever under its tame, male founding editors, and the censors did not monitor it closely. For a few months Mme de Beaumer took advantage of their negligence, using the journal to propagate her feminist, egalitarian, cosmopolitan message. But one censor, De la Garde, already mistrusted her, and although the *Journal des dames* was censored by François Marin, she knew she had little time before she would be muzzled again. Her tone was therefore urgent, her rhetoric bombastic. She needed to show nothing less than that the subjugation of women was a universal tragedy, that mutual respect between the sexes would lead to the same between social classes and eventually between nations, that a revolution in *moeurs* would thus result in social harmony and international peace. Even if only briefly, she now had listeners, a captive audience of subscribers. Making the most of the opportunity, her approach was frontal, demanding, belligerent.

"The honor of the French nation is intimately linked to the continuation of the *Journal des dames*. . . . Let no one think this statement singular, ridiculous, or absurd. . . . Be silent, all critics, and know that this is a *woman* addressing you!" With these strident words Mme de Beaumer launched her campaign to vindicate women's rights and persuade the world that her newspaper was of profound and far-reaching importance. "My only merit is to know the full worth of my sex. . . . How I would rejoice to rid the whole earth of the injurious notion [that we are inferior], still held by some barbarians among our citizens, who have difficulty acknowledging that we can think and write." An invitation was extended to women from the provinces and throughout Europe to send their works to the *Journal des dames*, where

21. For De la Garde's censorship activities, see Catherine Blangonnet, "Recherches sur les censeurs royaux et leurs places dans la société du temps de Malesherbes (1750 – 1763)" (Thèse de l'Ecole des chartes, Paris, 1974), 153, copy in Archives nationales (henceforth AN) AB XXVIII (210). De la Garde was a somewhat unusual censor in that he granted far more *permissions tacites*, presumably for questionable works, than privileges, where his signature would have had to appear on the approbation. For his refusal of Mme de Beaumer's manuscript, see Bibliothèque nationale, Nouvelles acquisitions françaises (henceforth BN nouv.acq.fr.) 3346, fols. 311–15.

they could set in motion a truly international exchange of ideas. Beyond these outside contributions, Mme de Beaumer promised to provide articles that would exemplify the glory and potentialities of women past and present, thus inspiring confidence and restoring dignity. She would of course amuse, but her primary goal was to instruct. Utility was an obsession for her. Even science would be included in the *Journal*, for stripped of its "pedantic charlatanism" it could be understood by women as well as men. Mme de Beaumer was sure that her female readers were ready for more intellectual fare. After all, the success of her ambitious venture depended on them, "my first judges, my true protectresses." [22]

Mme de Beaumer stressed that beauty is fleeting but wisdom lasting, that women must take advantage of their opportunities to advise and influence men, but that to do so they must abandon vain frivolities, throwing themselves instead into vigorous work or study, improving their characters as they honed their minds. Unfashionable as it was, Mme de Beaumer sang the praises of marriage and sexual fidelity, called for new standards of behavior, relationships based on equality, companionship, and trust. "Let it be firmly *resolved*," she declared, "that women will henceforth be enlightened and intelligent." Their talents, art, and genius will hold men in thriving unions, whereas relationships based on superficial attraction wilt like cut flowers. If women become as knowledgeable as men, Mme de Beaumer proposed, "if we educate ourselves, men will recognize that we are not only useful but indispensable." It is sad but true that "we are physically weaker . . . that war and peace are made without us." But wisdom in counsel could make women powerful nevertheless. By cultivating their minds, she urged her readers, they could form and shape the character of their families, instruct them in all matters, become the very backbone of society, and bring about world harmony. To succeed, however, women must get rid of mirrors and look instead within themselves. Their friends should be frank and critical, their partners not vain flatterers or empty-headed seducers, but men of virtue and substance. Only then would relationships between individuals be based on strong, durable foundations, and only then would the same be possible between nations. "Courage, women, no more

22. *JD*, Oct. 1761, "Avant propos," i, iv.

timidity. Let us prove that we can think, speak, study, and criticize as well as [men]. . . . I await this revolution with impatience. I shall do my utmost to be one of the first to precipitate it." [23]

Mme de Beaumer's bombastic entrance upon the journalistic scene occasioned instant ridicule, which only reinforced her determination to continue fighting for long overdue reforms. Male readers mocked her seriousness of purpose and ethic of decency, expecting her to falter, yield to their advice, and, as she said derisively, be "métamorphosée en Elégante." She announced in her second issue that she would ignore these detractors. "I shall henceforth close my ears to you, *messieurs les critiques*. We women think under our coiffures as well as you do under your wigs. We are as capable of reasoning as you are. In fact, you lose your reason over us every day." [24] Mme de Beaumer would continue to rail against conceited dandies bent on perpetuating flirtatious, superficial relations between the sexes. It was they who stood in the way of her mission's first step, the nurturing of feminine self-respect. "Women everywhere must scorn these useless encumbrances. Disdain is the only answer they deserve." [25] Determined to ignore them, she pursued her campaign.

To demonstrate the greatness of women at all levels of society, Mme de Beaumer did not confine herself to eulogies of famous queens, although she did make a point of praising Princess Anne of The Hague, daughter of King George II of England, as a chance to recommend the Orangist cause and republican Holland.[26] Less illustrious women were just as worthy of attention. She argued that any woman could understand practical subjects perfectly. Panning a new book, *Les Journées physiques,* an attempt to popularize physics for female readers based on Fontenelle's classic model, she strenuously objected to the author's sugary style. Science was "the most useful of the arts," and women needed serious instruction, not watered down drivel.[27] She pointed out Mesdames Dacier, du Bocage, and du Châtelet as examples of women with great intellectual accomplishments. She herself reviewed books on a wide range of subjects. She traced the roots of a novel by Tiphaigne de la Roche to the occult Rosicrucian tradition and displayed her familiarity with his free-thinking, *libertin* predecessors, among them Cyrano de Bergerac and the "comte de

23. Ibid., 79, 80.   24. *JD*, Nov. 1761, 103–5.
25. *JD*, Aug. 1762, 192. See also Sept. 1762, passim.
26. *JD*, Dec. 1761, 244ff.   27. Ibid., 199.

Gabalis." [28] She found a book called *Le Gentilhomme cultivateur* far more useful, however, because it advocated practical activities for aristocrats and because it dealt with agriculture, which had an importance and a value for humanity that women as well as men could recognize.[29]

But Mme de Beaumer's greatest enthusiasm was reserved for obscure female artists, merchants, artisans, and musicians from the lower classes. This abundance of capable, talented women, who were everywhere and too numerous to name, seemed to confirm all her arguments. Industrious and motivated from within, women succeeded at all tasks even without recognition and honor; with some well-deserved encouragement, these commoners would rise to ever-greater challenges, providing the world with the energy it now lacked. The senseless war had put Europe to soul-searching. It had dragged on for years, proving only that the "civilized" eighteenth century was as barbaric as any other despotic age. *Esprit* alone was worthless. A revival of commitment and *chaleur* was needed, the kind that had led the Romans to work virtuously for their society. What good were lofty philosophical systems? Maupertuis was impractical, and Rousseau was negative, seemingly determined to spew "paradoxes," put humans "back on all fours," and discourage both men and women in their quest for progress.[30] Mme de Beaumer did approve of one recent idea by a man, a proposal that the poor receive free legal assistance; but until realized, the idea was inert.[31] The editor strongly preferred practice to theory and was impatient to replace ivory tower speculations with industry and public service. She called commerce "the motor nerve of all great legislation." [32] But unlike the *Encyclopédie*'s glorification of the useful arts, Mme de Beaumer's stressed the crucial economic role played by women. Looking about, she saw large numbers of creative yet modest women busy at tasks, a ready, energetic force within society waiting to be tapped and challenged. She provided notices about female painters, shopowners, science illustrators, engravers, miniaturists, naturalists, sculptors, rugmakers, clockmakers, lensgrinders, collectors, taxidermists, weavers, chemists, and singers. Some of them had already begun to make their mark upon the world. A Mme de Moutiers had drawn for the famous biologist Réau-

28. *JD*, Nov. 1761, 105.   29. Ibid., 123.   30. *JD*, Oct. 1761, 62–63.
31. Ibid., 50–52, "Sur l'institution des avocats et procureurs des pauvres."
32. *JD*, Feb. 1762, 180.

mur, a Mlle Biheron, who molded artificial anatomical parts out of
wax, had actually won praise from the Académie des sciences. Such
steady, self-reliant, productive women—not the exception but the
rule—proved themselves the equals of men. Mme de Beaumer held
up their example in her answers to letters sent by idle readers searching for advice. If all women would throw themselves into useful,
constructive activity, the precedent for respect would be established.
And this was the essential first step in her "revolution."[33]

Mme de Beaumer's views were reflected in a poem written to her by
the poet and Mason Baculard d'Arnaud, "Couplets à Mme** sur l'Air
des francs-maçons," which she printed in the December 1761 issue of
the *Journal des dames*.[34] D'Arnaud was the orator at two Masonic
lodges, one at the Hôtel de Soisson, the other called the Loge de la cité.
Most of the members of these fraternities were merchants, bourgeois
whose sympathies were devoutly Jansenist and who believed deeply
in the solidity and value of the family. Baculard d'Arnaud brought to
Mme de Beaumer's paper his support for fidelity, industry, and wisdom, with all their Masonic overtones.[35] In general the editor espoused
the ideals of Masonry. She may have been a Mason herself. In The
Hague, where she spent much time, at least one coeducational lodge
had existed since 1751. Many of its members were actresses at the
Théâtre Français in Holland, and the *Journal des dames* carried a letter
from one such actress about her youth in La Rochelle. The paucity of
nobles in this Huguenot refuge gave the wives of *négociants* unprecedented power, and the letter described with obvious relish the inver-
sion of the traditional social order.[36]

But whether a Mason herself or not, Mme de Beaumer embraced
the Masonic vision of universality more vigorously, more literally,
than most journalists of her day. She reserved her highest praise for

33. *JD*, Oct. 1761, 78–79, 94–96; Nov. 1761, 190–92; Dec. 1761, 254–65, 281–84; Jan.
1762, 95–96; Feb. 1762, 201–3; Apr. 1762, 106–7; May 1762, 202–3; June 1762, 283–88.
34. On Baculard d'Arnaud, see Pierre Chevallier, *Histoire de la franc-maçonnerie
française* (Paris, 1979), vol. 1, *La Maçonnerie, école de l'égalité (1725–1799)*, 65–68. On
the commitment of Masonry to marriage and sexual fidelity, see Margaret C. Jacob, *The
Radical Enlightenment: Pantheists, Freemasons, and Republicans* (London, 1981), 206–8.
35. *JD*, Dec. 1761, 276.
36. Margaret C. Jacob, "Freemasonry, Women, and the Paradox of the Enlightenment," *Women and History*, 1984, no. 9: 69–93. The "Lettre de Mlle*, actrice au Théâtre
Français de ———" is in *JD*, Apr. 1762, 62–76, an issue published while Mme de
Beaumer lived in self-imposed exile in The Hague.

people with "l'esprit de l'univers." [37] Convinced that her message applied to all people in all places, she advertised a list of eighty-one booksellers in as many cities throughout France, Germany, Switzerland, Holland, Spain, Italy, Portugal, Russia, Sweden, and England where the *Journal des dames* was for sale. Published at the beginning of the December 1761 issue — her third — where the list filled several pages, such fanfare could not fail to catch the eye and make its point. No other paper had anything like it. And in an additional effort to show her journal's popularity, Mme de Beaumer cautioned her readers to avoid counterfeit versions, "to accept only those papers bearing her signature." [38]

The list of international distributors was a sham, a publicity stunt, and cannot be taken at face value, as a recent historian of the press has done.[39] Copies of the paper may indeed have been sent by the over-eager editor to some of these bookdealers, but not in response to any real demand. Mme de Beaumer mistook her own fiction for fact in her desire to make it come true. Her desperate financial situation, which she would soon reveal to Malesherbes, showed there were no takers for these international mailings. In her determination to impress her readers, she had misled herself into imagining and reaching out to a market that did not exist. The *Mercure*, considered to have an unusually broad circulation, reached only forty-six cities in 1762, mostly in the French provinces. But however fictitious, the list in the *Journal des dames* nonetheless awakened the slumbering authorities, who suddenly took action against Mme de Beaumer. Although we have no record of their previous charges against her, there was plenty here to disturb them and convince them that Mme de Beaumer needed disciplining. She was allegedly doing business with France's enemies, London and Berlin, and even with Saint Petersburg (Russia, in a sudden turnaround at the czarina's death, had just joined forces with

37. *JD*, Jan. 1762, 62.
38. The longest list is in *JD*, Dec. 1761. Mme de Beaumer's signature and the notice about counterfeiting appeared in her first issue, Oct. 1761, 96, and was repeated in every subsequent one.
39. See Caroline Rimbault, "La Presse féminine de langue française au XVIIIe siècle: Production et diffusion," in *Le Journalisme d'ancien régime*, ed. Pierre Rétat (Lyons, 1982), 199–216. On p. 215, Rimbault provides a map of the *Journal des dames*'s distribution under Mme de Beaumer; Rimbault concludes that the paper was "broadly international." But a look at Mme de Beaumer's private letters revealing her financial desperation and the frantic "pay up" notices in her early issues of 1763 show that this list indicating a worldwide market was far more dream than reality.

Frederick of Prussia against France). She conspicuously left out the Hapsburg cities with which France was allied. Mme de Beaumer had never been sufficiently patriotic, but she now seemed to be broadcasting her hostility to the Austrian alliance so dear to the duc de Choiseul. Her list was tantamount to treason.

Mme de Beaumer's daring up to this point can be explained partially by her residence in the sheltered *enclos du Temple*—the home address she gave in her first issues of the *Journal des dames* — one of the *lieux privilégiés* of Paris where the court's police could not penetrate and therefore something of a refuge for outlaws. The Temple, a walled enclave in the Marais housing about four thousand souls, was presided over by Louis-François de Bourbon, prince de Conti, cousin of the king, head of the chevaliers de Malte, Grand Prieur de France. Although a prince of the blood, Mme de Beaumer's protector Conti was a freethinker, libertine, and active Mason, who attracted within the walls of his safe haven numerous skeptics, Protestants, Jansenists, and fugitives. Conti, a *frondeur* leader, had always strongly supported the parlements against the king. He hid Rousseau in the Temple at several periods, harbored forbidden presses for the Jansenists' clandestine *Nouvelles ecclésiastiques* and for the *Courrier d'Avignon,* and allowed the selling and possibly the copying of *frondeur nouvelles à la main.*[40] "His love of independence," wrote a contemporary about Conti, "displeased the government with which he often fought. At the Temple he lived freely, far from the intrigues of the court where he ceased making appearances. . . . He liked to descend from the lofty rank where an accident of birth had placed him."[41] Within the close quarters of the Temple's walls, the high and the low did indeed rub shoulders. Next to the several grand *hôtels* ran narrow streets lined with crowded barracks, tiny studios, and workshops full of artisans. In the many little courts, merchants ran a lively market. The cafés were filled with a mixture of workers and people of rank. But the Temple was best known as a refuge for insolvent debtors. Furnished rooms were sublet to people who needed a place to stay while they restored order to their affairs. For 5 livres and a few sous they could request a

40. See E. J. J. Barillet, *Recherches historiques sur le Temple* (Paris, 1809), especially 46 – 47. On Conti's harboring of Jansenist presses, see BN ms.fr. 22093, fols. 384, 421. See also Frantz Funck-Brentano, *Figaro et ses devanciers* (Paris, 1909), 155, 288. On Conti's sheltering of Rousseau, see, for example, Bachaumont, *Mémoires secrets,* 2:275.
41. Barillet, *Recherches historiques,* 194 – 95.

permission de séjour of three months, during which creditors could not harass them. If this proved to be insufficient time to solve their financial problems, the *séjour* was generally renewed. The Temple was a world unto itself. "Here one lived under one's own laws. . . . It was like being in a foreign country yet in the heart of one's own land." [42] "It is good," wrote Louis-Sébastien Mercier, biographer of Paris and a subsequent editor of the *Journal des dames*, "that there should be in a city a sanctuary for victims of the agitations and vicissitudes of human life; here people and art have a kind of liberty too often fettered and denied them elsewhere." [43]

Certainly Mme de Beaumer qualified on a number of counts as needful of asylum. Her *frondeur* ideology was sufficiently at variance with French foreign and domestic policy to make it prudent to stay out of reach of the authorities. Her letters from this period reveal that she had incurred debts of 9,000 livres for the *Journal des dames* — perhaps simply buying it from the previous editor had necessitated her taking refuge in the Temple — but in Conti's haven she was safely protected from her creditors, for, as Mercier explained, "here the sheriff's exploits become null and void, arrest warrants expire on the threshold." [44] In this teeming, colorful microcosm, Mme de Beaumer could mingle inconspicuously with the crowds, and she obviously felt comfortable. Nearly every issue of her paper carried poems by the Temple's resident poet, the anticlerical abbé Mangenot, and publicity for Temple artisans and merchants whom she described with admiring affection.[45] She had chosen the safest place in Paris from which to launch her crusade.

But even in the Temple, where her person was out of danger, Mme de Beaumer could not escape the threat that her *Journal des dames* would be silenced, once it and she were perceived as political liabilities. Her printer, after all, was not within the walls. Sometime in December 1761 she must have been dealt a harsh warning, because her paper was henceforth drastically transformed. Although the *Nouveau Journal des dames*, as it was called after January 1762, continued her feminist campaign, it was suddenly intensely patriotic and royalist.

42. Ibid., 123–24. See also *Le Provincial à Paris, ou Etat actuel de Paris* (Paris, 1787), vol. *Quartier du Temple*, part 2, 155–56.

43. *Tableau de Paris*, ed. Gustave Desnoiresterres (Paris, 1853), 306.

44. Ibid., 305.

45. See, for example, *JD*, Oct. 1761, 94; Nov. 1761, 190, ads for Mme Martin and Mme Ravysi.

She was even persuaded to write a *Histoire militaire, ou Celle des
régiments de France dédiée à son altesse monseigneur le maréchal prince
de Soubise*. She announced in the January issue her project to "immor-
talize the deeds of those who gave their lives for the king, the *patrie . . . the state.*" [46] The prospectus for this work, hot off the press,
was sent to Malesherbes with a letter soliciting his goodwill. [47] The
same prospectus then appeared in the March issue of the *Journal des
dames*. France must win the war, Mme de Beaumer now argued, for
the glory of King Louis XV, "the love, the delight, the father of his
people, and the veneration of all the earth." Mme de Beaumer admitted that writing the *Histoire militaire* was difficult for her, since the
cause of women interested her far more than male heroism in battle.
But she would sacrifice all for the immediate needs of her *patrie*. [48]

We know from Mme de Beaumer's *Oeuvres mêlées* that she found
military history totally abhorrent. She must now have been persuaded
that drastic measures were necessary if she wished to maintain her
lifeline with her *Journal des dames* readers. Another English and Dutch
sympathizer, the abbé Raynal, had just been pressed into service for
France, "commissioned by government orders" to write an *Ecole militaire* which the *Mercure* applauded for "using the lives of great war-
riors to inspire and animate the young to defend our *patrie*." [49] For
Raynal's willingness to be tamed, he had even been rewarded with a
3,000-livre pension. [50] Mme de Beaumer sorely needed money and
must have thought her gesture foolproof. In an extra bid for approval,
she even dedicated her *Histoire militaire* to the prince de Soubise, the
king's closest friend and Mme de Pompadour's favorite general,
against whom public opinion had turned because the well-liked general de Broglie had been exiled for France's humiliating defeats while
Soubise continued to enjoy royal favor. [51] Grimm, pointing out the
similarities between Raynal's work and Mme de Beaumer's, implied
that too many such efforts could backfire. All these panegyrics seemed

46. *JD*, Jan. 1762, 58.   47. BN ms.fr. 22085, fol. 57.
48. *JD*, Mar. 1762, 289ff., "Prospectus pour l'*Histoire militaire*," 2–9. For a brief
discussion of Malesherbes's insistence that subjects demonstrate affection for their
ruler, see George A. Kelly, "The Political Thought of Lamoignon de Malesherbes,"
Political Theory 7, no. 4 (Nov. 1979): 485–508.
49. *Mercure*, July 1762, 66.   50. *Mémoires secrets*, 1:69.
51. See, for example, the mocking songs about Soubise in *Mémoires secrets*, 1:48–49,
57, 62–63.

almost impertinent when France's soldiers were performing no heroic deeds.[52]

During these months, Mme de Beaumer's feminism was permitted to continue, probably as a result of her political concessions to the authorities (she had even agreed to suppress entirely her list of eighty-one cities). She praised works by women, welcomed letters from readers supporting her efforts to make this the "siècle des dames,"[53] and adopted the suggestion of one subscriber who urged her to reclaim the French language from the men who had ravished it. "The career you pursue puts you in the unique position and gives you the right to use and make acceptable the feminized form of *author* and *editor*. . . . It is in fact a dishonor for women that such words are not in common parlance . . . since women have shown in literature that they can equal and surpass men." Delighted to accept the innovation of her sympathetic neologist, Mme de Beaumer henceforth referred to herself as *autrice* or *éditrice*, "since this question concerns the prerogatives of my sex, whose rights I uphold."[54] Mme de Beaumer continued to brandish her journalistic career as proof that women could do even the hardest jobs. To those who had expected the *Journal des dames* to be a mindless time killer, a triviality, she protested, "That is precisely what I am determined to avoid!" She portrayed herself as a teacher, guide, and *porte-parole*. "I love my sex; I have resolved to support and vindicate its honor and its rights."[55] She would show that women could be great historians and journalists. "We are daring enough to try and courageous enough to pursue careers." The very use of the term *autrice* she knew would offend male "purists and caustics" who, "jealous of our glory," could never admit women capable of independent thought. It was even rumored that a man was ghostwriting her own *Journal des dames*. This made her furious. "I am not and have never been the *dame* of any man; when one speaks of productions under my name, one should realize they are completely my own."[56]

In March 1762 Malesherbes and Mme de Beaumer's censor Marin, newly promoted to *censeur de la police*, suspended the *Journal des*

52. Friedrich Melchior Grimm, *Correspondance littéraire*, ed. Maurice Tourneur, 16 vols. (Paris, 1877–82), 5:76.

53. *JD*, Jan. 1762, 31–34; Feb. 1762, 195–97.   54. *JD*, Feb. 1762, 126–31.

55. *JD*, Mar. 1762, 223–24.

56. Ibid., "Prospectus pour l'*Histoire militaire*," following 288, especially 6–7.

dames. They refused to divulge their specific reasons to the editor, preferring to wear her down and break her spirit rather than confront her directly. A series of frantic letters from Mme de Beaumer protesting that she did indeed respect her superiors suggests that the general charge had been insubordination. The authorities simply did not trust her. She was indeed speaking glowingly of the king and the *patrie* in her paper now,[57] but her praise was fulsome, not reverential, and she had failed to write her promised *Histoire militaire.* Refusing to keep appointments with her, her censor sent her to Malesherbes, Malesherbes sent her to the police chief Sartine, Sartine sent her back to Marin, until the runaround put her in a frenzy. The *Journal des dames* was being delayed for months, costing her thousands of livres and numerous subscribers. "Why are you punishing me?" she asked Malesherbes, whose liberality towards men of letters was legendary. "I almost believe some evil genie has biased you against me. . . . The fatality that pursues me is without example. . . . I suffer deeply from your injustice."[58] She begged for a new censor, the busy but reputedly lenient Christophe Piquet.[59] When Malesherbes refused, she threatened to abandon her efforts in France and leave for a "freer foreign land." It may have been this threat that convinced Malesherbes to allow the *Journal des dames* to resume publication, although only under a substitute editor, a young man named Pierre Barnabé Farmain Du Rozoi. Perhaps the book-trade director reasoned that if Mme de Beaumer still had some stake, however benign, in a Parisian paper, she might not start up another, fiercer one in exile.

After April 1762 Mme de Beaumer's *Journal des dames* had left Conti's protection, and she listed her new address "at the home of M. le comte de Jaucourt, rue Mêlée, near the porte Saint Martin."[60] Houses on the rue Mêlée ran along the ramparts and backed onto the *boulevards,* the wide, newly popular promenades at the edge of the city where courtesans and countesses walked alongside each other in a crowded spectacle of street clowns, freaks, acrobats, merchants, and

57. See, for example, *JD,* Mar. 1762, 225–26.
58. Mme de Beaumer's letters from this period are in BN ms.fr. 22151, fols. 71–76.
59. On Piquet's activities, see Blangonnet, "Recherches sur les censeurs," 200–215. Of the 283 works he censored, nearly half were given *permissions,* indicating they were too dubious to receive a privilege but that Piquet still thought they should be read.
60. This was the address given for Mme de Beaumer in *JD* from April 1762 until April 1763, when she gave up the paper. In 1792 another feminist and republican, Mary Wollstonecraft, would live on the rue Mêlée and watch from her window as Louis XVI was wheeled by on the way from his prison in the Temple to his trial.

thieves. This new location was undoubtedly as much to Mme de Beaumer's liking as the Temple, for here was another neighborhood open to all estates, where the high- and lowborn mingled freely. Mme de Beaumer's new protector, a Huguenot nobleman with numerous relatives in Holland, was a direct descendant of Philippe du Plessis-Mornay, the probable author of *Vindiciae contra tyrannos*, a radical political treatise of the sixteenth century that proclaimed violent opposition to absolutism. Although much tamer than his ancestor, Comte Pierre de Jaucourt was active in his own right helping French Protestants fight for their civil liberties.[61] He was *premier gentilhomme* of the king's Protestant cousin Louis Joseph de Bourbon, prince de Condé, and the *Journal des dames* was now suddenly dedicated to Condé's daughter. How strenuously Jaucourt helped Mme de Beaumer is not clear. His main home, called the "Hôtel des Huguenots," was located on the rue de Grenelle in the prestigious faubourg Saint Germain. Mme de Beaumer probably visited there — in February her paper started carrying notices for female artisans on the rue de Grenelle — but she was not housed in the primary residence. Jaucourt was undoubtedly sympathetic to her cause. His younger brother, the chevalier de Jaucourt, was one of the most radical and outspoken male critics of women's historic subordination, as can be seen in his article "Wife" in the *Encyclopédie*. The comte de Jaucourt seemed willing to provide a base for Mme de Beaumer's travels and correspondence between Paris and Holland. By giving her a secretary, facilitating her Dutch connections, and putting a roof over her head, Jaucourt did more than anyone else for her, but he could not force the book-trade authorities to deal directly with her. And as long as they refused to see her, there was no point in her staying in Paris.

Du Rozoi, the ambitious nineteen-year-old to whom Mme de Beaumer now temporarily lent her paper, supported political positions that were antithetical to hers; he would spend his life in the service of the monarchy. He had probably volunteered to help with her *Histoire militaire*, for which his interest, unlike hers, was genuine. Later, under the protection first of Choiseul and then of Vergennes, he would edit a *Journal militaire* for the Ministry of Foreign Affairs in a labor of patri-

61. On Pierre de Jaucourt, see the introduction to *Correspondance du comte de Jaucourt, ministre intérimaire des affaires étrangères avec le prince de Talleyrand pendant le Congrès de Vienne publiée par son petit fils* (Paris, 1905). See also Jacob's *Radical Enlightenment*, 226–27.

otic love. During the Revolution his passionately royalist *Gazette de Paris* would round up hostages willing to exchange their lives for the imprisoned and condemned Louis XVI.[62] When he took over the *Journal des dames* in April 1762, he was already beginning to demonstrate his ability to charm the powerful. He eschewed ideological controversy and filled the paper with his own courtly poems and plays, delighted with the chance to advertise himself. The suspended paper was immediately allowed to resume publication under a new censor, the abbé Rousselet, who could find nothing objectionable in its light, affable tone. Mme de Beaumer appears not to have sold Du Rozoi the paper or taken him on as an official partner. Rather, she turned things over to him informally and temporarily, allowing him to use the paper for his personal aggrandizement as long as he kept it alive for her eventual return.

Meanwhile Mme de Beaumer rekindled her courage in Holland, collecting evidence that women were on the brink of an intellectual and social breakthrough. She may even have visited the spirited Lady Mary Wortley Montagu in England, whose reminiscences on smallpox inoculation and the place of women in society were featured in the *Journal des dames.*[63] Shortly after the Peace of Paris in 1763, Mme de Beaumer slipped back to France to give her paper one more try. She dismissed Du Rozoi and resumed her previous technique of simultaneously placating and jousting with the censors. She flattered Marin, "a man who never loses sight of those injured by blind fortune," and sang the greatness of the Bourbon name "written on the Book of Destiny," [64] but then she renewed her claim that the women's revolution was gripping the entire world. Her paper was an international affair, she boasted, essential for posterity, for the very survival of humanity. "The universe is my domain; I mean to sweep the horizon! My journal is widely known in every country of the world where the French language is spoken! Men everywhere are being forced to recognize that Nature made the two sexes equal." [65]

62. On Du Rozoi, see Jean Sgard, ed., *Dictionnaire des journalistes, 1600–1789* (Grenoble, 1976), 328 – 29; and Marc Martin, *Les Origines de la presse militaire en France à la fin de l'ancien régime et sous la Révolution (1770–1799)* (Château de Vincennes, 1975), 38 – 44 and passim. The only detailed account of his life is filled with serious inaccuracies. See, with caution, P. d'Estrée, "Farmin Du Rozoi," *Revue d'histoire littéraire de la France,* 1918: 211–42, 408 – 22, 562 – 79; 1922: 409 – 32; 1928: 24 – 29.
    63. *JD*, Aug. 1762, 161 – 80.   64. *JD*, Jan. 1763, 45 – 51; Apr. 1763, 61.
    65. *JD*, Jan. 1763, 39, 63, 67; Mar. 1763, 196 – 200.

Marin, displeased that Mme de Beaumer had returned to the scene, tried at first to belittle the problem by ridiculing the eccentric *"autrice,* as she styles herself,"* and pretending that she posed no serious threat. He shot off a letter to Malesherbes explaining that his usual techniques with women failed him now. "She has appeared this morning in my chambers, a large hat on her head, a long sword at her side, her chest (where there is nothing) and her behind (where there is not much) covered by a long culotte, and the rest of her body in a worn, narrow, black habit. Interrogated about the disguise, she replied that since she runs her paper alone, relying only upon herself, she dresses thus for reasons of economy and to be admitted to the [all male] parterre to review the latest play for 20 sous." The censor was frustrated that her lack of endowments prevented him from teasing that "the gentle curves of her stomach and the smoothness of her legs . . . would betray her." [66] But this levity belied the fact that Marin had come to view "the Beaumer woman" as an "offense to public morality," a writer of "uncommon rashness" and "singular indiscretion." [67] He had humored her in her feminism, but she was a political menace whose rantings he could no longer ignore. After failing to persuade her to repudiate the principles of a lifetime and convert the *Journal des dames* into a fashion magazine,[68] Marin found a technicality that served as an excuse to stop her. As a result, Mme de Beaumer's printer, Valleyre, paid her a visit explaining that "orders from higher up" prevented him from continuing to put out her paper, since she had sold it illegally from her home. This occasioned Mme de Beaumer's final letter to Malesherbes, a diatribe against privileged publishers and printers as government pawns, only the latest symbols in a never-ending saga of oppression. "I know their monopolies: that is why I have decided to renounce my paper." Why must authors, disseminators of truth, hold the beggar's pan, while corrupt booksellers feast on oysters? "It is pathetic to work like poor wretches [*misérables*] only to be ruined in the end." [69]

Mme de Beaumer had hoped, like Queen Christina of Sweden whom she greatly admired, to "make a mark upon the world." [70] But

66. BN ms.fr. 22135, fol. 90.

67. See Antoine Ricard, *Une Victime de Beaumarchais: Marin* (Paris, 1885), 52.

68. *JD*, Mar. 1763, 204–6, 306–7; Apr. 1763, 95.

69. BN ms.fr. 22135, fol. 91. Mme de Beaumer had earlier clashed with another *libraire,* from whom she had withdrawn her registers. See *JD*, Mar. 1762.

70. *JD*, Feb. 1762, 186.

she now sacrificed her pursuit of her own glory for her cause, realizing that personal animosity toward her threatened to thwart her *Journal des dames* entirely. This paper was an essential channel of communication that, however narrow, needed to remain open. She disappeared to Holland, never to be heard from again. Before she left, however, she found a worthy successor, a woman sufficiently connected in *le monde* to win the book-trade authorities' blessing yet daring enough to serve as *prête-nom* for the increasingly *frondeur* fare supplied by her male collaborators. Mme de Beaumer had set a precedent, linking the cause of women to far broader social and political reforms. Never again would the *Journal des dames* be benign.

Mme de Maisonneuve, who bought the paper from Mme de Beaumer for 3,000 livres in cash in April 1763, took an altogether different but equally courageous approach to her journalistic career. She had an impeccable sense of timing, understood the flow of politics, and meant to advance the cause of women by riding with, not against, the tide. She wanted success, not martyrdom, and was motivated less by ideological zeal than by her desire to pilot the *Journal des dames* to glory. As time went by, however, Mme de Maisonneuve became increasingly willing to make her life more exciting by taking risks. That she got involved at all with Mme de Beaumer's discredited paper shows from the outset a readiness to live dangerously.

In fact Mme de Maisonneuve was bored. Her testament shows that she had married a man in financial circles named Joubert — although she kept her maiden name and identified strongly with female family members — and that her brother was a valet in the king's wardrobe.[71] She had climbed from a home in the sleepy Saint Avoye neighborhood through a series of moves to a house on the prestigious rue Saint Honoré in a *quartier* dominated by the Palais Royal, the Louvre, and the magnificent newer mansions of the financial nobility.[72] Yet she

71. A sketch of Mme de Maisonneuve's testament is in a *registre de décès* at the Archives de la Seine, DC⁶256, fol. 64ᵛ.
72. These successive addresses are given in Mme de Maisonneuve's volumes of *JD* for May/June/July 1763, Mar. 1764, and Nov. 1764. On the atmosphere of the different *quartiers*, see Pierre-Thomas-Nicolas Hurtaut and Magny, *Dictionnaire historique de la ville de Paris et ses environs* (Paris, 1779), 4:186 – 97. For an excellent discussion of the migrations of Paris's social-climbing financiers, whose pattern Mme de Maisonneuve followed exactly, see Yves Durand, *Les Fermiers généraux au XVIIIᵉ siècle* (Paris, 1971), especially his chapter "L'Espace quotidien," 445 – 503, 645. Mme de Maisonneuve was in an ideal position to benefit from both her brother's and her husband's perquisites. The latter, a *commis au ferme*, could have been greatly helped by her brother's associa-

found the life of the idle, rich woman intolerably dull, as she explained in the early issues of her *Journal des dames*. She envied boys whose studies challenged them, prepared them for adversity, and stocked their minds.[73] She may not have seen herself shuttling about Europe in a black suit fomenting a feminist revolution, but she felt stifled in an atmosphere that required no more of her than a smile, a beautiful gown, and the kind of gracious hostessing described by an admirer to whom she had once most delicately served pears.[74]

The new editor deftly used her social station to achieve her goal. Unhampered by her predecessor's fierce independence and suspicion of male helpers, Mme de Maisonneuve welcomed whatever assistance she could get from men sympathetic to "the woman question." She would contribute her name, money, and protection to the enterprise, but she saw an association with men of letters as a necessity, not because she felt inferior but simply because she was new at the game. She also chose a propitious moment for this journalistic debut. Her brother was rewarded frequently by the *maison du roi* with extra pensions and vacations in foreign lands, and this royal generosity peaked just when she took on the *Journal des dames*.[75] Mme de Maisonneuve now became another beneficiary of monarchical goodwill. Choiseul's wife subscribed to her paper, and in June 1765 the proud editor had the personal honor of presenting it to the king at Versailles. Mme de Maisonneuve herself was made a *pensionnaire du roi* to the tune of 1,000 livres a year.[76] The *Mémoires secrets* predicted that her paper would soar in popularity, and the *Mercure* dignified the now competi-

---

tion with the royal household. See Durand, 87, 118. A delightful song described the scenario of success (ibid., 233):

> On voyait des commis
> mis
> Comme des princes
> Après être venus
> nus
> De leurs provinces

73. *JD*, May/June/July 1763, 36. Mme d'Epinay's similar frustrations are discussed in G. Roth, ed., *Les Pseudo-Mémoires de Mme d'Epinay: Histoire de Mme de Montbrillant* (Paris, 1951), 1:239.

74. *JD*, Jan. 1764, 31.

75. See AN F4 1940 d and F4 1941 g for some pensions awarded Jean-Baptiste de Maisonneuve in 1758 and 1759, and O¹108, fol. 162, "Brevet lui permettant d'aller en Espagne et d'y rester six mois" (22 Apr. 1764).

76. *JD* of May 1765, which appeared two months late, announced on p. 119 that the newspaper's April issue had been presented at court on Friday, 21 June. The Dec. 1765 issue printed on the title page that Mme de Maisonneuve was now a *pensionnaire du roi*. The poem for which she was awarded this pension appeared in the July 1765 *JD*, 5–6.

tive *Journal des dames* with a law suit.[77] Meanwhile, Mme de Maisonneuve announced triumphantly to the world and to Sartine, Malesherbes's successor as director of the book trade, that a woman had
finally achieved spectacular journalistic success.[78] In less than three
years, she had managed to quadruple the worth of her paper; having
bought it for 3,000 livres, she sold it for 12,000. How had she turned the
moribund *Journal des dames* into a thriving business, sound enough to
attract the canny *libraire* Panckoucke?[79]

Things had been hard at the start. Although Malesherbes approved
her as the paper's new editor, the directors of the postal service set
down stringent and expensive terms for her provincial and foreign
subscriptions. Their experience with Mme de Beaumer's erratic mailings to *libraires* in her imaginary worldwide following, for which
neither she nor the recipients paid, led them to try to recover some of
the funds owed to them. But they cast themselves in a policing role as
well. Had Mme de Beaumer perhaps been sending clandestine *nouvelles*, manuscript *notes à l'épingle* inside her bound volumes? The
poste now insisted that the new editor send each issue *sous bande*,
securely wrapped, and stipulated that no other papers could be
slipped in. Thirty different postal officials were to receive free copies
of each month's issue to examine. "This subscription," the document
concluded ominously, "will last only as long as it pleases the gentle-
men of the postal firm to grant it." [80]

Soon, however, Mme de Maisonneuve persuaded the authorities
she was above suspicion. The *poste* was converted from watchdog to
benefactor, allowing the new editor special discount rates for the
Journal des dames sent jointly with other periodicals.[81] Yet Mme de
Maisonneuve's paper was anything but bland. The secret was her

77. Bachaumont, *Mémoires secrets*, 16:274, 294; BN ms.fr. 22085, fols. 9 and 10,
describe the reasons for the *Mercure*'s suit and show that there was indeed a scramble
for the issues of 1765, which became rare collector's items.

78. BN ms.fr. 22085, fol. 7, and *JD*, Jan. 1765, "Avertissement," especially 4.

79. Charles-Joseph Panckoucke, who had one of the best noses for commercial
success in his day, was principal distributor of *JD* from October 1764 to December 1765.

80. "Extrait de la soumission que MM. les fermiers généraux des postes ont fait
souscrire à Mme de Maisonneuve," in *JD*, Nov. 1763, 117. The paper also continued to
carry notices urging Mme de Beaumer's former subscribers to pay their debts. See, for
example, *JD*, Dec. 1763, 119; Feb. 1764, 120.

81. *JD*, Oct. 1766, 103. For an excellent discussion of the ways the *poste* could assist in
periodical diffusion and distribution, see René Moulinas, *L'Imprimerie, la librairie, et la
presse à Avignon au XVIIIᵉ siècle* (Grenoble, 1974), 379ff. See also E. Vaillé, *Histoire
générale des postes françaises*, vol. 6 (Paris, 1951–53). Unfortunately, Vaillé's promised
volume on the *poste* and the *presse* never appeared.

confident, measured tone and the fact that, even though she treated piquant issues, she stayed always within fashionable limits, striking the perfect balance of spice and respectability. There was none of her predecessor's belligerent rhetoric. She made strong claims for women's intellectual abilities, but when letters from subscribers indicated her tone was too intimidating, she responded graciously, saying her paper was intended to satisfy all classes of female citizens.[82] She nevertheless insisted that her paper treat serious matters, although she was careful not to take sides. It discussed the philosophes, who were back in favor now that France's paranoia in the Seven Years' War had eased. The *Journal des dames* followed the activities of Marmontel, d'Alembert, and Choiseul's friend Voltaire and praised Catherine of Russia's special support of Diderot, for which the empress actually thanked Mme de Maisonneuve with a golden snuffbox. The paper came out loud and clear in favor of Calas's pardon and religious toleration, a topic in style with the philosophes.[83] But the editor did not push cosmopolitanism and *philosophie* too far. The powerful Choiseul, whose wife subscribed to the *Journal des dames*, was still smarting from the humiliations of the war. He had just been instrumental in suppressing the "too-worldly" Jesuits and, as a secret supporter of the parlements and their constitutional claims, was eager to rekindle French patriotism. The paper therefore printed a number of long articles on the education of patriots, to encourage even "citoyens sans fortune" to love and sacrifice for the state. Courses and services were advertised reaching beyond the moneyed elite. "All people are not made to be philosophes," stated the *Journal des dames*, "but all are made to be active citizens."[84]

Mme de Maisonneuve, determined to use her paper to bring current issues to the fore, thus reflected all the fashionable and sometimes inconsistent currents of the day. There was something for everyone, and this diplomacy was rendered into a delicious confection with plentiful *pièces fugitives*, music articles, theater reviews, and flattery for Marin.[85] She was assisted by a young Lyonnais, Mathon de la Cour,

82. For Mme de Maisonneuve's strong feminist claims, see *JD*, May/June/July 1763, "Nouveau prospectus," 7–9; Aug./Sept./Oct. 1763, 93; Jan. 1764, 106; June 1764, 33–45; Oct. 1764, 46; Oct. 1765, 9. For her accommodation of women "less occupied by serious study," see *JD*, Jan. 1764, 106; Feb. 1764, 99.

83. *JD*, Nov. 1763, 68; Dec. 1763, 10; Apr. 1765, 56, 71–86.

84. *JD*, Sept. 1764, 29–35; Feb. 1765, 56–65; Mar. 1765, 32–38; Apr. 1765, 41–46.

85. *JD*, Nov. 1763, 75; May 1765, 88–103; June 1765, 58.

who had come to Paris to seek his literary fortune and whose fledgling
Lettres à Mme*** sur les peintures had won the approval of Mme de
Pompadour. Mathon, from a family of magistrates and academicians,
had good looks, good manners, and an easy intelligence. Together he
and Mme de Maisonneuve concocted a paper that appealed to readers
and authorities alike. And from 1763 until the end of 1765, Mathon was
satisfied with that.

The year 1766 was a turning point for the *Journal des dames*. The
privileged *Mercure*'s successful suit against it, "to curtail [its] progress . . . and to limit the amount and kind of material [it] could
treat," [86] deprived the paper of its sugar coating. No longer could the
editors print theater reviews and *pièces fugitives*, no longer could they
hide behind such camouflage. Mme de Maisonneuve, perhaps wanting to avoid direct policy decisions at this crossroads, turned the paper
over completely to Mathon, but she trusted him enough to insist that
her name remain on the title page and that she be able to continue
presenting the paper to "the crowned heads of Europe." [87] Panckoucke, who had been publishing the paper since October 1764, now
dropped the distribution of the *Journal des dames*, doubtless sensing
that its honeymoon was over and that Mathon's articles, forced to
stand naked and unadorned, might be too controversial. After all,
Mathon came from a family of Jansenist magistrate patriots in Lyons. [88]
He could play the debonair Parisian only so long; as the *remontrances*
of the parlements against the Crown reached fever pitch in the
mid-1760s, his true provincial loyalties emerged. He chose to sell the
Journal des dames through the Durand family, daring publishers considered by the police inspector Joseph d'Hémery to be among "the
most sly and suspect of the book trade." [89] Documents also show that
he found himself a new, sympathetic censor, Arnoult, himself the son
of a magistrate, who lived in 1767 with the Gilbert de Voisin family,
famous judges and lawyers fighting for the civil rights of Protestants. [90]

86. Bachaumont, *Mémoires secrets*, 16:294; BN ms.fr. 22085, fol. 10.
87. BN ms.fr. 22085, fol. 10.
88. For the scant biographical information on Mathon, see *Archives historiques et
statistiques du département du Rhône* 6 (1827): 300–305; occasional references to him and
his father in Louis Trenard, *Lyon, de l'Encyclopédie au préromantisme* (Paris, 1958),
especially 1:127, 137–39, 177, 216–17, 226, 246, 282; and Leon Vallas, *La Musique à
l'Académie de Lyon au XVIIIᵉ siècle* (Lyons, 1908), 175, 178–80, 189, 193–200, 227.
89. See Micheline Zephir, "Les Libraires et imprimeurs parisiens à la fin du XVIIIᵉ
siècle" (Thèse de l'Ecole des chartes, Paris, 1974), 275, copy in AN AB XXVIII (208).
90. BN ms.fr. 21993, fol. 54, no. 815, shows that Arnoult had become Mathon's
censor. The *Almanach royal* for 1767 (405–8) shows his residence *chez* Gilbert de Voisin.

Then Mathon, with Mme de Maisonneuve's blessing, used the *Journal des dames* far more boldly.

Mathon had hinted earlier, in one of the paper's poems, that he himself was "destined for the bench," the most "austere but honorable career" a citizen could undertake in pursuit of liberty and justice.[91] He did not become a member of the bar, but his interests grew increasingly serious. He filled the *Journal des dames* with articles on the great legislator Lycurgus, on the glories of Spartan and Roman values, on the republican ideas of Rousseau (whom he may even have met in 1767).[92] He attacked *le luxe* and pushed the "public good," the "commonweal." Mathon later portrayed Paris as "a monstrous vampire that sucks, saps, and devours the rest of the state";[93] already in the *Journal des dames* he sympathized openly with people who wished to cut the profligate spending of the court and spread wealth throughout the realm. He wrote on the importance of commerce and industry.[94] He praised the Physiocrats' periodical, the *Ephémérides du citoyen*, for its open criticism of flaws in society.[95] When Laverdy—a frugal, hardworking parlementaire and Jansenist who with Conti and Conti's bailiff Le Paige had orchestrated the Jesuits' expulsion — became controller general, Mathon paid him a verse tribute in the *Journal des dames*, praising his efforts to curb royal extravagance.[96] Mathon knew and admired Benjamin Franklin and the republican "friends of man" with whom Franklin was associated. Mathon's later *Journal de Lyon* was strongly pro-American, and he wrote *Testament de M. Fortuné Ricard* in the 1780s, a hymn to public utility and frugality that was often attributed to Franklin.[97] Franklin and Mathon, whose father had written on music and mathematics for the Académie de Lyon, shared a love for science, inventions, and instruments. The *Journal des dames* became full of descriptions of scientific "curiosities," and the only

91. *JD*, June 1764, 16–17.

92. See the issues of *JD* for Sept. 1766, Jan., July, Aug., and Sept. 1767, and Jan. 1768.

93. *Discours sur les meilleurs moyens de faire naître et d'encourager le patriotisme dans une monarchie* (Paris, 1787), "Avertissement" and 13–14, 46–50, 53, 55. In spite of his republican leanings, Mathon could never bring himself to favor the king's beheading and was guillotined for insufficient radicalism in November 1793.

94. *JD*, June 1765, 31–33.   95. *JD*, Dec. 1765, 69.

96. *JD*, May 1764, 3. For Laverdy's *frondeur* activities, see Dale Van Kley, *The Jansenists and the Expulsion of the Jesuits from France, 1757–1765* (New Haven, 1975), especially 45, 52, 85, 128, 133–36, 231.

97. For Grimm's favorable review of Mathon's *Testament de M. Fortuné Ricard* and its similarities to Franklin's projects for Philadelphia and Boston, see *Correspondance littéraire*, 14:188.

illustration in its fifty-odd volumes was a beautiful foldout engraving of Franklin's glass harmonica. It may even have been Franklin who interested Mathon in Freemasonry, for now the *Journal des dames* published Masonic poems, reviewed books on Masonry, praised the late journalist-Mason Pierre Clément's *Cinq Années littéraires*, and lauded the Masonic virtues of *zèle, douceur, candeur, honnêteté*, and, above all, *bienfaisance*.[98]

Mathon's journalism became bold for other reasons as well. Despite his auspicious beginnings, he had failed to make it in *le monde*. He had come to resent Paris snobbery and identified more and more with the ostracized and persecuted Rousseau. Grimm had a heyday mocking the "provincial vulgarity" of the spin-off of the *Journal des dames*, the *Almanach des muses*, an annual poetry anthology that Mathon and his friend Sautreau de Marsy started up in 1765.[99] He had been competing for years in the essay competitions of the Académie française and losing each time to the philosophes' darling, La Harpe. The "republic of letters," it seemed to him, was deaf to new talent. And he had become impressed by the young Louis-Sébastien Mercier, another unsuccessful contender for academic honors, whose writings Mathon found fresh, vigorous, energetic, gutsy, intense. Mercier, he argued, was far more vital and original than the "feeble, prosaic, and cowardly" La Harpe who got all the honors.[100] While Grimm and the literary establishment branded Mercier a base and vulgar outsider, Mathon filled his *Journal des dames* with thirty- and forty-page excerpts of Mercier's work, attacking tyranny, social inequality, and the hoarding of grain for profit while peasants starved. "The liberty, comfort, and happiness of subjects," wrote Mercier in a typical passage, "are more important than the glory, grandeur, and power of the realm." [101] Mathon now fiercely attacked writers, like his former friend the poet Claude-Joseph Dorat, who wrote for "fun" rather than committing themselves to a useful cause.[102] Artists were citizens first; they

98. *JD*, July 1765, 61; Oct. 1766, 31–54; Dec. 1766, 50. For Mathon's involvement in Masonry in Lyons, see his *Discours prononcé dans la loge d'adoption du patriotisme* (Lyons, 1785), discussed in Trenard, *Lyon, de l'Encyclopédie*, 1: 177–78.

99. Grimm, *Correspondance littéraire*, 4:433, 473; 7:224–25; 8:445–46.

100. For criticisms of La Harpe, see *JD*, Dec. 1764, 116; Jan. 1765, passim; Apr. 1766, 85.

101. *JD*, June 1768, 35–63, especially 49–51, 60–61. For more praise of Mercier, see *JD*, Sept. 1765, 74; Sept. 1766, 46; Oct. 1766, 61–79; Mar. 1767, 66–67. For Grimm's negative remarks on Mercier's writings of this period, see, for example, *Correspondance littéraire*, 7:300, 309, 377.

102. *JD*, July 1766, 89.

should work not for personal recognition but to stretch human potential and improve the world. He attacked the *Nécrologe des hommes célèbres* for being too elitist, for glorifying men whose high birth distinguished them but who did nothing for humanity. The *Nécrologe* responded by accusing Mathon of political irresponsibility, of wanting to diminish the distance between the greats and the "most vulgar of men" and of therefore being "completely mad."[103]

Mme de Maisonneuve had continued to lend her name to the *Journal des dames* throughout Mathon's progressive rebelliousness. She had watched him unabashedly declare his support for parlement's fight against "despotism," for *frondeur* writers like Mercier, for academic rejects and establishment outcasts in general. She had even overlooked for years his chronic lateness and chaotic handling of the business — far from appearing at regular monthly intervals, Mathon's issues were as much as six months behind schedule. He had also failed to pay her an agreed-upon pension. All this she had tolerated apparently without embarrassment, because she liked his politics and admired the various philanthropic projects he was setting up in Lyons — trade schools, farming collectives, water purification experiments.[104] As long as Choiseul remained powerful, the *Journal des Dames* had little to fear, but as the political climate turned hostile to him in the late 1760s, Mme de Maisonneuve's position became untenable. The new chancellor, René de Maupeou, an ardent royalist, was already planning the suppression of the refractory parlements. In January 1769 Mathon's *permission* to continue the paper was denied by Sartine, and its publication was suspended, the documents say vaguely, by "superior orders." As much for Mathon's protection as her own, Mme de Maisonneuve never "exercised her right to relaunch it."[105] In the heyday of the Jansenist triumph after the expulsion of the Jesuits, she had made clear in her paper her hostility to the *dévots*, denouncing them as "hypocrites."[106] But now the political pendulum had swung completely. With Mme Du Barry, the new ministry, and the arch-

103. JD, Apr. 1768, 78–79. For the response, see *Nécrologe des hommes célèbres*, 1769:247–53.

104. See *JD*, Nov. 1767, "Avis" and 61. That Mathon's issues were extremely late can be seen by comparing the official dates on their title pages with the date at the bottom when they were *achevé d'imprimer;* see also BN ms.fr. 22085, fol. 10. For descriptions of Mathon's philanthropic projects, see *Archives du Rhône* and J. B. Dumas, *Histoire de l'Académie des sciences, belles-lettres et arts de Lyon* (Lyons, 1839), 1:329–31.

105. BN ms.fr. 21993, fol. 154, no. 815; BN ms.fr. 22085, fol. 10.

106. JD, May 1764, 78.

bishop of Paris all favoring the dispersed Jesuits, it seemed best to keep quiet. The conservative Marin, Mme de Beaumer's old foe, had been catapulted to power by Maupeou and now, as editor of the official *Gazette de France*, was paid 10,000 livres a year to uphold the absolutist thesis.[107] Mme de Maisonneuve favored reform, but not political suicide: so long as Maupeou and his despotic "triumvirate" reigned, that is, until 1774, the *Journal des dames* remained silent.

The last female editor, the baronne de Prinzen (or Princen or Prinzenne — all three spellings appear), was the widow of a German nobleman and a protégée of the teenage dauphine Marie Antoinette. Born Marie Emilie Mayon in Aix-en-Provence in 1736, she described herself as "plus que bourgeoise, sans être de qualité," the daughter of "respectable parents who struck a happy medium between the idle nobility and the laborious commoners."[108] Marriage to a much older baron had forced her into a social whirl at court, a life of "perfumed parties and pleasures" that she disliked as much as her husband adored them. His extravagance soon exhausted their fortune. According to her story, he literally died of shame (being a "weak soul"), but she welcomed the return to more modest circumstances, the "freedom" of being unattached again, the chance to care for her little daughters.[109] In October 1774 she married again, becoming Mme de Montanclos, but this union was no more successful than the first. Documents reveal that within months of the wedding the couple legally separated, and she went to live in her own house in Paris on the rue des Bernardins near the place Maubert, while he retired to Troyes in Champagne.[110] The ambitious and independent Mme de Montanclos had something of Mme de Beaumer's fiery spirit, although she

107. Denise Aimé Azam, "Le Ministère des affaires étrangères et la presse à la fin de l'ancien régime," *Cahiers de la presse*, July 1938:428–38. See also Charles Aubertin, *L'Esprit public au XVIIIᵉ siècle* (Paris, 1889), 276–77.

108. *JD*, Dec. 1774, 194. This appears in an anonymous but largely autobiographical piece, "Réflexions d'une solitaire aux Iles d'Hyères." Although the baronne de Prinzen never claimed these as her own in the newspaper, she later included them in her two-volume *Oeuvres de Mme de Montanclos* (Paris, 1792) and published them again separately. See A. F. Delandine, *Bibliothèque de Lyon: Catalogue des livres qu'elle renferme dans la classe des belles-lettres* (Paris and Lyons, n.d.), 2:263, 313.

109. *JD*, Dec. 1774, 194–205. In *Biographie universelle des contemporaines* (Paris, 1834), 3:647, Alphonse Rabbe appears to have based his brief notice on Mme de Montanclos, which does not cite any sources, on this account.

110. See AN Minutier Central (hereafter MC), étude 85, liasse 652 (19 Apr. 1775 and attached documents dated 11 Apr. 1775).

JOURNAL

DES

DAMES,

DEDIÉ

A MADAME

LA DAUPHINE,

Par Madame la Baronne DE PRINCEN.

JANVIER 1774.

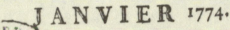

A PARIS;

Chez LACOMBE, rue Chriſtine.

M. D. CC. LXXIV.

Cover of the *Journal des dames*, January 1774.

was more polished and distinctly more maternal. "Ô, la cruelle chose d'être auteur femelle!" [111] she cried out in the midst of a conflict with the Comédie-Française. And she later confessed to Mercier, to whom she turned over the paper and whose close friend she remained, that whatever successes she had in life were won by "baring her teeth to men." [112] Still, familiarity with life at court had taught her how to curry favor, play games, and secure connections. She decided to use those skills to relaunch the *Journal des dames*.

The young dauphine Marie Antoinette, to whom the paper was now dedicated, was deeply hostile to Maupeou's triumvirate for having ousted her old friend Choiseul and for having barred her from any influence at court. The Austrian princess, out of boredom and frustration with her husband's sexual insufficiency, flirted with Comte Axel de Fersen and her brother-in-law, the comte d'Artois, and spent her idle hours enjoying the plays of Beaumarchais and Mercier, plays born of republican and even popular sympathies. Both of these writers were declared foes of Maupeou's ministry. During 1773 Beaumarchais, close friend of Mme de Beaumer's former protector the prince de Conti, had used a series of best-selling, seditious *mémoires* to pulverize the chancellor for his exiling of the parlements and his repressive censorship. Although the police tried desperately to confiscate them and discipline their author, Marie Antoinette fought to get his politically challenging *Barber of Seville* performed. The dauphine also loved the *drames* of Mercier, which the royally protected Comédie-Française refused to perform or even read. "Poor queen," wrote a commentator on her penchant for these two revolutionary writers, "she walked carefree, oblivious, and blind, never suspecting the venom, hatred, and revengeful anger hidden in the comic poet's laughter and the *dramomane*'s tears." [113] The *Journal des dames*'s shady past thus did not frighten Marie Antoinette; she was probably even pleased to sponsor a paper by a bright, outspoken woman twice her age who proposed to uphold her as an intelligent, virtuous model for the whole female sex.

The baronne de Prinzen had been biding her time, waiting for the right moment to start up her journal. By the end of 1773, in large part

111. Archives du Théâtre Français, dossier "Mme de Montanclos," letter dated 10 Feb. 1783. I am indebted to Sylvie Chevalley, former archivist of the Comédie-Française, for supplying me with additional information on the journalist's relations with the actors and, in particular, on their voting record on the plays she submitted.

112. BN nouv.acq.fr. 24030, fols. 87–88.

113. V. Hallays-Dabot, *Histoire de la censure théâtrale en France* (Paris, 1862), 140.

because of Beaumarchais's *mémoires*, it appeared that Maupeou was losing his grip. The clandestine *Journal historique*, whose author, Pidansat de Mairobert, later became a censor of the *Journal des dames*, had begun in October to report a widespread lack of support for the "despotic tribunal" of Maupeou. Maupeou's detractors, predicting his overthrow, had become more outspoken; he was now described as sallow and sickly, "sometimes yellow, sometimes green," "the horror of the nation," "the most repugnant countenance on which one could spit."[114] And there was another hopeful sign. A playwright named Jean-Baptiste Artaud, whom the baronne considered a kindred spirit, had just joined the ranks of royal censors.[115] Artaud had landed this post during a fleeting moment as protégé of the powerful duc de Duras, gentleman of the king's bedchamber and the head of the Comédie's governing board. But Artaud lost favor with Duras almost immediately, for he could not hide his republican sympathies, his love for street theater, his *frondeur* leanings. Artaud wrote a eulogy for the boulevard actor Taconet, a great man overlooked by the elitist *Nécrologe* because of his humble birth. In it, Artaud denounced high society and the exclusive "corps politiques de la littérature" in much the same terms that Mathon and Mercier had used.[116] The baronne de Prinzen felicitously arranged to get Artaud as censor for her *Journal des dames*'s first few issues, although his aversion to the capital was such that he left after a few months to become editor of the *Courrier d'Avignon*, a paper operating somewhat outside the system of French censorship and relatively challenging to the regime.[117]

The baronne de Prinzen tactfully refused to discuss the political reasons behind the "successive revolutions" and stormy past of the

---

114. J. de Maupeou, *Le Chancelier Maupeou* (Paris, 1942), 70, 72, 166, 192, and similar descriptions in Edgar Faure, *Le Disgrâce de Turgot* (Paris, 1961), 11. See also Charles Collé, *Journal historique* (Paris, 1807), 3:520.

115. Artaud's signature appeared at the end of the *JD* issues of early 1774. Although the paper still lacked a royal privilege, it had now a *permission de sceau* and so was formally processed and bore its censor's printed name for the first time since its founding in 1759. The baronne de Prinzen had first obtained a *permission tacite* (BN ms.fr. 21989, IIIe registre, fol. 48), but the status of the paper was then upgraded to a *permission scellée* (BN ms.fr. 22013, IIIe registre, no. 30). Artaud is mentioned briefly in Georges Grente, ed., *Dictionnaire des lettres françaises, XVIIIe siècle* (Paris, 1960), 1:112. See also the chevalier de Mouhy's *Abrégé de l'histoire du Théâtre Français* (Paris, 1780), 2:8. He appears in the *Almanach royal* as a censor only in the year 1774.

116. *Taconet, ou Mémoire historique pour servir à la vie de cet homme célèbre, article oublié dans le Nécrologe de 1775* (Amsterdam, n.d.), especially 11, 30, 42, 47, 51–52.

117. See Moulinas, *L'Imprimerie, la librairie, et la presse à Avignon*, and Jack R. Censer's article in this collection.

Journal des dames, and she did her best to set it on a solid foundation. She flattered not only the dauphine, whose help she needed in the "hazardous career" she had undertaken, but also the dauphine's favorite brother-in-law, Artois, and her confidante the comtesse de Noailles: "In your heart she finds her sweetest shelter. . . . Play Maecenas to Antoinette . . . for without her continued approval, I am nothing." [118] The editor then described approvingly the controversial *Iphigenia* by Gluck, the dauphine's former Viennese music master; she praised Choiseul, still exiled in Chanteloup, whom Marie Antoinette fervently wished to restore to power.[119]

But the journalist was too independent to find such elaborate courtship easy. Hustling at Versailles was exhausting and soon distasteful. She felt herself too old for such aggravation. Was it not ridiculous for a middle-aged woman with small children to be fawning over dissipated royal teenagers? The *Journal des dames* carried a poem to a helpful babysitter, Mme Marchais, who took care of the "troupeau" of Prinzen offspring at court while the baronne "romped" with people who preferred "pleasures and delights" to motherhood.[120] And sometimes her best intentions backfired, her most graceful overtures turned clumsy. When she heaped praise on a portrait of Marie Antoinette by the artist de Lorge that everyone else found unflattering, she felt obliged to make a public apology in the *Journal des dames*, explaining that she had seen the picture at the Tuileries before it became smudged in transit to Versailles where everyone else saw it.[121]

All of this took its toll on the journalist, a quick-tempered, emotional woman who found criticism at once infuriating and shattering. As the months went by, she worried less about pleasing her protectress in order to solidify her own reputation and more about being of service to her female readers. The topic of motherhood, though a delicate, even painful subject for Marie Antoinette, who was rumored to be barren, nevertheless received increasing attention in the *Journal des dames*, as did the idea that intellectually inclined women should be able to play a public role if they so chose.

Once the dauphine became queen in May 1774, the journalist expected her to take responsibility for social injustice and to help women

118. *JD*, Jan. 1774, "Dédicace," 7–9, 106, 113, 119.
119. *JD*, Oct. 1774, 223; Mar. 1775, 340–51; Jan. 1775, 80–81.
120. *JD*, Feb. 1774, 142.   121. *JD*, Mar. 1775, 384–89.

reclaim their dignity. The paper attacked court frivolity, moral dissi-
pation, and *le luxe* more forcefully than ever. That the new queen was
neither virtuous nor maternal did not stop the baronne de Prinzen
from calling on her to "reverse the *goût du siècle*" by making feminine
modesty, seriousness, and fidelity fashionable.[122] After the editor became Mme de Montanclos in the fall and moved to Paris, she made an
even more pronounced break with prevailing aristocratic values. Although the *Journal des dames* continued to carry advertisements for
cosmetics made by the Maille family, *vinaigriers du roi,* for outrageous
coiffures and bonnets designed by the fashionable M. Beaulard, and
foldout pages of *contredanses* with music, the paper was directed more
and more to *mères de famille* who had turned from vain pastimes to
tender parenting and had hence become solid *citoyennes.*[123]

Mme de Montanclos's feminism was more complex, subtle, and
many-sided than that of her two female predecessors, for it was combined with great admiration for Rousseau's works on both the political
and emotional levels. Curious as it may seem, Mme de Montanclos
believed that Rousseau had done a great deal for feminine self-esteem.
The *Nouvelle Héloïse* had just appeared when Mme de Beaumer was
handing over the *Journal des dames* to Mme de Maisonneuve in the
early 1760s, and the impact of its ideal of motherhood had not yet been
felt. Besides, the first two female editors appear to have been childless
— the first lived alone *au Temple* in a furnished room, the second
mentioned no children in her will — and probably never wrestled
with the problem of coordinating independent ambitions and family.
Both resented Rousseau's dim view of women's intellectual capacities
and could not appreciate his arguments for their moral superiority,
their unique role in forging bonds of affection and shaping character.
But since then, for over a decade, Rousseau's ideas had been working a
revolution in feminine psychology, and by the 1770s many women,
especially mothers, had come to see him as their champion rather than
their foe. They were among his most ardent fans and enthusiastic
readers. He made them feel socially useful. It was he who insisted
upon their special contribution of love and firm but gentle guidance to
the moral regeneration of society and to public felicity. The "mère

122. JD, Aug. 1774, 246–47.
123. See, for example, advertisements in JD, June 1774, 238; Jan. 1775, 135; Mar. 1775,
393. For more serious articles, see JD, Mar. 1774, 36; Dec. 1774, 257; Jan. 1775, 151; Feb.
1775, 266; Apr. 1775, 123, 128.

tendre" was of prime importance to the strength of the state. From
breast-feeding through sensitive, relaxed, yet practical home education of their young, mothers not only cemented their families but
provided the moral backbone of the *patrie*. Rousseau had of course
argued the inequality of the sexes and denied women any public role,
but he had greatly enhanced their status in the home, and his heroine
Julie symbolized pride and embodied his vision of the mother as a
spiritual reformer and a strong, virtuous individual.[124] Women, Rousseau stressed, must never try to be like men. They should nurture,
civilize, and tame their mates and children as only the female sex could
do, and they must believe this was not only a useful function but one
both dignified and essential. Through the home, the mother's empire,
she made her invaluable civic contribution.[125]

Mme de Montanclos's *Journal des dames* was profoundly influenced
by Rousseau. The editor, who had several small children, portrayed
them as joyful, precious little beings with whom it was a pleasure,
even a privilege to spend time.[126] She treated motherhood as a right
that women had to reclaim and show themselves worthy of exercising.
It was an awesome responsibility, but not a burden. Teaching children
could even be a shared delight. The educational theories of Fromageot
and Fourcroy, both disciples of Rousseau, received extended coverage. Mothers were shown how to teach their sons and daughters
themselves at home, rather than turn them over to "mercenaries."[127]
Because women, "nature's most cherished creation," could "join to
the light of philosophy the warmth of feeling," they could mold their
offspring with a unique blend of "wisdom, kindness, and pa-
tience."[128] Particular attention was given to the education of girls, as
future mothers who would themselves need to carry on the tradition.

In her paper, Mme de Montanclos admitted no conflict between her

124. See Jean H. Bloch, "Women and the Reform of the Nation," and P. D. Jimack,
"The Paradox of Sophie and Julie: Contemporary Response to Rousseau's Ideal Wife
and Ideal Mother," both in *Women and Society in Eighteenth-Century France: Essays in
Honor of J. S. Spink*, ed. Eva Jacobs et al. (London, 1979).

125. For an interesting discussion of the form in which Rousseau's ideas caught on
and permeated the literature of the 1760s and 1770s, see David Williams, "The Fate of
French Feminism: Boudier de Villemert's *Ami des femmes*," *Eighteenth-Century Studies*
14, no. 1 (Fall 1980): 37–56. A later edition of Boudier's work, his *Nouvel Ami des femmes*
(Paris, 1779), included a "Notice alphabétique des femmes françaises qui se sont distin-
guées dans les lettres, ou autrement," in which he listed Mme de Beaumer without
comment but raved about the baronne de Prinzen's *Journal des dames*.

126. *JD*, Mar. 1774, 34.
127. *JD*, Jan. 1774, 165–75; Mar. 1774, 34–36; Jan. 1775, 31.
128. *JD*, June 1774, 151; Aug. 1774, 115.

own decision to pursue a career and her motherhood. She had chosen to do something entirely unconventional but never thought of abandoning her private life for her public job. Women should be able to do both, as she hoped to show by her own example. Unlike Mary Wollstonecraft, for whom Rousseau's ideas were incompatible with feminism, Mme de Montanclos did not perceive these two views as mutually exclusive. She accepted Rousseau but went a step further, insisting that the "mère tendre" be also a "mère éclairée," that she be able to pursue her own interests and thus communicate to her children, especially her daughters, feelings of intrinsic worth and self-reliance. The *Journal des dames* held up the example of Laura Bassi, a determined bourgeoise who earned a doctorate in physics at Bologna; the editor hoped that soon women everywhere would reach the summit of scholarly recognition, so that such an event would no longer be considered extraordinary.[129] She rejoiced that "at last careers are open to both sexes."[130] Ultimately, however, women were to use their personal triumphs to enrich family interactions. Fanny de Beauharnais, whose lover Dorat would become the *Journal des dames*'s last editor, wrote a feminist *A tous les penseurs, Salut,* in which she argued that only educated, active, respected women could properly give of themselves and fulfill their roles as "wives, mothers, friends, daughters, and citizens."[131] The *Journal des dames* carried a long speech from the Académie de Dijon arguing that women were equally capable in science and mathematics and opposing the "unjust and destructive prejudice" that barred them from achievement and kept them confined to the domestic sphere. If given educational opportunities and professional recognition outside the home, mothers could enlighten their children, provide examples of happiness, multiply the resources of society, and inspire patriotism, the surest guarantee of the prosperity of states.[132] Intelligent motherhood, then, was depicted as a boon, not a predicament. The *Manuel des époux* was recommended to all readers, there were stories and poems on the joys of fidelity and marriage, breast-feeding was advocated as the best guarantee for healthy, happy babies, and Charles White's *Avis aux femmes enceintes et en couches* was praised for treating childbirth as a natural, beautiful process rather than a malady and a misfortune.[133]

129. *JD*, Mar. 1775, 381.   130. *JD*, Jan. 1774, 165–66.
131. *JD*, Feb. 1774, 177–89.   132. *JD*, June 1774, 127–53.
133. *JD*, May 1774, 47; July 1774, 229; Sept. 1774, 7–10, 97; Jan. 1775, 31; Mar. 1775, 401.

Behind the scenes, however, things were not easy at all for Mme de Montanclos. As her correspondence shows, she wrestled frequently with the conflicting demands and divided loyalties of her public and private lives. Her letters reveal an ambitious woman who drove herself hard, needed approval, and became ill when she lost her confidence. In a conflict with the Comédie-Française, which delayed giving her a verdict on a play she submitted, she wrote that "discouragement destroys the body as well as the mind." She wondered if her gentle, polite approach had invited the haughty *comédiens* to "victimize" her, to indulge in the "barbarous pleasure" of mistreating a woman. In a gesture of protest or impulsive anger, she withdrew the play and threw back in their faces her special privilege of free tickets to all performances. This act would be regretted much later, and when she was fifty-one years old she tried to reclaim her *entrées,* explaining that she had been so "weak from family troubles and the pains of maternity" that any obstacle thwarting her literary progress "turned my poor head." "Domestic embarrassments" combined with "fear of cabals" led to bouts of insecurity that nearly paralyzed her. Looking back, she perceived her children as "distractions" and "emotional obstacles" to creativity, although her commitment to them had saved her ego. She genuinely loved them and enjoyed watching them develop, but they had been an excuse to hide behind. When they were grown she felt ambivalent, "sadly free, because my children have all left," but frightened at the prospect of empty time that only literary inspiration, if it came, could help to fill.[134]

There were professional as well as domestic conflicts. Mme de Montanclos had a number of faithful female contributors to the *Journal des dames,* including the grandniece of Mme Dacier, and the marquise d'Antremont. Both of these women were raising and educating their own children and enjoying the double privilege of intellectual activity and motherhood, of being "woman truly woman, in every sense of the word."[135] But there were other women who turned hostile to the journalist, feeling she was too critical, too demanding and hard on her sex. Mme de Montanclos called a spade a spade. She refused to

134. Archives du Théâtre Français, dossier "Mme de Montanclos." See especially letters dated 3 July 1782, 21 Feb. 1783, 21 Mar. 1783, 15 Apr. 1787, and 9 July 1787.

135. This was how the marquise d'Antremont described herself earlier in Mathon's *Journal des dames,* Apr. 1768, 1–4. She and Mme d'H ———, grandniece of Mme Dacier, contributed articles and reviews to Mme de Montanclos's issues of late 1774 and early 1775.

give special dispensation to works "by or for women" unless they
served some purpose or had some artistic merit. She panned the *Par-nasse des dames*, an anthology of works by women from all periods and
all nations, for it seemed to do more harm than good, adding fuel to
the fire of women's detractors by "pulling from oblivion names that
should have died there." [136] Her failure to defend women writers
deeply wounded one Mme de Laisse whose works Mme de Montan-clos criticized in the *Journal des dames*. The offended author wrote
angry, sarcastic letters to the *Mercure* calling herself a "feeble mortal"
and the journalist a "wise divinity," impeccably tasteful and "univer-sally recognized for her fairness." [137] Although surely upset by these
attacks, Mme de Montanclos was determined to spare the public the
embarrassment of an ugly dispute between two women, and she did
not strike back. [138] She would maintain her professional dignity at all
costs.

Although she did not discuss political matters directly in these early
issues of the *Journal des dames*, Mme de Montanclos's rhetoric grew
increasingly legalistic after Louis XVI and Marie Antoinette ascended
the throne and became France's new hope in May 1774. In a bid for
popularity, the young king demolished the detested "triumvirate." By
August Maupeou's ministry was dismissed, and the nationwide clam-oring for the return of the exiled parlements led to their recall by
November. The *patriotes* rejoiced that law had been restored to the
land, and the *Journal des dames* reflected the juridical flavor of these
months, featuring the works of several *avocats* and casting the
"woman question" as more needful of legal definition and protection.
Mme de Montanclos wrote to the lawyer Jacques Vincent Delacroix
that she had proprietary rights to any writings by women appearing in
the press. When the *Mercure* published a poem by a Mme de Courcy,
she immediately reprinted it in the *Journal des dames* and felt vindi-cated that she had "insisted on justice being done" when these verses
won a prize from the Académie de Rouen. [139] Just weeks after Mau-peou's fall, and obviously encouraged by it, Mme de Montanclos
called on women to rebel against the "tyrannical laws of silence" that
had historically kept them "apathetic, tame, and mute." Her *Journal
des dames* was furthering women's advancement, and she praised

136. *JD*, Oct. 1774, 146–55.
137. *Mercure de France*, Aug. 1774, 180–85; Feb. 1775, 152–55.
138. *JD*, Feb. 1775, 241.   139. *JD*, July 1774, 88–89; Jan. 1775, 32.

judicial *mémoires* that tried to do the same, like one by Delacroix defending the crowning of virtuous girls at the ceremony of the Rosière de Salency.[140] In November, the very month the parlements were recalled amid wild rejoicing, the *Journal des dames*'s editor printed a special letter to her readers defending "the glory of a sex nearly always undervalued." "The particular purpose of this journal is to make known the virtues, intellect, and talent of the sex to which it is consecrated. It is not I who wish to shine, but I do swear it my intention to force men to guarantee women the justice they have previously refused them on whim. . . . We can know everything, for our minds are flexible and thirsty, and we can do all the good of which humanity is capable."[141] All along Mme de Montanclos had linked motherhood and patriotism. The recurring image of children as "Cornelia's jewels" recalled the Roman mother of the Gracchi brothers, classical republican heroes. Despite poverty, Cornelia had considered herself the richest, happiest woman alive because of her fine sons.[142] Now, in addition, the *Journal des dames* suggested that because of all their services to the state, women deserved the explicit protection of the law.

Mme de Montanclos's interest in the lawyer Delacroix indicated that her political tastes were becoming more daring even before she linked up with Mercier. She had at first taken on one obscure M. Rocher as a "coadjuteur littéraire," to help her with translations. Rocher was an acquaintance from her earlier life at court and an intimate of the comtesse de Bussi. He turned out to be a social conservative and a literary reactionary, waxing ecstatic over Homer but rejecting "le bel esprit moderne." He declared himself an *ancient* in a profession of faith to the *Journal des dames*, wrote reviews belittling women's intellectual capacities, and soon lost favor with the editor.[143] Delacroix, on the other hand, was a parlementaire, a friend of Mercier, a future Jacobin, American sympathizer, and translator of John

140. *JD*, Aug. 1774, 241–47.   141. *JD*, Nov. 1774, 8–9.
142. See, for example, *JD*, Mar. 1774, 34.
143. Rocher, who is not mentioned in any biographical sources, first appeared in *JD* in May 1774, 126. He contributed to the issues of July and August (see his antifeminist piece in *JD*, July 1774, 77) and declared the strains of his job in September (76–81); he had been dismissed by Mme de Montanclos by November (7–8). The fact that he no longer had any involvement with the paper was repeated in Feb. 1775, 201. Rocher published five poems in the *Almanach des muses* between 1772 and 1775, long after Mathon had left the publication. A M. Rocher was awarded a *terrain* in Montreuil for his good services in the *Garde des plaisirs du roi* (AN O¹ 114 [768]), but we cannot be certain it was the same person because no given names appear in *JD*.

Adams; he had attempted a periodical of his own during the Maupeou years. Six volumes of his *Spectateur français* appeared between 1772 and 1773 before the paper became one of the many journalistic victims of the "triumvirate." Delacroix had inserted among articles on *moeurs*, history, and fashion, others that were distinctly *frondeur*, in which he argued that the law must equalize conditions and protect the oppressed by providing public defenders, so that "the weak will no longer be abused, because they will cease to appear weak." He praised the *économistes* and the exiled Choiseul. His call for a new tribunal that would be "pure" and "fair" was an indictment of Maupeou's parlement, as was his plea that cases be opened up to "the public, which has the right to judge magistrates, ministers, and kings." Soon his paper was threatened and its subject matter circumscribed, but a paper devoid of serious content dismayed the *graves politiques* among his subscribers, and it also violated his own principles of what journalism should be. Bemoaning the fact that the editor of the English *Spectator* had been able to speak freely while his French counterpart could say nothing of his government's faults or duties, Delacroix refused to "pay servile court to *les Grands*." He left the corrupt ministers to their flatterers, saying they were unworthy of his truthfulness, but the stranglehold on the press made him fear for his *patrie:* "I do not know if it is possible for humanity to survive much longer in this state of degradation."[144]

In his own paper, Delacroix had devoted considerable space to women, who he thought had great influence over "general opinion." Although he felt they could benefit from protective legislation, he believed that they had already made enormous progress in society and had a right to a fulfilling life outside the home.[145] Mme de Montanclos saw him as an ally but nevertheless admonished him for referring to women as hummingbirds and men as eagles, to which he protested that he meant the word as a compliment, for these were the richest birds in nature. He genuinely admired the female journalist's gump-

144. Jacques Vincent Delacroix's *Spectateur français*, now lost, can only be consulted in the form of excerpts that the editor reprinted years later. The quotations in this paragraph come from two such abridged versions of the *Spectateur:* Delacroix's *Peintures des moeurs du siècle, ou Lettres et discours sur différents sujets* (Amsterdam and Paris, 1777), 1:97, 103; 2:3–4, 41–43, 92, 209, 254, 322–30 (a blatantly *frondeur* "Discours sur les mémoires"), 357–60; and Delacroix, *Le Spectateur français avant la Révolution* (Paris, l'an IV), iv, 209, 481.

145. For his views on women, see Delacroix's *Peintures des moeurs*, 1:89–93, 305–11 ("Sur la révolution arrivée dans l'existence des femmes"), and 2:85–87, 357–58.

tion in reviving the worthwhile *Journal des dames*. His own less happy experience taught him that such success required good timing, the proper connections, and restraint, for indeed Mme de Montanclos had so far steered clear of major controversy. Delacroix's own silenced *Spectateur français*, he told her now, "could benefit from one of your miracles of resurrection." [146]

Although Mercier published a poem in Mme de Montanclos's *Journal des dames* in May 1774, he only began to be featured centrally in the fall, after she left Versailles and took up residence in Paris on the rue des Bernardins, a few short blocks from his home on the rue des Noyers, facing the rue des Anglais.[147] This *quartier*, called Saint Benoît, was the "Latin Quarter," and although neither fashionable nor luxurious, it was described by the *Dictionnaire historique de la ville de Paris* as one of the oldest and most interesting.[148] Rents here were modest; one chose this area for good, lively, intellectual company, not prestige. As neighbors, Mme de Montanclos and Mercier became well acquainted after October 1774 and may even have begun to socialize regularly; by 1789 they saw each other frequently, when both had moved a little west on the Left Bank but still just a block apart, Mercier then on the rue de Seine and Mme de Montanclos on the parallel rue Mazarine.[149] Month after month, as the political climate lightened, Mercier's works and causes received an increasingly positive press in the *Journal des dames*. In October his play *Childeric* was praised, albeit judiciously, by the grandniece of the great writer Mme Dacier, who appreciated bourgeois *drames* and shared Mercier's love for English theater. The reviewer helped the playwright by pointing out flattering parallels between his heroine Bazine and "our august queen Marie Antoinette." She also underlined and endorsed his sympathy with the parlements and his hatred of despotism; she commended his insistence that citizens have protection under the law and that the tribunals of the nation be reestablished, as rumor held the parlements were about to be. Mercier had King Childeric say — and the quotation was repeated in the *Journal des dames* —"I will respect the liberty of the *patrie*. . . . [I pledge] to be the vigilant eye of the laws, to be the first to submit

146. *JD*, July 1774, 89–90.
147. These addresses can be found in *JD*, Nov. 1774 and May 1775, respectively.
148. Hurtaut and Magny, *Dictionnaire historique de la ville de Paris*, 4:195.
149. See the affectionate letter from Mme de Montanclos to Mercier about one of their frequent dinner engagements in 1789, BN nouv.acq.fr. 24030, fols. 87–88.

myself to their inviolable authority." The reviewer ended in admiration of Childeric, a king sufficiently secure not to fear admitting his
faults to his assembly.[150] In December, after the parlements had been
recalled, the same reviewer defended Mercier's *Le Déserteur,* which
showed the inhumanity of the death sentence for runaway soldiers
and was so blatantly republican that the *Journal encyclopédique* had
suggested it be called *Le Brutus français.*[151]

By Mme de Montanclos's second year with the *Journal des dames,*
Mercier's influence could be seen everywhere. In February 1775 there
was an article attacking carriages in Paris, one of Mercier's pet peeves
that would appear repeatedly in his *Tableau de Paris.* These carriages,
which created filth and caused accidents and "infernal noise," should
be either burned or taxed to benefit the poor. In a century the number
of carriages careening through the crowded capital had multiplied
from 100 to 1,400. They interfered with walking, thinking, working,
even sleeping, and each had its insolent but useless lackey, its "dandi-
fied do-nothing," who should be cultivating rather than cluttering
and encumbering the earth.[152] The March 1775 issue of the *Journal des
dames* carried a passionate review of Mercier's *Jean Hennuyer,* a play
that the police had explicitly forbidden about the atrocities of the Saint
Bartholomew's Day massacre of Protestants and the courage of one
man who stood up against Charles IX. Readers of the *Journal,* the
reviewer cautioned, might find this very harsh medicine, but it was
one of the greatest pieces of literature in the fight against religious
prejudice and fanaticism, a fight from which women should no longer
shy away.[153]

By 1775 Mme de Montanclos was deeply involved with additional
family responsibilities resulting from her new marriage and apparently satisfied with her job of relaunching the paper. She was ready to
turn it over completely to Mercier for his polemics on behalf of worthy
causes. She had made enough of a stir, she believed, to have left a
mark upon the public and to be remembered when she found the time
and energy to stage a comeback. She even paved the way for her
return to the literary scene in her last issue by promising her readers
that they would hear more from her in future, that she planned to be a

150. *JD,* Oct. 1774, 196–216.
151. *JD,* Dec. 1774, 230–31. See the collected reviews of *Le Déserteur* in the *Bibliographie parisienne,* 1770:87.
152. *JD,* Feb. 1775, 163–67.   153. *JD,* Mar. 1775, 315–23.

femme de lettres all her life, that she was simply taking time out for mothering; journalistic duties had tired her and sapped her strength. Meanwhile she was turning her paper over to someone whose "energy" and "force" would give it unprecedented importance.[154] Mme de Montanclos boasted that she had acquired a faithful and ever-growing readership; the number of subscribers continued to climb, and more material was being contributed each month than could possibly be accommodated.[155] Reassured that her *Journal des dames* had grown from shaky beginnings into a solid enterprise with a substantial following, Mme de Montanclos felt she had a worthwhile literary property to turn over to Mercier. Her paper could serve him as a mouthpiece. She could guarantee him readers. The problem was that in the eyes of the police, Mercier was suspect. Because they would never have approved his official takeover of the *Journal des dames*, it would have to be negotiated privately. But first, the paper would need to be placed on a still more secure footing, so that silencing it later would be difficult and it could never be suspended for hidden reasons as it had under Mme de Beaumer. For this purpose, Mme de Montanclos decided to get a royal privilege for her journal, which had existed for fifteen years without one.

Saying nothing of her plans to sell the rights for the paper, Mme de Montanclos applied for a privilege to the new *garde des sceaux*, Hue de Miromesnil, and the new chancellor, the comte de Maurepas. She was awarded it by *brevet* from her protectress's husband and the new king, Louis XVI, on 22 March 1775.[156] For the first time her paper had complete legal protection against unscrupulous counterfeiters. More important, it could only be stopped by an official government suppression and was no longer subject to suspensions, which censors were not obliged to explain. She proudly entered her *Journal des dames*'s new status with the book-trade syndicate on 29 March. Next, suspecting that her new husband, who had been unable to keep pace with her in the capital and had retreated to Troyes, would not approve her plan to let Mercier succeed her, she extracted from him a fascinating document. Although legally separated "in property," he was still her spouse and would normally have had the final word on any business

154. *JD*, Apr. 1775, 139.   155. *JD*, Nov. 1774, 8; Feb. 1775, 258.
156. See BN ms.fr. 21966, pp. 390–91, no. 559, for the full text of Mme de Montanclos's privilege and all the protections it afforded *JD*. See also BN ms.fr. 8132, p. 35, showing that her privilege would expire on 22 March 1781.

transactions in which she was involved. But she made him sign a statement in the presence of two notaries in Troyes and two more in Paris, permitting her to negotiate her literary property herself and handle alone all financial affairs regarding her paper. From what we know of Mme de Montanclos's independent spirit, this document was probably an ultimatum, a precondition for any further relationship between her and her husband. In response to her insistence on this carte blanche, he attested that he "declares . . . and irrevocably authorizes Dame Marie Mayon, my wife . . . to give and hand over to whatever person she chooses, for whatever price, terms, and conditions she judges appropriate, the privilege of the *Journal des dames*. . . . She may receive the payment, give receipts, contract whatever obligations, sign and witness whatever acts are necessary, and generally do whatever she deems correct, fair, and fitting." [157] One of the foremost jurists of the day, Robert Joseph Pothiers, had recently summed up the legal nonexistence of married women;[158] the enumeration of rights granted by her husband to Mme de Montanclos shows precisely what wives were normally not allowed to do. Brandishing her signed release from bondage, Mme de Montanclos knew she had no time to lose. Having secured the notarized documents in Troyes on 11 April, she had them countersigned by her own notary in Paris and then, in a private meeting, sold the *Journal des dames* to Mercier on 19 April.[159]

She sold it for a song, motivated not by profit but by an ideological kinship already demonstrated in over a year of editorial support. She had become such a staunch supporter of Mercier's that bequeathing him her paper seemed an honor. It was "henceforth his to use as he saw fit." It probably bothered her to ask even a pittance from this man who devoted all his time, as she described it, to fighting for worthy causes, to shaping a better future for mankind.[160] (This was no doubt a reference to his utopian *L'An 2440*, another of Mercier's forbidden books and police targets.) Mme de Montanclos virtually gave Mercier

157. MC, étude 85, liasse 652 (19 Apr. 1775). The documents dated 11 April signed in Troyes are attached.
158. *Traité de la communauté [et] de la puissance du mari sur la personne et les biens de la femme* (Paris, 1770). See also his earlier *Traité des obligations* (Paris, 1761) and *Du contrat de mariage* (Paris, 1768).
159. MC, étude 85, liasse 652 (19 Apr. 1775), "Cession de privilège de Mme de Montanclos à M. Mercier."
160. BN nouv.acq.fr. 24030, fols. 87–88.

the *Journal des dames*, asking only 1,500 livres, half of what Mme de Maisonneuve had paid Mme de Beaumer twelve years earlier, when the journal was in a sorry state and had no royal privilege. Mercier gave her 900 livres and his *libraire* was to give her 100 livres of annual *rente* for the next six years. Mme de Montanclos had already collected 300 livres from her *libraire*, her profit from the first one hundred subscriptions, but all the other money that had been paid by subscribers since January 1775 (the figure was not mentioned) was now Mercier's to claim as his own. He, anonymously, would assume full responsibility for the *Journal des dames* as of May 1775. Meanwhile she promised to pay all expenses for the April issue currently in preparation, the last to bear her name but already marked by her successor's determination to tackle the problems of the day head on.[161]

The issue of April 1775, a joint production, contained Mme de Montanclos's last plea for loving and responsible motherhood, "for I like to think that most women these days are devoting themselves to the formation of the hearts and minds of their children."[162] Advertisements continued for dentists, lessons, free books, and whatever might help *mères de famille*.[163] But the familiar poems and stories about maternal tenderness and the beauties of nature were now heavily message-laden and set against the background of the grain famine, about which Mercier was profoundly concerned. In one poem, a farmer's wife, with babe at her breast, was starving because crops did not suffice to cover taxes. Jacques Turgot, the new finance minister, was lauded for giving 100,000 écus to ease starvation in Limousin and for going personally to comfort the peasants. A letter allegedly from "les laboureuses de la paroisse de Noissy près Versailles, à la reine" begged the monarchs to buy for their wardrobe only French wool and feathers to strengthen the economy and bring down the price of wheat. There was also a plea for the elimination of the hated corvée.[164]

The *Journal des dames* had certainly come a long way from the *rien délicieux* that its male founding editor had meant it to be. Mme de Montanclos, like her two female predecessors, had come to see that the problem of women's subordination was one of many social injustices and that none of them would be solved without widespread political reform. For that reason, all of them supported the efforts of

161. MC, étude 85, liasse 652 (19 Apr. 1775).   162. JD, Apr. 1775, 23.
163. Ibid., 123–24.   164. Ibid., 85, 34, 37, 10–12.

male *frondeurs* in the pages of their paper and outside as well. Mme de Montanclos's journalistic experience and her friendship with Mercier reinforced her natural tendency to fight for rights and take the underdog's side in controversies. When, in 1776, Mercier's friend Le Tourneur was attacked by Voltaire and the Académie française for the "treasonous act" of translating the complete works of Shakespeare, Mme de Montanclos signed her name beside Mercier's on a list of Le Tourneur's supporters and subscribers, a gesture of protest against the elite establishment.[165] She fought fervently for fair treatment at the Comédie-Française in the 1780s when she felt the actors did not give her plays a chance. "If there is a way, messieurs, to enforce my rights and see that justice is done toward me, I will find it. If you have the right to sacrifice authors to your whims, you must show me legal proof."[166] Her poems, printed for the next several decades in the *Journal de musique, Journal encyclopédique, Courrier de l'Europe,* and *Almanach des muses,* often starred plucky, transparently autobiographical heroines, like the plain widow who turned down a wealthy suitor because he refused her terms for an egalitarian marriage.[167] Other poems defended the Jews, the poor, the elderly. Mme de Montanclos may have belonged to one of the female Masonic lodges that proliferated in the late 1770s and often had parlementaire leanings. Her letters reveal that she gave frequent readings to groups composed exclusively of Masonic *auditrices,* her *Journal des dames* had preached the same virtues — fidelity, discretion, modesty, purity, trustworthiness, charity — to which female Masonry was committed, and the *Journal de musique,* to which both she and Mathon contributed in 1777, was heavily Masonic.[168] She continued as a journalist for the *Correspondance des dames,* and her many plays, although panned by the mordant antifeminist Rivarol, were performed and favorably reviewed in the *Tribunal d'Apollon.* The journalist Clément-Hémery

165. Pierre Le Tourneur, *Shakespeare traduit de l'anglais* (Paris, 1776), 1: list of subscribers.

166. Archives du Théâtre Français, dossier "Mme de Montanclos," letter dated 21 Feb. 1783.

167. *Almanach des muses,* 1806: 120.

168. See Chevallier, *Histoire de la franc-maçonnerie,* 1:200–206, especially 201. There was much overlap of theme and vocabulary. *JD,* Mar. 1775, 402–3, advertised both Mathon's *Journal de musique* and his *Almanach musical.* The Rosière de Salency, a celebration of innocence and simple virtues that received much attention in *JD,* was also the model for female Masonry. The paper was often referred to as a *temple* (*JD,* Sept. 1774, 112; Nov. 1774, 12) and Mme de Montanclos as Minerva.

thought Mme de Montanclos's literary and professional accomplishments sufficiently impressive to list her as one of the great woman writers of all time, alongside Mesdames de Staël, de Sévigné, and de La Fayette.[169]

Mme de Montanclos would not have been pleased with her obituary in the *Journal des arts,* which flattered her but treated her intellectual efforts as an unfortunate deviation from the accepted feminine social course. "Author of many agreeable works, Mme de Montanclos was very beautiful. Her cast of mind was ingenious but also gentle, and although a *femme de lettres,* she managed nevertheless to be well liked." [170] It would have upset her far more, however, to know that a century later the attitude toward female journalists was still inhospitable. "If the advantages of modern progress are contestable on many points," wrote the author of a short sketch on the "bluestocking" Mme de Montanclos in 1913, "they are nevertheless evident in the press, where [progress] has rid us, or almost, of female journalists." [171] The three women who edited the *Journal des dames* initiated the combat against this attitude. That they found the fight lonely and exhausting, that each gave up her personal involvement with the paper very quickly, is not surprising. It was to be a bigger and longer battle than they could have imagined. But all three were impatient for the social and political changes that would improve their lot and therefore sympathized with men who challenged the regime, whose ideas of liberty filled them with optimism and hope. Mme de Montanclos called herself the "Jean-Jacques Rousseau of the female sex" [172] and put into the hands of Mercier a chance to use his pen as a sword. Mme Roland later considered him a "political zero" for voting against the king's execution, but in 1775 when he took over the *Journal des dames,* Mercier was regarded as a very dangerous man.

What Mercier did with the *Journal des dames* cannot be treated in this essay, but in his hands it became overtly *frondeur,* supporting the American insurgents, attacking slavery, upholding the "inalienable rights" of even the humblest citizen, and excoriating most of the

169. Antoine de Rivarol, *Petit Almanach de nos grandes femmes* (London, 1788), "Montanclos"; Albertine Clément-Hémery, *Les Femmes vengées de la sottise d'un philosophe du jour, ou Réponse au projet de loi de M. S**M***portant défense d'apprendre à lire aux femmes* (Paris, n.d.), 33.
170. A. Marquiset, *Les Bas-Bleus du Premier Empire* (Paris, 1913), 105.
171. Ibid., 93.   172. *JD,* Dec. 1774, 191.

entrenched institutions of the Old Regime. All this was done, Mercier explained, for the protection and liberation of "the people." His policy was to teach the reading public, including the lower classes, how to think for itself. The press would thus expose intrigue and lift the audience out of ignorance. Mercier went to court to fight for his right to speak his mind and was thus perhaps the first journalist to make a legal issue out of freedom of expression. He then inspired several other new journalists, with whom he established an informal network, to do the same. They were threatened, silenced, and eventually forced to expatriate themselves. Mercier, who fled to Switzerland, was back in France during the Revolution and became one of its most active journalists. The police had always recognized Mercier as a fierce, bizarre, and dangerous publicist, and when freedom of the press became a real issue in 1789, he threw himself into the fray. His experience on the *Journal des dames* had well prepared him.

The case of the *Journal des dames* suggests several new avenues for further research. The Old Regime press, even decades before the Revolution, was considerably more daring than has hitherto been believed. Even this journal, whose title seemed to disqualify it from serious consideration, acquainted its readers with social causes and familiarized them with such *frondeur* vocabulary as law, nation, parlement, citizen *patriote*, and human rights. It criticized, first obliquely but with increasing boldness, the Comédie, the Académie, and even the king's ministers. Journalists could make such attacks because of a surprising degree of tolerance in certain aristocratic circles, from which editors won both patronage and protection. The *Journal des dames* was supported in particular by such members of the Orléans branch of the royal family as the prince de Conti and the duc de Chartres, and even for a time by Marie Antoinette herself. Its editors used other new strategies as well to defend themselves: they cultivated and secured malleable, sympathetic censors; chose neighborhoods, like the Temple, where they could live out of danger; found distributors willing to take risks, like the booksellers in the Palais Royal; and negotiated the formal protection of privileges to replace the previous tacit permission to distribute their papers.

Women, we have seen, played a significant role in the fight for freedom of the press. The female editors of the *Journal des dames* recognized the potential of journalism to reach and sway an audience, and they willingly embarked on a career other *femmes de lettres* scorned. The disapproval was mutual, for the editors had no use for the salon set that played hostess to great men, arbitrated matters of literary taste, and made or broke reputations of aspiring male writers. The female journalists were genuinely concerned with bettering the lot of women. They wanted immediate, frequent, frontal, and reciprocal contact with a broad social spectrum of readers with whom they could discuss their cause. They were, however, ahead of their time. Women in their day were excluded from public office and from professions. An official edict of 1755, for example, had formally forbidden women to become doctors. Although many French intellectuals vaguely believed that women should improve their minds and even that the subordinate position of women in society was somehow wrong, few were ready to demand specific civil rights for women. Fewer still were receptive to such demands. The female journalists had hoped to show by their own example that women could manage a career. When persecution and pressure led to their failure, they put their paper into the hands of men who fought for an expansion of human freedoms. Even though the *Journal des dames* did not succeed as a vehicle for feminist reform, it became a weapon in the more general journalistic protest against an intransigent, repressive regime.

Chapter Three

The *Gazette de Leyde* and
French Politics Under Louis XVI

JEREMY D. POPKIN

On 24 June 1789, the day after Louis XVI's unsuccessful attempt to cow the members of the newly proclaimed National Assembly into agreeing to return to their earlier status as the deputies of the Third Estate at the Estates General,. the Chamber of the Nobility met for the next-to-last time. With the fate of the ancien régime's political institutions hanging in the balance, Duval d'Eprémesnil, the firebrand of the Paris parlement, rose to speak. He provided his listeners with a surprise: instead of a blast against the claims of the bourgeois deputies, he treated them to "long complaints against several articles from the

I would like to thank Keith Michael Baker, Jack R. Censer, and Carroll Joynes for their comments on earlier versions of this essay. Some parts of the contents were presented as papers at meetings of the Society for French Historical Studies, the Midwest Journalism History Association, and the Arbeitskreis für die Frühgeschichte der Presse; I am grateful for helpful suggestions from all three audiences. Research on this project was made possible by fellowship support from the American Philosophical Society (1980), the University of Kentucky Research Foundation (1982), the Newberry Library NEH Fellowship Program (1983), and the American Council of Learned Societies (1985), and by the assistance of the staffs of the Regenstein Library (University of Chicago), the Newberry Library (Chicago), the Leiden University Library, the Bibliothèque nationale, the University of Wisconsin Library, and the Margaret I. King Library (University of Kentucky). Finally, I would like to thank my good friend Judy Hansburg for first alerting me to the existence of the Luzac family papers in Leiden. Of course, neither she nor any of the other people and institutions who have supported my work over the years bear any responsibility for the results presented here.

Gazette de Leyde."[1] His public attack on the paper marked both the high point and the end of this remarkable periodical's role in French political life. Like d'Eprémesnil himself, the *Gazette de Leyde* had done much to expose the weaknesses of the old order and set the revolution in motion. Ironically, the revolution d'Eprémesnil opposed was about to deprive both him and the newspaper he denounced of their power and influence.

The biweekly newssheet known throughout the civilized world as the *Gazette de Leyde* was one of the dozen or more French-language newspapers published outside France in the last decades of the eighteenth century. Like its Dutch competitors, the *Gazette d'Amsterdam* and the *Gazette d'Utrecht,* the *Gazette de Leyde* dated back to the arrival of French Huguenot refugees in Holland under Louis XIV; the earliest known copies are from 1677.[2] The paper had been founded by one Huguenot family, the De la Fonts; in 1738, it passed into the hands of Etienne Luzac, senior, the son of another Huguenot refugee, whose family retained control of it until the French invasion of the Netherlands in 1795.[3] Like the other French-language international newspapers of the eighteenth century, it offered regular reports of international affairs, particularly wars and diplomatic negotiations, and some coverage of domestic politics in the major European states, especially England. Under the editorship of Etienne Luzac, senior, between 1739 and 1772 and his nephew Jean Luzac from 1773 to 1798, the *Gazette de*

---

1. *Gazette de Leyde* (hereafter cited as *GL*) 7 July 1789 (reporting Chamber of the Nobility session of 24 June 1789). The actual title of the *Gazette de Leyde* was *Nouvelles extraordinaires de divers endroits;* since the paper was universally known as the *Gazette de Leyde* at the time, it would generate more confusion than precision to use the actual title. Holdings are catalogued in American libraries under the title of *Journal politique,* a name imposed on the paper during the Napoleonic period, just before it went out of business in 1811.

GL was counterfeited in several other European cities during the 1780s. Only one number of one of these counterfeit editions has been identified to date, and so it is not known whether their content is identical with the original edition. All references in this study have been verified in the copy owned by the Regenstein Library of the University of Chicago, the most complete run of the paper in America and equaled only by the copy of the British Library, London. The University of Chicago copy, which runs from 1739 to 1811, is a special presentation copy on high-quality paper, with unusually wide margins, similar to one that the editors were required to present to the city government of Leiden as one condition of their exclusive privilege for the publication of a French-language gazette there.

2. W. P. Sautijn Kluit, "De Fransche Leidsche Courant," in *Mededelingen gedaan in de Vergaderingen van de Maatschappij der Nederlandsche Letterkunde te Leiden* (Leiden, 1870), 5. Until 1680 the paper bore the title *Traduction libre des gazettes flamandes et autres.*

3. Ibid., 21.

Leyde built up a reputation for timely, accurate, and impartial reporting that elevated it above its many rivals: like the *London Times* in the
nineteenth century or the *New York Times* today, it was the major
international newspaper of record. And, from the early 1750s down to
the outbreak of the French Revolution, it played an important role in
French domestic politics.

A periodical edited and printed in the sleepy Dutch university town
of Leiden could occupy a major position in the politics of France
because of the strange disjunction of theory and practice in French
public affairs. Theoretically, France was an absolutist polity in which
the king and his government controlled the flow of politically significant information. Through a comprehensive set of censorship regulations, the government prevented the publication of unauthorized material; through its privileged news publications, particularly the
Gazette de France, it gave the French nation the information it wanted
to circulate. In practice, however, the government had never succeeded in imposing complete control over the flow of news, and in fact
it actively connived in undermining its own legal monopoly over it.
The *gazettes de Hollande* and their imitators from Germany, Switzerland, England, and Avignon were openly tolerated throughout most
of the century. They could be publicly advertised in France; they were
delivered, clearly marked by their distinctive address labels, through
the royal mails; the Paris bookseller David had an official privilege for
their distribution; and the income from delivering them was a regular
item in the calculations for the level of the *ferme des postes*.[4]

These papers were tolerated despite the fact that they frequently
carried news and information that the French government sought to
keep out of circulation. In contrast to the official French papers, which
covered only the public actions of the king and purveyed an image of
royal authority that insisted on the monarch's absolute power over

4. The best overview of the French-language press in the eighteenth century remains Eugène Hatin, *Les Gazettes de Hollande et la presse clandestine aux XVIIe et XVIIIe
siècles* (Paris, 1865). Hatin reprints a list of ten such papers that were advertised publicly
in 1779 (p. 49). The most recent brief surveys of the subject are Jerzy Łojek, "Gazettes
internationales de langue française dans la seconde moitié du XVIIIe siècle," in *Modèles
et moyens de la réflexion politique au XVIIIe siècle* (Lille, 1977), 1:369–82, with an incom-
plete list and an attempt at ranking the importance of the various papers; G. C. Gibbs,
"The Role of the Dutch Republic as the Intellectual Entrepôt of Europe in the Seventeenth and Eighteenth Centuries," *Bijdragen en Mededelingen betreffende de Geschiedenis
den Nederlanden* 86 (1971): 323–49. For the inclusion of income from such papers in the
contract of the *ferme des postes*, see Eugène Vaillé, *Histoire générale des postes françaises*
(Paris, 1951–53), 6:105.

events, the foreign-based journals openly revealed the workings of a different system of politics, one in which the royal will was frequently contested and sometimes defied. These journals regularly reported the internal debates of the sovereign courts or parlements in the major cities, the assemblies of Estates in some of the provinces, the Assembly of the Clergy and other corporate bodies. They recorded the resolutions and challenges to royal authority of institutions that appeared in the official papers only when their representatives humbly presented their respects to the king. And no publication devoted itself to this task more than the *Gazette de Leyde*. More restrained than the genuinely clandestine pamphlet press that circulated inside France itself, the *Gazette de Leyde* nevertheless conveyed a wealth of supposedly illegal information to readers both inside and outside the kingdom. Unlike the pamphlets, it arrived promptly and predictably, covering events as they happened and adjusting itself to unanticipated changes, shaping its readers' views of French political life steadily and imperceptibly.[5]

Had the *Gazette de Leyde* merely reprinted the views of groups contesting royal authority in France — together, of course, with the government's responses — it would already have played a significant role in increasing the flow of political information in France. But the paper went beyond the role of impartial narrator. From the time of the refusal-of-sacraments controversy in the early 1750s, when a Jansenist-inspired *patriote* faction first used the parlements to challenge royal authority and defend a constitutionalist interpretation of the French monarchy, down to the eve of the Estates General in 1789, the paper held to a consistent editorial position: it favored those people who claimed that France was governed by certain fundamental laws that bound the monarch and his ministers. To be sure, the paper did not

5. The relationship is complex between publicly sold newspapers like *GL* and the manuscript newsletters that circulated in France during the late eighteenth century, such as the *Correspondance secrète* known as "Métra" (most often referred to on the basis of a reprint edition published in London from 1787 to 1790) and the *Mémoires secrets* known as "Bachaumont." François Moureau has recently shown that much of the content of the "Bachaumont" *Mémoires secrets* for the late 1760s actually appeared first in a publicly distributed foreign-based newspaper, the *Courier du Bas-Rhin* ("Les Mémoires secrets de Bachaumont, le *Courier du Bas-Rhin*, et les 'bulletinistes' parisiens," in *L'Année 1768 à travers la presse traitée par ordinateur*, ed. Jean Varloot and Paule Jansen [Paris, 1981], 58–79). A comparison of *GL* with "Métra" and "Bachaumont" shows that the "secret" news bulletins did contain some current political information that was not in the Dutch paper, but their specialty was salacious anecdotes about individuals in the news. The chief difference between these two genres of periodicals in such periods (the late 1760s, 1785–89) was that *GL* presented French politics as a serious contest over constitutional issues, while the secret papers depicted it as a clash of ignoble personal ambitions.

thunder against ministerial despotism in each and every issue: its views were expressed only in passing remarks inserted in its narrative of events in France and in rare articles devoted to leading figures in the *patriote* movement. But these oblique hints added up over time, and no regular reader could have been in much doubt about the editors' own views.

Since the *Gazette de Leyde* printed not just a random selection of information about French politics but a systematic narrative reflecting a definite point of view, it is important to determine who controlled the choice of news that the paper printed. Ultimate control over what to print rested with the paper's owner, who was, for most of the reign of Louis XVI, also its editor: Jean Luzac (1746–1807). Nephew of Etienne Luzac, senior, Jean Luzac took over the running of the paper in late 1772; his brother, Etienne, junior, handled the actual printing.[6] Jean Luzac was well qualified to edit an international newspaper. Fluent in at least six languages, he was professor of classical languages and of Netherlands history at the University of Leiden for many years. He was also a man of strong political views. His sympathies went to movements for liberty, wherever they might appear. The great cause of his life was the American Revolution; he was an early and energetic supporter of the American envoy John Adams in his campaign to win Dutch recognition for the new nation, and he not only translated Adams's most important pieces of propaganda but contributed his own money to support the colonists.[7] But Luzac's enthusiasm for liberty was not limited to the Americans. Like his uncle, he was a firm supporter of Polish independence,[8] and he played a major role in Leiden city politics during the unsuccessful Dutch Revolution of 1784–87, although he opposed the radical democratic current that controlled the city in 1786–87.[9]

6. Kluit, "Leidsche Courant," 81–82. The two brothers obtained full legal control over the paper in 1783.

7. Jean Luzac's personal papers are in the Leiden University Library. On his role in generating Dutch support for the cause of American independence, see Jan Willem Schulte Nordholt, *The Dutch Republic and American Independence,* trans. H. Rowen (Chapel Hill, N.C., 1982).

8. The extensive role of the French-language press in Polish affairs in the eighteenth century has been analyzed in Jerzy Łojek, *Polska inspiracja prasowa w Holandii i Niemczech w czasach Stanislawa Augusta* (Warsaw, 1969; in Polish with French notes, documentation, and summary), and the same author's "International French Newspapers and Their Role in Polish Affairs During the Second Half of the Eighteenth Century," *East Central Europe* 1 (1974): 54–64. GL played an especially important role in publicizing the Polish king's efforts to ward off the country's partitions in 1772–74 and 1791–94.

9. Jeremy D. Popkin, "Luzac, Jean," in *Dictionnaire des journalistes,* ed. François Moureau, supplement 4 (Grenoble, 1985).

Jean Luzac, editor of the *Gazette de Leyde*, 1773–1798.

Not surprisingly, Luzac gathered around himself an editorial staff that shared his views. Although not too much is known about the other collaborators of the *Gazette de Leyde*, several other activists in the Dutch Patriot movement worked for it. The most important of these was Antoine-Marie Cerisier (1749–1828), a minor French diplomatic agent in the Netherlands at the time of the American war who subsequently launched a very successful career as a pro-Patriot journalist in Holland. In 1785, he deserted his own journal, the *Politique hollandais*, to take over the editorship of the *Gazette de Leyde*. Forced to flee to

France after the Prussian invasion that crushed the Dutch Revolution in September 1787, Cerisier promptly became involved in French politics as a member of the *Société des amis des noirs*; eventually, he founded a newspaper of his own in Paris, the *Gazette universelle*, which was an important constitutional-monarchist organ until its suppression after 10 August 1792.[10] Like Luzac, Cerisier had clear political opinions. In 1779, in a pamphlet admittedly intended for circulation primarily in the Netherlands, he had called for major constitutional reforms in France, including the summoning of the Estates General.[11] But his connection with the French foreign ministry and his subsequent career in Paris, where he had close ties with the court, raise the most difficult problem in interpreting the origins and intent of the *Gazette de Leyde*'s coverage of French affairs: the extent to which it reflected the views of the French foreign ministry.

Given the known backgrounds of Luzac and Cerisier, it is no surprise that the *Gazette de Leyde*'s coverage of affairs in France consistently favored the *patriotes*, normally supported the parlements, and usually opposed arbitrary ministerial measures. What is surprising is that the narration of French events in which these views appeared was prepared, in large part, in Paris, and in all probability had the approval of important figures in the French government. At least for most of the 1780s, the major part of the *Gazette de Leyde*'s reporting on French domestic affairs was not assembled by correspondents working specifically for the newspaper but by a news bureau in Paris that also served other foreign-based publications. A comparison of the contents of the *Gazette de Leyde* and another major international newspaper, the *Courier du Bas-Rhin*, published in the Prussian enclave of Cleves, shows that the two journals normally printed identical articles from Paris, a practice that is all the more surprising since the underlying editorial positions of the two papers were usually in sharp opposition.[12] Thus the crucial process of selecting material for the paper's French news stories did not actually reflect Luzac's or Cerisier's direct

10. Jean Sgard, ed., *Dictionnaire des journalistes, 1600–1789* (Grenoble, 1976), 81.
11. Antoine-Marie Cerisier, *Suite des observations impartiales d'un vrai Hollandais* (Arnhem, 1779), 18.
12. I have been able to verify the appearance of identical articles on French affairs in the two papers from January 1786 through July 1789, but there is no reason to doubt that the practice began earlier. In general, these articles appeared first in *GL* and then in the *Courier du Bas-Rhin* (hereafter cited as *CBR*), which was printed one day later, but *CBR*'s editor was not simply plagiarizing from his Dutch rival, because there are occasions when the German paper published certain material first (for example, *CBR*'s article of 30

intervention at all, even though the end product closely corresponded to their known personal views.

The source of this French correspondence was a *bulletiniste* named Pascal Boyer, working under the direction of the comte de Vergennes, French foreign minister from 1774 to 1787. Pascal Boyer was certainly involved with the *Gazette de Leyde* and Cerisier at the time of the Revolution: he is identified in some of Luzac's correspondence from 1789 and 1790, and he coedited the *Gazette universelle* with Cerisier, eventually ending up on the guillotine as a result. He had been arrested briefly and *embastillé* in 1781, but he was released on Vergennes's orders, with the promise that Vergennes would "give him the greatest opportunities to expand his correspondence and his foreign connections." [13] The notion of a government-tolerated news bureau was certainly in the air at the time,[14] and it seems likely that Boyer was running such an operation. The *Gazette de Leyde* relied on Boyer for most of its news from France, although it cannot automatically be assumed that the paper knew the full extent of its correspondent's connections with the French government. Even if it did, however,

---

Aug. 1786 appears in *GL* for 1 Sept. 1786). Considering the consistent hostility between the two publications, it is hard to believe that Luzac would not have drawn attention to *CBR*'s plagiarism if he had had exclusive rights to the articles. The papers were on opposite sides in the Dutch Revolution, and *CBR* was consistently hostile to the French parlements before the Revolution. Each paper did publish some information about France that did not appear in the other; *GL* was especially rich in reprints of documents, such as parlementary *remontrances*, which *CBR* usually just summarized, while *CBR* printed a variety of attacks against individuals, such as its denunciation of the pro-parlementaire pamphleteer Nicolas Bergasse for his role in the famous Kornmann case (2 July 1788).

13. Boyer was the compiler of the Paris news for *GL* from 1780 to 1789 (Archives nationales [Paris], F7 4615,d.2 [Pascal Boyer]). His brief arrest and his pact with Vergennes are described in a document cited in Frantz Funck-Brentano, *Les Lettres de cachet à Paris* (Paris, 1903), 406. Boyer remained associated with *GL* during the early years of the Revolution, and Luzac's prorevolutionary friends blamed him for the hostile tone of the paper's coverage (Filippo Mazzei, letter to Luzac, 22 Mar. 1790, in Luzac Archives, carton 29). On Boyer's leading role in editing the Paris *Gazette universelle* from 1789 to 1792, see the contract between his heirs and the owner of that paper's successor, the *Nouvelles politiques*, signed on 16 Dec. 1794, in Archives nationales, F 7 3463.

14. The academician and journalist Jean-Baptiste Suard had tried to get Vergennes's permission for one of his friends to write such a correspondence for one of the Dutch papers during the early 1780s, promising that the letters would include only "publicly known events, with no reflections," but Vergennes turned him down on the grounds that if it became known that the French government was tolerating such a correspondence, "le public et les particuliers . . . imputeront au gouvernement toutes les impertinences des gazetiers étrangers" (Pierre Manuel, *La Police de Paris dévoilée* [Paris, 1791], 1:211–14). Vergennes probably used this argument as a pretext to protect his own favored *nouvelliste*, Boyer.

there is little reason to think that Luzac would have been upset. The paper had a clear policy of rejecting financial subsidies from foreign governments, but it never showed any aversion to relying on government-furnished information.[15]

In the case of the paper's French coverage, government-furnished *nouvelles* would have normally satisfied Luzac. There was a fairly close match between his personal views and Vergennes's policies, and Vergennes understood that the paper could only achieve credibility if it was given a certain amount of leeway. Both Luzac and Vergennes had favored the retention of an independent Poland in the 1770s, both favored the American bid for independence, and Vergennes tilted toward the Dutch Patriot movement, although he avoided giving it official French backing. Vergennes did not personally favor radical reform in France itself, but some of his subordinates in the foreign ministry did; on the other hand, Vergennes was frequently at odds with other ministers over specific issues and sometimes used the press to make his position clear.[16] Whatever Vergennes's personal views of the issues discussed in the *Gazette de Leyde*, the toleration of such publications was already a long-established French tradition. Successive ministers had recognized the impossibility of completely suppressing either the manuscript newsletters that were produced in Paris or the printed versions of them that often appeared in the foreign French-language press.[17] At the end of the 1750s, Lamoignon de Malesherbes, then *directeur de la librairie*, outlined the French administration's dilemma in a long *mémoire*. Despite his reputation for liberalism, he was anything but indifferent to "the abuses that stem from the freedom that the foreign gazettes, especially those from Holland, have allowed themselves for the past several years." But he saw no real solution to the problem.

The papers' habit of printing materials from all parties in interna-

15. In the late 1760s and early 1770s, the paper had rejected an offer of Polish subsidies but accepted a regular supply of information furnished by King Stanislas II supporting his policy of limited concessions to the partitioning powers in order to preserve some measure of Polish independence. The paper had, however, insisted on its right to publish information about Poland from other sources as well. Łojek, "International French Newspapers," 57, 61.

16. On Vergennes's policy, see especially Orville Murphy, *Charles Gravier, Comte de Vergennes* (Albany, 1982).

17. On examples of this practice as early as the 1730s, see Françoise Weil, "Les Gazettes manuscrites avant 1750," in *Le Journalisme d'ancien régime*, ed. Pierre Rétat (Lyons, 1982), 94–95.

tional disputes was a well-established custom with which it would be dangerous to interfere; the unspoken thought in Malesherbes's mind was undoubtedly that any pressure on the gazettes in this area would backfire and discredit the French government's own claims. To limit the papers' intervention in French domestic affairs, Malesherbes considered the possibility of banning them altogether. He concluded, however, that even if the French government allowed a domestic reprint of all that they contained in the way of foreign news, "such truncated gazettes would be purchased only by those people who could not obtain the real ones, and there are a thousand ways to smuggle in a printed sheet . . . and the gazetteer, annoyed by a ban that would reduce his sales, would allow himself even more freedom." The best suggestion he could come up with was to abolish the bookseller David's exclusive privilege for the sale of the foreign gazettes in France, in the hope that a free market would drive subscription prices down and bring the foreign publishers to the point where they would offer the French government concessions to get the old arrangements restored. But Malesherbes resigned himself to the fact that he would never manage to get the distribution monopoly repealed. His ultimate conclusion was that the French government's only practical recourse against the papers was the traditional one of lodging complaints with their host governments, "always an embarrassing move" because it invited counterdemands from the other side and forced the ambassador to waste his time and prestige on "a miserable libel." Ideally, Malesherbes was sure it would be preferable to "speak commandingly to the author and influence him by the attraction of the profit the free circulation of his paper in France will give him."[18]

For the most part, ministers after Malesherbes were guided by the same logic. The "triumvirate" of Maupeou, Terray, and d'Aiguillon, the hard-line ministers who carried out the coup of 1771 against the parlements in a final effort to end the domestic conflict that had plagued Louis XV since 1752, attempted to implement the policy of rigor that Malesherbes had outlined but rejected. They banned the foreign gazettes, considered a privileged domestic paper to supplement the *Gazette de France*, and opened negotiations with the editors

18. "Mémoire sur la gazette d'Hollande donné à M. le chancelier au mois de mars," n.d. but probably 1759, in Anisson-Duperron Collection, Bibliothèque nationale, Manuscrits français (hereafter BN ms.fr.) 22134, fols. 227–31.

of the foreign papers.[19] But there was no convincing answer to the reply Etienne Luzac, senior, made to the ministry's approaches in 1772. Luzac countered French complaints about the paper's refusal to limit itself to reprinting items from the *Gazette de France* by pointing out that "this would alert the French public that we were holding things back and produce an effect just the opposite of what is hoped for."[20] Ironically, if the government-approved *nouvelles* in a paper like the *Gazette de Leyde* were to do the government any good, they had to appear to come from an independent source. The paper had to be allowed to mention the parlements and other known centers of opposition to government policies, lest it become too obvious that the ministry was controlling what it could say.

A close analysis of the paper's content suggests a general rule that probably governed the Paris news bureau's conduct until the time of Vergennes's death and the beginning of the pre-revolutionary crisis in early 1787: it was free to mention events that were more or less public knowledge in Paris, even if they were unfavorable to the ministry; it could summarize and even reproduce the texts of official documents emanating from institutions such as the parlements provided they were already circulating in printed form in Paris itself.[21] But the paper was not to attribute personal motives to the political actors it mentioned. The government could console itself with the thought that the damage was already done. Further publicity through the foreign-based press, arriving several weeks later, would not substantially add to the harm. The news the *Gazette de Leyde* carried about French domestic affairs was thus a reasonably full summary of the public

19. Parts of the Maupeou ministry's press policy can be followed in the antiministerial news bulletins later printed as the *Journal historique de la Révolution opérée dans la constitution de la monarchie françoise, par M. de Maupeou, chancelier de France, Nouvelle édition, revue, corrigée, et augmentée* (London, 1776). On 15 Oct. 1771 the *Journal historique* noted that *CBR* had become the third foreign gazette to be banned since the exile of the Paris parlement (2:186); on 16 Oct. 1772 it mentioned the prospectus of a new *Journal historique et politique*, which was intended to replace the foreign gazettes by reprinting everything important they contained. "But one can already see that they are visibly mutilated and that, by choosing carefully from all the news only that which favors despotism . . . the intention is to shape all the peoples for servitude" (3:285).

20. Cited in Hatin, *Gazettes de Hollande*, 150.

21. GL's correspondence usually indicated that documents printed in the paper, even supposedly clandestine ones like parlementary *remontrances*, were reproduced from printed copies obtained in Paris. In cases where the originals were said to be in manuscript, reference was often made to other, inaccurate versions said to be circulating in France, implying that the paper's official sources had decided to print their version to combat these rivals.

statements of all political actors enjoying some recognized right to discuss government policies under the Old Regime, overlaid with a thin veneer of editorial commentary applied in Leiden.

The extent of the *Gazette de Leyde*'s influence in French politics depended not only on the range of news and information it could print but on the extent of the audience it could reach inside France itself. During the period from 1752, when the paper first began to give extensive treatment to domestic French political dissensions, until the outbreak of the American war, the paper's circulation was quite modest. An exchange of letters between Luzac and his French distributor in the 1770s suggests that the paper could not have had more than about 400 French subscribers in the 1750s. There were 287 in 1767 and 300 in 1773. French sales had increased dramatically to 2,560 in 1778, reflecting interest in the American war, but then they slumped to 1,490 after the peace treaty in 1783.[22] This was a sizable part of the paper's total press run, which was around 4,200 in 1785. The paper's circulation probably rose toward the end of the decade, since its profit showed a healthy growth from 19,500 Dutch florins (almost 40,000 livres) in 1786 to a peak of 29,400 florins in 1789. Although some of these extra sales were in other countries, there were clearly more French readers than there had been before 1770.[23] The Maupeou coup of 1771 and its aftermath, together with the American War of Independence, stimulated public interest in current political news, and a number of new foreign-based papers were formed in the late 1760s and 1770s. It is not clear whether the *Gazette de Leyde*'s new readers were people who had not subscribed to a paper before the mid-1770s or people who had formerly supported another paper. Nevertheless, the paper's outspokenness, compared to other foreign gazettes, about such issues as the refusal-of-sacraments controversy should have given it an advantage in attracting readers.[24]

22. Kluit, "Leidsche Courant," 87. In 1779 the paper had a dispute with the postmaster of Antwerp over the rate for forwarding its bundles of copies to France. The postmaster asserted that the bundles had grown from 5 or 6 Dutch *pond* in the 1750s to 35 *pond* by 1779. If the latter weight represented approximately 2,500 copies (the circulation for 1778), then the total number of copies shipped to France in the 1750s would have been between 300 and 400 (ibid., 76).

23. Ibid., 166.

24. After the foundation of the major Dutch gazettes in the 1660s and 1670s, no similar enterprises were created until the 1730s, when the *Gazette de Cologne* and the *Courrier d'Avignon* appeared. No further French-language papers were created along these lines until the appearance of *CBR* in 1767, followed by the *Gazette de Deux-Ponts* in 1770, the *Courrier de l'Europe* (London) in 1778, and the *Journal générale de l'Europe*

The *Gazette de Leyde*'s French subscribers were spread throughout the kingdom, even though those in southern France must have received their copies long after they received the *Courrier d'Avignon*, the only quasi-independent newspaper in that region.[25] Most of the *Gazette de Leyde*'s other competitors were located near France's northern borders, like the gazette itself. They would have had an advantage in timeliness only in a narrow area close to their point of arrival in France. Theoretically, the French bookseller who had the privilege for the sale of foreign gazettes had a monopoly on the distribution of subscriptions in the country, but a notice in the *Gazette de Leyde* in December 1784 listed nineteen cities besides Paris where subscriptions could be ordered directly. With the exception of Bordeaux and Lyons, these were all towns north of Paris; presumably, readers in these localities did not want to wait for their copies to travel to Paris and back.[26]

Socially, the *Gazette de Leyde*'s readers belonged to France's upper classes. An annual subscription to the paper cost 36 livres, more than twice the price of the *Gazette de France* and far more than any peasant or artisan could have spared. One regular reader was Louis XVI; another the philosophe Condorcet, even though he criticized the paper's pro-parlementaire position.[27] The letters published in the paper in 1787, 1788, and 1789 do not provide a representative sample of the total readership — they came almost exclusively from people who had been mentioned in the paper. Nevertheless, they show that the readers included many members of the nobility, including the *pairie*

(Liège) in 1785. It has been known for a long time that the American War of Independence stimulated general interest in political news. The role of domestic political controversies, particularly the Maupeou coup, is emphasized in Durand Echeverria, *The Maupeou Revolution* (Baton Rouge, 1985).

25. The *Courrier d'Avignon* was published in the papal enclave in southern France. Since it required French permission to circulate at all, it was more tightly controlled than any of the other international papers, but it did have the advantage of arriving much earlier in southern France. On the *Courrier*, see the excellent study by René Moulinas, *L'Imprimerie, la librairie, et la presse à Avignon au XVIIIe siècle* (Grenoble, 1974). There is also a mediocre American master's thesis on the paper, which summarizes its political content under Louis XVI: Charles F. Hinds, "The *Courrier d'Avignon* in the Reign of Louis XVI" (M.A. thesis, University of Kentucky, 1958; based on the extensive run of the paper in the University of Kentucky library, the best surviving collection of this important publication).

26. *GL*, 24 Dec. 1784. The paper was also sold in Geneva.

27. The Dutch Patriot Dumont-Pigalle asserted that Louis XVI "reads only that gazette." Letter of 22 Aug. 1786, in Rijksarchief, The Hague, Dumont-Pigalle Collection, carton A. For Condorcet, see letter to Mme Suard, n.d. but from 1774, Bibliothèque nationale, Nouvelles acquisitions françaises (hereafter BN nouv. acq. fr.) 23,639, fol. 191.

— the ducs de Charost and de Rohan — the robe, represented by d'Eprémesnil, the diplomatic service, and the army. Foulon, the aristocratic intendant massacred in July 1789, had posted a letter to Leiden just days before his death.[28] Commercial advertising, which occupied about 5 percent of the paper's total space, was also slanted toward a wealthy clientele. The most common advertisements were for auctions of large private libraries and art collections, redemptions of bonds sold through the Amsterdam banks, patent medicines, and such luxuries as tulip bulbs, chocolate, and perfumes. The readers of the *Gazette de Leyde* in France were thus primarily members of that mixed elite of aristocrats and wealthy bourgeois who played the crucial role in the launching of the revolutionary movement between 1787 and 1789.[29]

Most recent discussions of this group have stressed their common interest as owners of landed property, which was increasingly coming to override differences in social status. But they were also defined as a group by their literacy and access to information.[30] During the reign of Louis XVI, the *Gazette de Leyde* and its competitors played a key role in giving this elite the information it required in order to assert itself in politics.

For the *Gazette de Leyde* as well as for many of France's political institutions, the beginning of Louis XVI's reign had meant the end of the authoritarian measures and reforms begun in 1771 by the ministers Maupeou, Terray, and d'Aiguillon. As Carroll Joynes's contribution to this collection shows, the gazette carried extensive coverage of the struggle between royal authority and the *parti janséniste* in the 1750s, and it continued to follow the details of French internal politics throughout the 1760s as well. But this coverage, which included regular publication of parlementary *remontrances* and other antiministerial propaganda, came to an abrupt end with the issue of 2 August 1771. For the next several years, the *Gazette de Leyde* did little more than reprint the contents of the *Gazette de France*; it was not able to publish

28. Joseph-François Foulon protested against the paper's report that he had helped plan the unsuccessful counterrevolutionary coup leading to Necker's dismissal on 11 July 1789. His letter appeared in *GL*, 28 July 1789, along with the report of his death.

29. For this "revisionist" view of the social origins of the Revolution, see William Doyle, *The Origins of the French Revolution* (New York, 1980); and Patrice Higonnet, *Class, Ideology, and the Rights of Nobles During the French Revolution* (New York, 1981).

30. Elizabeth Eisenstein, "Who Intervened in 1788? A Commentary on *The Coming of the French Revolution*," *American Historical Review* 71 (1965): 97.

the wealth of information from antiministerial sources that supporters of the parlement gathered inside France and circulated in manuscript form. Jean Luzac's assumption of editorial control at the end of 1772 did not change this situation. The paper devoted most of its columns to news from England and other countries where it could gather information of real interest; indeed, Stockholm, where Gustavus III staged his coup against the Swedish aristocrats in 1772, considerably surpassed Paris as a source of news in that year.[31]

By early 1774 the aftereffects of the Maupeou coup were beginning to diminish. The *Gazette de Leyde* was able to carry occasional articles that went beyond the bounds of officially approved discourse, such as a letter from the leader of the antiministerial movement in the Parlement of Rennes, La Chalotais, justifying himself for violating the terms of his exile to Saintes. This appeared with an editorial comment noting approvingly that the government was easing its treatment of the members of the pre-Maupeou parlements who had been dismissed in 1771.[32] The unexpected death of Louis XV offered the paper a chance to really resume its old role in reporting French affairs. The paper relied entirely on official sources for its coverage of the old king's death; there was not a hint of the popular hostility to Louis XV that made the government afraid to move his body to Saint-Denis by way of Paris. But semiofficial reports from court circles immediately began to reach the paper, as different factions jockeyed for position under the new monarch. Some of these stories, such as the ones reporting the exile of the much-hated Mme Du Barry, served the interests of the new ruler by dissociating him from the sins of his predecessor.[33] No doubt, they appeared with governmental blessings. Others explaining the reasons for the dismissal of the duc d'Aiguillon and claiming that Maupeou would be retained doubtless came from the embattled minister himself or sources close to him.[34] Still other letters pressed the claims of Choiseul, who had retained many supporters including the queen, after his disgrace in 1770.[35]

But the *Gazette de Leyde*'s overriding concern was the fate of the old parlements, exiled since 1771. Officially, the recall of the Paris parle-

---

31. An analysis of the content of *GL* for 1772, based on a sample of every fifth issue, shows that 53½ columns were printed with a London dateline, 34 from Stockholm, 24½ from Paris (and an additional 1½ from Versailles), and 24 from Warsaw.
32. *GL*, 25 Feb. 1774.   33. *GL*, 24 May 1774.
34. *GL*, 31 May, 10 June, 14 June 1774.   35. *GL*, 21 and 24 May 1774.

ment was not announced until November 1774, but the *Gazette de Leyde* had clearly expected such an action since the fall of Maupeou and Terray, which it had reported on 2 September 1774. At that time, it had also noted public approval of "the release given to M. de La Chalotais," a leader of the Patriot opposition in the 1760s who had been arrested under Maupeou. An editorial comment in the issue of 6 September noted, with clear reference to Maupeou's dismissal, that "there is an end to all things," and a story in the issue after that, datelined Brussels, reported the public rejoicing about the parlements' imminent recall and praised La Chalotais and his colleagues, "whose patriotism and attachment to the kingdom's laws had caused their disgrace." [36] There was thus every indication that the *Gazette de Leyde* would resume its old role as a major ally of the parlementaire-led opposition to ministerial "despotism."

The fall of Maupeou coincided with the appointment of a new ministry, dominated by the comte de Maurepas, the young king's "mentor," and Jacques Turgot, the enlightened reformer. It was to be expected that Jean Luzac, the warm supporter of the American revolutionaries, would welcome a man like Turgot. In fact he did, but this welcome was initially based on the notion that Turgot's planned reforms would implement the constitutionalist ideas that the parlements themselves had incorporated in their rhetoric in the 1750s and 1760s. The paper saw a clear parallel between the French parlements and the American colonial assemblies. It observed that if Turgot carried out his rumored plan to allow each French province to tax itself, as suggested earlier by the Parlement of Rouen, "it would not be one of the least remarkable singularities of our century that France should return to the nation the right of taxing itself, a right that is so sacred and that should be inalienable for every unenslaved people, while England works to take it away from its American subjects, who certainly did not go to clear the wastes in order to lose the rights of citizens and of Englishmen." [37]

This article reflected views that the paper was to adhere to steadily down to the Revolution. So far as the *Gazette de Leyde* was concerned, the essential issue at stake in French domestic politics was not reform in the direction of greater efficiency, although this was desirable. It was rather freedom and the right of participation in government.

36. *GL*, 9 Sept. 1774.   37. *GL*, 16 Sept. 1774.

Among the "languages" used to discuss politics in pre-revolutionary France, the paper opted decisively for the vocabulary of freedom, justice, and "rights," not for rationality and efficiency.[38] Although hardly blind to the shortcomings of the parlements, the paper accepted their importance in the limitation of absolute authority in France and gave them the aura of genuine representative institutions that they had long sought to claim for themselves. Unlike many of the parlementaires, the paper was willing to shift its allegiance to more genuinely representative bodies if and when they came into existence. But in their absence, its policy was clear: the parlements were for France what the colonial assemblies were for America — true representatives of the popular will and defenders of freedom.

Although the paper's initial enthusiasm for the parlements underwent a certain transformation during the two years of Turgot's ministry, Luzac seems to have fully appreciated the Turgot reforms only at the moment when the minister was about to fall. The paper offered something less than a ringing endorsement of Turgot's attempt to enforce free trade in grain, asserting that "a middle course would probably be, in this as in all things, the most sure," but adding "that no fair-minded man can fail to be convinced of the patriotic intentions and wise views of the controller general."[39] By the spring of 1776, it had lined itself up somewhat more forcefully with the minister and was more critical of both the selfish interests that objected to his attempt to abolish the guilds and the parlement's opposition to him. The paper praised a pamphlet believed to be inspired by the minister, *Inconvéniens des droits féodaux*, which the Paris parlement condemned,[40] and it continued to praise Turgot's intentions. But it never clearly explained the goals of his reforms, nor did it give very timely publicity to his own statements of his views contained in the preambles to his major reform edicts. It was well informed about the machinations leading to Turgot's fall, pointing to d'Eprémesnil as the instigator of the campaign against him, and it repeatedly asserted that public opinion was against the parlement, a comment obviously in-

38. For the notion of the conflicting "languages" available for the discussion of French politics in this period, see Keith Michael Baker, "A Script for a French Revolution: The Political Consciousness of the Abbé Mably," *Eighteenth-Century Studies* 14 (1981): 235–63.
39. *GL*, 9 May 1775.
40. *GL*, 8 Mar. 1776. The background for the condemnation of this pamphlet is explained in Edgar Faure, *La Disgrâce de Turgot* (Paris, 1961), 443.

tended to influence the outcome of the struggle going on in France.[41] But its support for Turgot became clearest when the battle was over. In an article following his dismissal the paper commented, "Even though his ministry was not of long duration, he has at least the satisfaction of leaving it with a reputation that is not always given to *hommes d'état*, that of a true patriotism and the most complete probity." [42] Once Turgot was gone, the paper fought a rearguard action, assuring readers that the king still meant to see Turgot's policies implemented. It was realistic about his lack of support, noting that "the major commercial cities seemed to oppose the principle of general free trade," [43] and it held no apparent grudge against the parlements. The *Gazette de Leyde* demonstrated during the Turgot years that it was willing to free itself from its traditional loyalty to the parlements if it were convinced that there was a better option for the advance of freedom. Despite Turgot's concern for enlightening the public, however, he himself did little to cultivate the paper and made no effort to use it to shape public opinion in his favor, leaving it to rally to his side only when it was too late to offer much help.[44]

Turgot's dismissal was followed in 1777 by the appointment of Jacques Necker, who attempted to trim wasteful expenditures instead of launching major social and economic reforms. Necker's promotion roughly coincided with the French decision to support the American colonists in their war against England, and the consequences of this decision greatly overshadowed French domestic events in Luzac's pages. From 1776 to 1783, the American war and its naval extension were the *Gazette de Leyde*'s principal concern, and diplomatic news from Versailles overshadowed both Necker's reforms and the other internal issues of the period. Luzac was among the leading Dutch supporters of the American cause. Consequently, there was a natural congruence of interests between the *Gazette* and the French foreign minister, Vergennes, who had decided to use the American revolt to weaken France's major enemy. With its close connections among the Americans and at Versailles, the *Gazette* was in an excellent position to

41. *GL*, 26 Mar. 1776.   42. *GL*, 24 May 1776.
43. *GL*, 28 May and 31 May 1776.
44. Edgar Faure, the closest student of Turgot's ministry, notes repeatedly that he was not an effective propagandist and relied on pamphleteers who showed little sense of timing or of effective ways to frame arguments. Faure, *Disgrâce*, 52, 79, 524–25. *GL*'s treatment of his administration confirms this view.

NUMERO XXVI.

NOUVELLES EXTRAORDINAIRES

DE

DIVERS ENDROITS

du MARDI 1. Avril, 1777.

De PARIS, *le* 24. *Mars.*

LE Parlement vient de rendre & faire publier un Arrêt, lequel, fur l'appel *à minimâ* de la Sentence du Bailliage d'*Orléans* du 22. Mai 1776. condamne au carcan & au banniffement plufieurs Particuliers de la dite Ville, convaincus d'ufure, quelques-uns pour avoir escompté ou prêté fur gages à 20. Sous par Louis par mois. Parmi ces Ufuriers font un Commiffaire de Police, un Chirurgien, un Apothicaire, un Huiffier. Le même Arrêt décharge d'accufation le Prieur de *Saint-Laurent*, Chanoine de la Cathédrale d'*Orléans*, & le Curé de la Paroiffe de *St. Donatien* de la même Ville. Il ordonne " que les Loix, citées dans l'Ar-
„ rêt, depuis le Capitulaire de *Charlemagne*
„ de l'année 789. jusqu'à l'Arrêt de la Cour
„ du 27. Août 1764. feront exécutées felon
„ leur forme & teneur. En conféquence,
„ fait défenfes à toutes Perfonnes d'exercer
„ aucunes efpèces d'ufures prohibées par les
„ Saints Canons reçus dans le Royaume, Or-
„ donnances, Arrêts, & Réglemens de la
„ Cour, en quelque manière que ce foit ou
„ puiffe être, & même fous apparences fein-
„ tes & controuvées de faits de Commerce,
„ &c. " Cet Arrêt eft d'autant plus remarquable, qu'on fe rappelle que, malgré les repréfentations du Parlement, les pourfuites dans une pareille affaire contre des Particu-

liers d'*Angulême* ont été annullées par des Arrêts du Confeil au rapport de Mr. *Turgot*, alors Contrôleur-Général, dont le fyftème étoit, qu'il falloit, pour l'avantage du Commerce, regarder l'Argent comme Marchandife, fujet conféquemment à une variation de prix telle qu'elle a lieu pour les Denrées ou pour le cours des Effets à la Bourfe, &c.

On dit, que le Sr. *Tort* veut fe pourvoir au Confeil en caffation de l'Arrêt du Parlement, du 19. Mars, dont nous avons déjà rendu compte (*l'Ordinaire dernier*:) Cependant, comme nous venons d'en recevoir un Précis plus ample, nous croyons devoir le donner à nos Lecteurs. Le voici.

Le Procès de M. le Duc de Guines *a été jugé le 19. de ce mois par quarante-cinq Juges. Il l'a gagné tout d'une voix. La plainte de* Tort, *en ce qu'il impute à M. le Duc de Guines de l'avoir fait jouer dans les Fonds d'*Angleterre, *& de l'avoir fuit fuir, déclarée injurieufe & calomnieufe. M. le Duc de Guines & M. de* Montval *déchargés de l'accufation.* Tort *blâmé, (ce qui s'exécute en faifant mettre le condamné à genoux & lui difant: La Cour te blâme & te déclare infame:* Va-t-en.) *Condamné en outre en des dommages-intérêts envers M. le Duc de* Guines, M. de Montval *& M. de* Saudray, *par forme de réparation civile, applicables de leur confentement aux pauvres Prifonniers, & à tous les dépens du Procès, (qui emportent prifon.) Enjoint à* Roger *&* Delpech *d'être plus circonfpects à l'avenir, leur écrou ou acte d'emprifonnement fubfiftant; & les dits* Roger *&*

Front page of the *Nouvelles extraordinaires (Gazette de Leyde)*, 1 April 1777.

provide readers with an extremely well documented account of the war. It assembled the scattered evidence of covert French involvement on behalf of the Americans in 1777, predicted the public announcement of a treaty between His Most Christian Majesty and the Continental Congress for several weeks before the news was made official, and offered European readers the first printed texts of this treaty and the related Franco-American treaty of commerce in 1778 and 1779.[45] The paper used British published sources extensively to cover the war — because of British control of the seas, American accounts had a much harder time reaching the Continent — but it worked diligently to counter the impression that things were going badly for the Americans, and this naturally served the interests of the French government as well.

Because of his deep commitment to the American cause, Luzac was hardly likely to go out of his way to obtain material about French domestic affairs that would offend the French government. In any event, French political life after Turgot's dismissal was considerably less dramatic than it had been at any period since the beginning of the refusal-of-sacraments controversy in the early 1750s. The *Gazette* did cover various minor issues involving the Paris parlement, such as its clash with the rival Grand Conseil in 1777. It retained sources in the parlement, as indicated by occasional references to *remontrances* or the mention of an abortive effort at internal reform in 1783.[46] But the parlement could not be the centerpiece of French news coverage during these years because that body itself was relatively quiescent. It did not publish its *remontrances* illegally inside France during these years, and consequently the *Gazette de Leyde* did not publish them either. Nor did the occasional coverage of bodies like the Estates of Brittany, also fairly peaceful during this period, constitute a real challenge to ministerial authority.

In fact, as long as Necker remained in office, he himself seems to have been the main source of news for the paper, and it was respectfully "ministerial" in tone. Luzac — or his Paris correspondent — praised the controller general for financing the war without raising taxes and for abolishing unnecessary court sinecures. The paper gave favorable notice to Necker's creation of provincial assemblies, like the one he created in Berry.[47] All these stories tended to be quite brief,

45. On GL's coverage of the American war, see Bernard Faÿ, *L'Esprit révolutionnaire en France et aux Etats-Unis à la fin du XVIIIe siècle* (Paris, 1925), 35–36; and Peter Ascoli, "The French Press and the American Revolution: The Battle of Saratoga," in *Proceedings of the Fifth Annual Meeting of the Western Society for French History*, ed. Joyce Duncan Falk (Santa Barbara, Calif., 1977), 46–55. The text of the Franco-American commerce treaty appeared in *GL*, 23 Oct. 1778; the text of the treaty of alliance appeared in *GL*, 19 Feb. 1779, based on a copy published in the Providence, R.I., *Gazette* of 19 Dec. 1778.

46. *GL*, 25 Mar. 1783. On this attempt to limit the fees charged to litigants (*épices*), see Bailey Stone, *The Parlement of Paris, 1774–1789* (Chapel Hill, N.C., 1981), 46–47.

47. *GL*, 23 Mar., 27 July, 1 Jan. 1779.

although they were sometimes accompanied by the texts of the relevant edicts; a minor naval engagement in the ongoing war was sure to receive much more elaborate coverage. Necker's opponents, who kept up a vigorous pamphlet war against him at home, received no coverage in the paper, which gave the impression that his policies enjoyed nearly universal support.

The most dramatic moment of Necker's first ministry was its end, in the four months between the publication of his sensational *Compte rendu* and his abrupt dismissal. When Turgot's ministry was nearing its fall, the *Gazette de Leyde* had stepped up its coverage of French affairs. In the last stages of Necker's regime, the paper simply became less and less informative. It announced and praised Necker's *Compte rendu* and offered readers extracts from it, but it gave only a very sketchy impression of the opposition forming against him, attributing it vaguely to "people who found their private advantage in general disorder."[48] As matters moved toward a climax, the paper tried to persuade its readers that the minister's position was solid, noting "the harmony between the ministerial administration and the magistrates" that seemed to rule out a campaign by the parlement against the controller general.[49] The paper understood the probable impact of the unauthorized publication of Necker's private memorandum on provincial administration; it referred to the memorandum in its issue of 1 May 1781, but it still claimed that the king supported Necker's policies.[50] It then lapsed into silence for several issues before giving a one-sentence announcement of Necker's dismissal, supplemented by a two-sentence "explanation" that told readers almost nothing.[51] It was clear that the *Gazette de Leyde* was simply not being allowed to report events in France as it had been up to 1777.

This muzzling of the paper seems to have been part of a crackdown on the Paris *bulletinistes*, masterminded by Vergennes and mentioned in several contemporary sources.[52] Faced with the difficult diplomatic

48. *GL*, 23 Feb., 2 Mar., and 13 Mar. 1781.
49. *GL*, 30 Mar. 1781. In fact, the Paris parlement played a major role in undermining Necker. Robert Harris, *Necker* (Berkeley, 1979), 238–39.
50. *GL*, 8 May 1781.   51. *GL*, 29 May 1781 (two separate reports).
52. See, for example, Mathurin François Adolphe de Lescure, ed., *Correspondance secrète inédite sur Louis XVI, Marie Antoinette, la cour et la ville, de 1777 à 1792* (Paris, 1866), 1:363 (1 Feb. 1781); and the report from Paris in the Hamburg *Politische Journal*, Apr. 1781, 391–92, whose correspondent noted that the intrigues against Necker were freely discussed in Paris coffeehouses and salons.

task of winding up the American war, the foreign minister probably wanted to minimize the repercussions of the intrigues that had forced Necker out. Neither Vergennes nor the naval minister Sartine had any particular affection for the controller general, whose efforts to rationalize French finances had interfered with military and naval expenditures.[53] For its part, the *Gazette de Leyde* could only have defied Vergennes at the cost of separating itself from the minister most responsible for supporting the American cause so dear to Luzac's heart, in order to embrace a minister whose reforms it had approved but who had never wholeheartedly supported French involvement in the war. Another consideration was economic: the *Gazette de Leyde*, like the press in general, was enjoying extraordinary sales in France during the war, thanks to its wealth of information about the fighting. To risk a ban at this precise moment would mean losing precious readers to rival papers, as well as giving up the inside information on French diplomacy and military operations that Vergennes provided. A variety of considerations thus led the *Gazette de Leyde* to reduce its coverage of French domestic affairs and to deny Necker a real chance to state his case in its columns.

The two years that followed Necker's dismissal were even duller for the paper. French domestic politics in 1782 and 1783 had virtually ceased to generate news: the new controller general, Joly de Fleury, undertook no important initiatives and the parlement was uncharacteristically calm. The American war had ended in accordance with French designs, and the ministry could enjoy a rare moment of popular favor. The financial crisis brewing as a result of Necker's wartime loans was not yet apparent. There was thus less news than usual from the "supply side." At the same time, Vergennes continued his rigorous campaign against *nouvellistes* and pamphleteers. Robert Darnton has noted his measures against the authors of scandalous *libelles* during these years and the general dip in book production they caused;[54] the *Gazette de Leyde* and competitors like the *Gazette de Cologne* suffered under the same restraints. Even the *Gazette de France* became more monotonous than usual — a difficult feat. The *Gazette de Leyde* was more and more absorbed with events closer to home. Jean Luzac was

---

53. Murphy, *Vergennes*, 324–25.
54. *The Literary Underground of the Old Regime* (Cambridge, Mass., 1982), 191–95.

increasingly involved with the events of the Dutch Revolution, and his paper carried an ever-growing number of documents from various town assemblies and provincial estates in his native country.

The lull in the coverage of French domestic politics was not destined to last long. As usual, the impetus to renewed attention came from inside France itself, and, indeed, from the institutions that had always enjoyed privileged access to the paper: the parlements. The paper had continued to keep up contacts with the Parlement of Paris even during the quiet years from 1777 to 1783; one can detect the hand of d'Eprémesnil behind a number of seemingly minor news items. But it was the Parlement of Bordeaux that first turned to the *Gazette de Leyde* to renew the practice of using the paper as a means of waging war against the court and the ministry. Around 1784 several long-simmering controversies involving that body reached the point where the Bordeaux judges decided to publicize their point of view. The Dudon affair, which involved their attempt to prevent the son of one of Maupeou's appointees from inheriting his father's seat in the parlement, inspired the first of these illegally published *remontrances*.[55] It was followed by a succession of other events in which the contestatory image of French politics was revived for the first time since 1776. The Parlement of Paris soon took up some of the issues sparked by the Parlement of Bordeaux's protests, and later stories in the *Gazette de Leyde*, such as the letter from Paris in the issue of 13 August 1784, revived the paper's old practice of summarizing the parlement's internal debates and indicating just how fully that body was opposing ministerial policy. The issue of 21 September 1784 included the first text of a Paris parlementary *remontrance* since 1776. The issue was the arrest of the mayor of Bordeaux, the vicomte de Noë, who had been called before a military court. The text was a vigorous denunciation of such arbitrary procedures and a ringing defense of citizens' rights and the need for due process: "Where these forms cease to reign, everything that makes men happy and secure — the distinctions of powers, public liberty, personal security, legitimate authority, civil laws, natural law — all is shaken, all disappears."[56] Readers of the *Gazette de Leyde* were once again exposed to the radical constitutionalist rhetoric

55. *GL,* 18 May 1784; on the Dudon affair, see William Doyle, *The Parlement of Bordeaux and the End of the Old Regime* (New York, 1974), 191–95.

56. *GL,* 28 Sept. 1784 (*remontrance* of 31 Aug. 1784).

of the sovereign courts, and the specter of ministerial despotism was conjured up again as it had been in the 1750s and 1760s.[57]

There was nothing accidental about this development. An unusual letter from Bordeaux, dated 17 September 1784 and published in the *Gazette de Leyde* of 28 September 1784, charged that supporters of the government had tried to discredit the Bordeaux parlement's *remontrances* in the Dudon *fils* affair by using its official propaganda organs to claim that the protests had never been approved by the parlement as a whole. To foil this maneuver, the author of the letter asked Luzac to print an *arrêté* confirming the *remontrances* issued by the parlement on 23 July 1784, which the *Gazette de Leyde* duly included. It was thus clear to all that the Parlement of Bordeaux was furnishing the Dutch paper with material and deliberately choosing it as a vehicle for its political polemics with the ministry.

This renewed skirmishing between parlements and ministers indicated that the tight rein on news coverage of French affairs had been lifted. The *Gazette de Leyde*'s columns gradually filled with more controversial material from France. Necker's defense of his administration in his *Administration des finances* and the resulting controversy with Charles-Alexandre de Calonne received considerable attention, but it is not clear whether it was this issue or some other problem that resulted in a temporary ban on the paper in March 1785.[58] The various financial scandals simmering in Calonne's administration produced other stories.[59] The death of the old *patriote* firebrand and leader of resistance to royal authority in Brittany, Caradeuc de La Chalotais,

57. Several recent studies have reevaluated the significance of the political ideas articulated by the parlements' representatives in the 1750s and 1760s and shown that they were not just ideological smokescreens for narrow special interests but anticipated many of the fundamental political ideas of the revolutionary period. See especially Dale Van Kley, *The Jansenists and the Expulsion of the Jesuits from France, 1757–1765* (New Haven, 1975) and *The Damiens Affair and the Unraveling of the Ancien Régime, 1750–1770* (Princeton, 1984); Keith Michael Baker, "French Political Thought at the Accession of Louis XVI," *Journal of Modern History* 50 (1978): 279–303, and "On the Problem of the Ideological Origins of the French Revolution," in *Modern European Intellectual History*, ed. Dominick LaCapra and Steven Kaplan (Ithaca, 1982), 197–219; and D. Carroll Joynes, "Jansenists and Ideologues: Parlementary Opposition in the Parlement of Paris, 1750–1774" (Ph.D. diss., University of Chicago, 1981).

58. The ban on the paper is mentioned in Lescure, *Correspondance*, 1:546 (17 Mar. 1785), and in Kluit, "Leidsche Courant," 97. Kluit indicates that the French embassy in The Hague quickly assured Luzac that the ban would be lifted; he incorrectly states that it remained in force until August 1788.

59. See, for example, *GL*, 12 July 1785 (an article about speculation in the shares of the Spanish Bank of St. Charles); 14 July 1786, defending the speculative activities of the abbé d'Espagnac.

was the occasion of a warm eulogy.[60] But the story of the year, and the one that enabled the paper to break free of all restraints on its coverage of French politics, was the arrest of the cardinal de Rohan on 15 August 1785, the first public event in the Diamond Necklace affair.

The Diamond Necklace affair was a journalistic sensation: the cardinal de Rohan, a member of the peerage, stood accused of having used the queen's name to obtain a fortune in jewels, with the notion that she might reward him with her most intimate favors. It involved high-ranking people, bizarre characters, sex, money, and power. It also became a major news story because all the major actors decided to take their stories directly to the public, and the *Gazette de Leyde* was more than willing to help them. The initiative in supplying the paper with information came from the highest possible quarters. Marie Antoinette had been disturbed by the ugly rumors being spread about her. Determined to make the cardinal the scapegoat, she arranged for his arrest with the connivance of her adviser, the Austrian ambassador Mercy d'Argenteau, and sprang it on most of the ministers without advance warning.[61] The first stories about the case to appear in the paper were strongly unfavorable to the cardinal and particularly insistent on clearing the queen's name. It is virtually certain that they emanated directly from the queen and probably were furnished to the press by Mercy. The paper even published a purported transcript of a private conversation, in which the king and the queen confronted the cardinal with their accusations for the first time. (This text was later incorporated into the supposed *mémoires* of Mme de Campan, the queen's lady-in-waiting.)[62]

But the court was not to have everything its own way in the papers for very long. The cardinal might be the symbol of everything that was rotten with the French Old Regime, but he was also a great noble, a prince of the Church, and a friend of d'Eprémesnil, one of the Paris parlement's masters of publicity. The revelation of the cardinal's associations with the charlatan Cagliostro and the adventuress Mme de la

60. *GL*, 9 Aug. 1785.

61. Frances Mossiker, *The Queen's Necklace* (New York, 1961), 266 – 67.

62. *GL*, 30 Aug. 1785; Jeanne-Louise Genet de Campan, *Memoirs of the Court of Marie Antoinette* (London, 1851), 2:21–22. The text of Campan is identical to that published in the paper except for one significant passage. In the *GL* version, the king confronts the cardinal with a letter he is supposed to have written to the jewelers who sold the necklace; in the Campan version, he is confronted with a letter from the queen to Mme de la Motte that the king accused him of forging. The Campan version was obviously more incriminating for the cardinal.

Motte that spilled across the *Gazette*'s columns in September 1785 did nothing to make him look more presentable. But the case raised serious legal issues, and the cardinal gathered some eminently respectable supporters who were as adept at using publicity in his favor as the queen had been in organizing a barrage against him. The famous lawyer Target, who had always supported the parlementaire struggle against ministerial despotism, took up the case. The cardinal chose to be tried as a peer by the parlement, which was thus presented with an opportunity for asserting its independence of the Crown and defying the clergy such as it had not enjoyed since its restoration in 1774.[63] Rohan's supporters' view of the case was summarized in the *Gazette de Leyde*: "His Eminence is not guilty of any wrongdoing; he was misled by his excessive credulity and his excessive trust in others."[64]

The focus in the propaganda war over the case shifted from the extraterritorial papers back to Paris, where the major parties began to issue *mémoires* and uncensored statements of their own arguments. The *Gazette de Leyde* collected many of these items, including the statements of the jewelers who had sold the ill-fated necklace, several pieces on behalf of the cardinal, and the sensational *mémoire* of Cagliostro. The paper's news source in Paris recorded the views of the defendants as they issued contradictory accusations against each other, but he remained fundamentally persuaded of the cardinal de Rohan's innocence throughout the affair. By defying the pope's instructions and turning to the Paris parlement, a lay court, for his vindication, the cardinal had succeeded in cloaking himself with the mantle of the Jansenist and Gallican resistance to Roman meddling in French affairs. Consequently, the cardinal emerged as something of a patriotic hero, battling to win back his good name against the intrigues of the queen. He also invoked the principle of a government of laws, where private hatreds could not lead to the imprisonment of an innocent man.

"Ministerial despotism" was not the issue in the case; the ministers had had nothing to do with the accusations against Rohan, and the *Gazette de Leyde*'s *nouvelliste* made a point of indicating Vergennes's role in producing several of the key witnesses who helped absolve the

63. On the background of the Cour des Pairs, see the excellent unpublished study by Martin Mansergh, "The Revolution of 1771, or the Exile of the Parlement of Paris" (D. Phil. diss., Oxford University, 1973).
64. *GL*, 9 Sept. 1785.

cardinal. When the parlement handed down its verdict, ruling that Rohan was not guilty and rejecting the *gens du roi*'s request that he at least be censured for his conduct, the *Gazette de Leyde*'s editor commented, "If one of the most pleasant duties of the reporter is to render justice to the truth, he cannot remain indifferent when he sees oppressed innocence triumph over fraud, artifice, imposture, and ingratitude all combined together."[65] The Paris news bureau on which the paper relied reflected the views of those members of the parlement who voted to acquit Rohan altogether; the reporter gave the names of all forty-eight members of the Grand Chambre who had voted on the verdict and their votes — the only occasion when he ever provided such a roll call of the parlement.[66]

The Diamond Necklace affair, as the *Gazette de Leyde* presented it, was less a demonstration of the corruption of French high society than a vindication of such basic libertarian principles as the right of an accused defendant to a fair trial by his peers and the need for a government of fixed laws, immune to influence even from figures as highly placed as the queen. Once again the great issue of liberty, the *Gazette de Leyde*'s chief concern, had come to the fore, and once again the Parlement of Paris had taken the key role in defending it. The cardinal's affair was thus the opening shot in the continuing string of controversies that led directly to the creation of the National Assembly.

This sensational judicial affair coincided with a growing number of reports in the paper about protests against Calonne's financial administration and the renewal of parlementary *remontrances* against his measures. Even though the paper, true to its habit of publishing contradictory material from a variety of sources, continued to alternately attack and defend many of Calonne's measures, it was clear to its readers by the end of 1786 that France was in a troubled state. To add to the purely political turmoil, the paper had reported several instances of social unrest and especially the revolt of the Lyons silk weavers in August 1786.[67] The *Gazette de Leyde*, as well as its journalistic competitors, had recovered from the repression of 1780 – 83, and French

65. *GL*, 9 June 1786.   66. *GL*, 13 June 1786; *CBR*, 14 June 1786.
67. Three different letters from Lyons, all dated 15 August, appeared in *GL* of 25 Aug. and 1 Sept. 1786, together with a fourth report incorporated in the paper's regular letter from Paris. Only the latter report appeared in *CBR*. For a brief description of the riot, see Louis Trenard, "La Crise sociale lyonnaise à la veille de la Révolution," *Revue d'histoire moderne et contemporaine* 2 (1955): 5 – 45.

readers were once again treated to the spectacle of their king and his ministers being openly thwarted by other forces in the country.

By the end of 1786, the *Gazette de Leyde* was transmitting to its readers a detailed picture of a country dotted with hot spots of unrest and a capital filled with intrigues, many of them aimed against the dominant minister, Calonne. But, in contrast to the 1750s and 1760s, the situation had not resolved itself into a straightforward contest between two parties, one of which the paper supported and one of which it opposed. On the contrary, the reports printed in the *Gazette de Leyde* covered a maze of seemingly unrelated issues. On the one hand, they celebrated the Parlement of Paris for its absolution of the cardinal Du Rohan. On the other, they were critical of its refusal to render justice to the criminal-law reformer Dupaty in the case of three peasants of Chaumont who were accused of murder.[68] Similarly, the paper publicized accusations against Calonne and his replies evenhandedly.

The role of the *Gazette de Leyde* in French politics during the years of the pre-revolutionary crisis from 1787 to 1789 evolved away from a relatively unconnected narration of events toward a more consistently partisan stance, in which the paper backed the efforts of what it saw as a *patriote* party on the model of the American revolutionaries and Polish patriots against the maneuvers of a government flirting with "despotism." The *Gazette de Leyde* no longer saw the parlements as providing France with the representative institutions that would make it a constitutional polity. But it continued to look to the parlementaires and the anti-absolutist tendencies they embodied as the best hope of achieving such a polity, and the paper continued to provide the parlementaire patriots with a powerful medium for addressing their French compatriots. Especially during the crisis caused by Loménie de Brienne and Chrétien-François Lamoignon's eleventh-hour attempt to suppress the sovereign courts in May 1788, the Dutch paper was not only an excellent chronicle of events in France's political life but a major force in molding French public opinion.

As the amount of French news it carried expanded during the last years before the Revolution, the paper's sources diversified as well. It

68. On 22 Aug. 1786 *GL*'s report from Paris noted that the parlement had been unexpectedly severe toward Dupaty. "The dispute . . . will inevitably pit philosophy, which seeks reform of our criminal laws, against the judges, who do not believe that it is absolutely necessary." On 25 Aug. the paper's article said that "all of Paris will accompany Dupaty to the parlement, and his cause will be defended as much by public opinion as by his speech."

continued to rely heavily on its regular source in Paris, who had close contacts with the *patriote* parlementaires. Especially after the death of Vergennes in February 1787, this compiler took an increasingly independent line, often critical of ministerial policy. The *Gazette de Leyde* also continued to have a close relationship with the French foreign ministry even after Vergennes's death; it printed items forwarded through the French embassy in The Hague and, conversely, French diplomats intervened on its behalf when it ran into trouble in Versailles.[69] The paper had long had direct links with sources in Brittany, which were revived in 1788 when that province again became the focus of resistance to ministerial authority. News items from major ministers — in particular from Necker when he resumed office in 1788 — and sometimes from key court figures reached Leiden either directly or through the Paris news bureau. The paper also received a flood of unsolicited material from political activists inside France, which enabled it to keep up with such non-Parisian developments as the reform movement in Dauphiné.

Particularly important were the *remontrances* and other official documents issued by the parlements that the paper reprinted in full in 1787, 1788, and 1789. Between January 1787 and July 1789, it published sixty-seven such texts, in which the magistrates denounced ministerial usurpations of authority, expatiated on the necessity of adhering to fixed constitutional laws, asserted the sovereignty of the nation, demanded guarantees for individual rights, and claimed that only the people, acting through the Estates General, could approve taxes. Thirty-eight of these documents came from the Parlement of Paris, but the provincial courts were not neglected: seven pieces each came

69. Aside from whatever official connections Boyer continued to have in Paris, the French government influenced the paper through a regular correspondence between Luzac and Antoine-Bernard Caillard (1737–1807), who became secretary of the French embassy in The Hague in 1786. Caillard's letters suggest that he was assigned to win Luzac's confidence, which he set out to do by assuring him that GL was "superior to everything else in the way of public papers" (letter of 31 Mar. 1786). From there, he rapidly progressed to forwarding short articles, adding urgent requests that they be printed and often indicating that they had been sent directly from the foreign ministry in Paris. The direction in which this pressure was applied, however, was not always in line with French ministerial policy; Caillard, who characterized himself as a disciple of Turgot, was vehemently opposed to the pretensions of the parlements and skeptical of Necker's ability to resolve the crisis at the time of his recall (letter of 4 Sept. 1788). He also passed along to Luzac a copy of the abbé Sieyès's *Préliminaires de la constitution,* with an approving comment (letter, n.d. but between Oct. 1788 and Feb. 1789). Most of the articles Caillard asked Luzac to print dealt with diplomatic affairs (Caillard Correspondence, Luzac Archives, carton 29).

from Bordeaux and Rouen, three from the Parlement of Toulouse, and others from Besançon, Rennes, Grenoble, Aix, the Paris cour des aides, the Chambre des comptes, and the Châtelet. If the paper rarely added its own editorial comments to these texts, it hardly needed to: they constituted a sweeping campaign against the Brienne ministry and the fundamental operating principles of the Old Regime. In addition, the paper carried the full texts of numerous other documents opposing ministerial policy: twenty-one resolutions from the different bureaus of the first Assembly of Notables in 1787 and nine more from the second session of that body in late 1788; a variety of protests from provincial Estates, assemblies of nobles, and other groups opposing the Lamoignon reforms of 1788, resolutions from the various provincial assemblies that met in Dauphiné in 1788, and the like. Altogether, 139 texts appeared in full in the paper in the last two and one-half years of the monarchy, and many more were summarized. This was only a small fraction of the total number of such documents circulated inside France itself, but it included more than enough items to document the crisis of the regime.[70]

Despite Luzac's distance from the scene, he remained well informed about French events, and his paper chronicled them fully. There were few French men or women, even in Paris, who knew more about the internal politics of their own country during this period. Luzac needed his wide network of informants because the events leading up to the Revolution were exceedingly complex, far surpassing parliamentary politics in England, for example. He had to synthesize his account from reports of happenings in Versailles, Paris, and a number of provinces, and he could not draw on local newspapers to help him: authorized French periodicals remained virtually mute about the country's political crisis until well into 1789. If the *Gazette de Leyde* overlooked some key features of the pre-revolutionary crisis — the extent of peasant unrest, the growth of political clubs in the capital — it must nevertheless be given credit for having put together a remarkably detailed picture of the traditional elite politics of the pre-revolutionary years. In fact, for some critical episodes of the last years of

70. Ralph Greenlaw, who has made a thorough study of the pre-revolutionary pamphlet literature, has found at least 1,348 documents published by corporate bodies inside France between Jan. 1787 and May 1789. I would like to thank him for permission to use these statistics, based on unpublished revisions to his article "Pamphlet Literature in France During the Period of the Aristocratic Revolt (1787–1788)," *Journal of Modern History* 29 (1957): 349–54.

the Old Regime, its chronicle remains the fullest or indeed the only reliable source. Largely freed from government-imposed restrictions and aided by the growing number of French people who wanted to tell their story to the public, the *Gazette de Leyde* achieved with genuine distinction one of the greatest tasks taken on by an eighteenth-century news organ.

The pre-revolutionary crisis became public with the summoning of the first Assembly of Notables, which the *Gazette* reported on 9 January 1787. The paper also published an officially supplied encomium of this measure, stressing its radical implications: "Such an extraordinary and courageous act can only be universally applauded. The nation will see with delight that its sovereign deigns to approach it and to bind himself more and more closely to it. Nothing will do more to raise the level of enthusiasm with which it is already imbued; nothing will do more to strengthen patriotism." [71] Although the meetings of the assembly were not intended to be public, the *Gazette de Leyde*'s sources had no difficulty obtaining a great deal of inside information about it: the list of participants, the agenda, the text of the letters of convocation.[72] Nor was there any doubt about what the paper hoped the convocation of the assembly would accomplish. Not only did it anticipate significant fiscal reforms, but it hoped the results of the meeting would "lead the ministry to a further stage, closer to the ancient constitution of national assemblies." [73] Although Calonne did not intend his handpicked assembly to open the way to genuine representative government in France, Boyer—or whoever dictated the correspondence the *Gazette de Leyde* used—took the opportunity to push for such a result.[74]

The actual assembly, of course, proved to be a disaster for Calonne. The notables greeted his reform proposals with a suspicion that was not unwarranted in view of the many questionable financial maneuvers he had patronized or permitted before throwing himself on the mercy of the notables. Calonne attempted to use the power of publicity to outflank the reluctant notables: he eventually had the texts of his

71. *GL,* 9 Jan. 1787; this passage also appeared in *CBR,* 10 Jan. 1787; according to Aimé Chérest, *La Chute de l'ancien régime* (Paris, 1884–86), 1:231, it also appeared in the official domestic press, including the *Journal de Paris* and the *Mercure de France.*

72. *GL,* 9 Jan., 12 Jan., and 16 Jan. 1787.   73. *GL,* 30 Jan. 1787.

74. On Calonne's intentions in summoning the assembly and his opposition to the creation of a genuine representative assembly, see Jean Egret, *The French Pre-Revolution,* trans. Wesley D. Camp (Chicago, 1977), 4.

proposals published and widely disseminated, and the notables accused him of trying to give the public the impression that they had already consented to many of the key proposals that were still under discussion.[75] But Calonne's opponents had their own means of publicity, and the *Gazette de Leyde* became one of their major resources. The paper eagerly collected all the information it could about the assembly. It was furnished with the text of what eventually became the official procès-verbal of the sessions, which it printed, but this primarily gave the ministers' speeches.[76] The paper's correspondent supplemented the account with a running summary of what was actually going on in the sessions, explaining, for example, that Necker's partisans were harassing Calonne.[77] Most important, however, was the fact that, despite Calonne's initial plea that the discussions be kept secret, Louis XVI eventually permitted the various bureaus into which the assembly was divided to print their *arrêtés*. Twenty-one of these resolutions appeared in whole or in part in the paper, nearly all of them critical of the minister's proposals.[78] Together with the *Gazette de Leyde*'s summary of the most important polemical pamphlets generated by the Assembly of Notables, this extensive coverage of the meeting made it quite clear why Calonne was finally dismissed.[79]

There were some important aspects of the politicking in the sessions that the paper did not clarify. Although, for example, it mentioned Necker's role in stimulating opposition to Calonne, it never men-

75. *GL*, 17 Apr. 1787.

76. The text of *GL*'s coverage of the opening ceremonies and public speeches is identical with the subsequently published *Procès-Verbal de l'Assemblée des notables, tenue à Versailles, en l'année 1777* (Paris, 1788) (see *GL*, 9 Mar. 1787 and subsequent issues). The paper also had information about the assembly that was not in the officially published documents. For example, the issue of 6 Mar. 1787 summarizes the opening session of the assembly and mentions that the draft of Calonne's speech had been burned the night before and he had had to speak from notes. This episode is not mentioned in the official procès-verbal, but it is confirmed in the "Journal du bureau de Monsieur" published in Pierre Chevalier, ed., *Journal de l'Assemblée des notables* (Paris, 1960), 24.

77. *GL*, 23 Mar. 1787.

78. *GL*'s coverage of the assembly's proceedings had included a few short quotes from speeches opposing the ministry and some excerpts from the discussions of Calonne's proposals in the bureaus before they were given official permission to publish their resolutions on 2 Apr. 1787. The first text it published under the new regulations appeared in the issue of 6 Apr. 1787 (30 Mar., *arrêté* from bureau de Monsieur). The paper thus slightly exceeded the bounds officially set for publicity about the assembly but essentially followed its normal pattern of publishing only material that was already in circulation in Paris. For the government's policy about publicizing the bureaus' resolutions, see Chérest, *Chute*, 1:189.

79. *GL*, 20 Apr. 1787.

tioned Loménie de Brienne, whose ambition to replace Calonne made him one of the controller general's most dangerous opponents.[80] But on the whole, the paper had seized the opportunity Calonne offered to air the government's problems and had given the French their first taste of what an assembly brought together to debate reforms would look like. Profiting from the fact that, even if Calonne did not wish to carry on such debate in public, the other parties to the assembly were eager to propagate their views, the *Gazette de Leyde* and its competitors opened up the proceedings to its admittedly limited but nonetheless significant French reading audience. The age of parliamentary journalism in France had dawned.

Calonne's dismissal and the dispersal of the notables shifted the focus of the *Gazette de Leyde*'s reporting back to the traditional centers of its interest: the parlements and the ministry, now headed by Loménie de Brienne, a man for whom the paper never showed much enthusiasm. The new ministry went ahead to promulgate several of the major reforms discussed during the Assembly of Notables, in particular the creation of provincial assemblies and the extension of the *vingtième* tax to ward off a financial collapse. The resulting confrontations with the parlements provided the *Gazette*'s Paris *nouvelliste* with the occasion to state clearly his own views on the direction France should take, and the publicity the *Gazette* gave to the parlements powerfully aided their campaign against Brienne. In essence, the paper's articles urged France's decision makers to come to a compromise that would move the country directly toward the creation of functioning representative institutions. In a general review of the Assembly of Notables's meeting, the paper's correspondent praised virtually all of the participants, concluding that, compared to its most recent predecessor in 1626, "this assembly gives the highest impression of the nation's energy as well as the progress made in knowledge and enlightenment." On the other hand, the paper noted, France now had ministers "who do not believe that the science of government is a secret, nor that they should keep matters to themselves alone."[81] In effect, then, the conditions were right for the creation of a regular representative assembly. The paper welcomed the new provincial

80. On Brienne's role in the Assemblée des notables, see Chérest, *Chute*, 1:182; Egret, *Pre-Revolution*, 20, 23–24. The first specific reference to him in *GL* was the announcement of his appointment as minister, *GL*, 11 May 1787.

81. *GL*, 15 June 1787; most of this account also appeared in *CBR*, 13 June 1787.

assemblies, without discussing the crucial question of whether they should be elected or appointed, but it quickly sensed that they raised the problem of what the role of the parlements was to be in any new order of things.

On several occasions in the summer of 1787, the paper took editorial positions that indicated its evolution away from the classical parlementaire position that the sovereign courts themselves were a satisfactory representation of the national will. When the members of the Paris parlement themselves called for the convocation of the Estates General, the paper's correspondent wrote:

It is good to see the parlement now recognizing this grand principle. Less than twenty years ago, the very mention of the Estates General was too much for it, as it has been for all the ministers since Cardinal Richelieu. Times have certainly changed. The parlement no longer claims to be a "miniature Estates General." It has been blamed so often for exceeding the bounds fixed by the nature of its function that, if its wish is accepted and the nation gains protectors in the form of its natural representatives, the parlement seems ready to limit itself from now on to administering justice. It will leave to the assembled nation the right to examine and pass taxes, and it will no longer incur the criticism it has sometimes received of having sacrificed the interests of the population. Here is, without a doubt, the most complete proof that the parlement has given up all its old prejudices: that it is far from resisting royal authority for the sole pleasure of showing its power and that it deserves, more than ever, the confidence and the gratitude of the nation for its attachment to the old constitutions of the nation.[82]

This semiofficial judgment reflected Brienne's initial hope that the parlements would cooperate with his reforms as well as his willingness to play the Estates General off against the parlements. It also foresaw a limitation of ministerial power that neither Brienne nor the king had yet accepted. Subsequent articles pursued the same tack. While applauding the Paris parlement for its ringing declaration that only the Estates General could impose new taxes, the paper wished the members had not rejected the proposed stamp tax, which it felt would be the least severe for the poor.[83] Even though the French people had an interest in the restoration of their primitive "constitution," they were no less concerned about their "national honor, the credit of the kingdom," which required an adequate government revenue.[84]

82. *GL*, 31 July 1787; *CBR*, 1 Aug. 1787.   83. *GL*, 3 Aug. 1787.
84. *GL*, 10 Aug. 1787.

The parlement's refusal to compromise on the tax edicts and the government's decision to exile it to Troyes, announced in the paper on 24 August 1787, naturally dashed any hopes of a compromise. The *Gazette de Leyde* once more offered considerable aid and comfort to the Paris parlementaires and their provincial colleagues by printing and praising the *remontrances* and other declarations of the embattled magistrates at a time when the government was using severe measures to try to prevent their dissemination.[85] Whatever its criticisms of the parlements at other moments, the paper was never prepared to publish stories favoring an authoritarian program that simply dismissed such deeply rooted traditional institutions. The paper did publish some of Brienne's propaganda against the parlements, notably by reproducing a pamphlet he had commissioned that claimed that it would be dangerous to assemble the Estates General in the midst of such a pressing crisis.[86] But throughout the months up to Brienne and Lamoignon's coup against the parlements on 8 May 1788, the paper's coverage was so heavily tilted toward the protests of the sovereign courts — not just the Paris parlement but also its sister courts in Bordeaux, Rouen, Rennes, and Toulouse — that Luzac felt compelled to make a special point of it when he devoted some space to the views of the other side, acknowledging that his paper had an obligation, after all, "to represent the contest from all angles."[87] The exceptional nature of this article suggests that in reality the paper was quite content to leave most of the talking to the parlements and that it expected its French audience to approve of its generally antiministerial tone; the publication of a strongly worded critique of the parlements, in which they were accused of using constitutionalist rhetoric merely to defend the interests of wealthy privileged groups, required special explanation.

The *Gazette de Leyde* thus served to strengthen the parlements' resistance to Brienne even though, on other issues that arose during the same period, the paper's stories were sometimes at odds with the judges' positions. As befitted a Dutch descendant of the Huguenots,

85. *GL*, 18 Sept. 1787, reported the arrest of Kersaulan, the son of a *conseiller* of the Parlement of Rennes, for carrying messages from the exiled Paris parlement in Troyes to the capital.

86. *Lettre d'un avocat. GL*, 28 Aug. 1787, attributed the work to the abbé Morellet, a longtime associate of Brienne; Chérest, *Chute*, attributes it to the abbé Maury, the future counterrevolutionary spokesman in the National Assembly.

87. *GL*, 21 Mar. 1788.

Luzac strongly supported Malesherbes's edict granting civil rights to Protestants, issued in December 1787 and debated at length in the Paris parlement during the following months. In this case, the paper found itself urging the parlement, rather than the ministers, to bow to the wishes of public opinion and carry out "this so universally desired registration, which has in its favor, so to speak, the unanimous support of the public." [88] The parlement was far from being equally unanimous, as the paper soon noted: d'Eprémesnil, the member whose activities it had always covered most extensively, took the lead in organizing an ultimately unsuccessful party to oppose the proposal. When the parlement finally did vote to register the edict, the *Gazette* claimed that d'Eprémesnil had lost much of his popularity by opposing "a law that only gives men, Frenchmen, what belongs to them by the law of nature." [89] D'Eprémesnil was sufficiently stung by the paper's singling him out in this way to route a protest to the editor through the Paris correspondent, explaining that he, too, favored granting civil rights to Protestants but wanted to make sure that any such law could not be stretched to include deists or atheists and that it would not undermine the special legal position of Catholicism.[90] D'Eprémesnil, who had repeatedly used publicity in the foreign press to oppose the ministers, had now discovered that this weapon could be turned against him.

Throughout the months of uncertainty prior to the Lamoignon coup, there were other issues on which the paper was critical of the parlement, such as its reluctance to accept the criminal justice reforms proposed in February 1788. In a general statement on the question of reform, the *Gazette* condemned the members of the parlement who feared that "in detaching a few stones from this edifice, one will make the whole magnificent monument fall down. . . . The rights of man, his natural liberty, and its connections with society had not been discussed and explored [in the past] as they have been by Montesquieu, Beccaria, Servant [*sic*], etc. In a word, although the spirit of innovation is dangerous, it is even more contrary to reason and the good of humanity to oppose every reform because one is afraid to touch what has been done by our ancestors, who had their passions, their prejudices, their errors, like their descendants." [91] If this seemed

88. *GL*, 18 Dec. 1787.   89. *GL*, 5 Feb. and 8 Feb. 1788.
90. *GL*, 4 Apr. 1788.   91. *GL*, 7 Mar. 1788.

to contradict the paper's expressions of respect for France's ancient constitution, the contradiction resulted from the optimistic assumption shared by the paper and reform-minded figures in the government that on fundamental constitutional issues, reason and tradition led to the same result: representative government.

Everything but the basic constitutional issue was swept aside on 8 May 1788. Frustrated in his efforts to get the parlements to yield on the issue of taxes, Garde de Sceaux Lamoignon decided to return to Maupeou's policy of 1771 and reform the refractory sovereign courts out of existence. The *Gazette de Leyde*'s Paris correspondent had been aware for several weeks that something drastic was in preparation. In fact, he had received an advance copy of the planned edicts, probably obtained by d'Eprémesnil, and sent it or a summary over to the paper, which published it in its edition of 2 May 1788.[92] Of course, the delays in transport meant that copies of this issue could not have reached Paris much before the government actually acted. As usual, the *Gazette* publicized the parlement's protests against the measures. In his first letter from Paris after the coup, the paper's Paris correspondent, who strongly opposed Lamoignon's plan, wrote, "The terrible conflict that has arisen between the Royal Power and the magistrature, reminding France of the shock she experienced eighteen years ago through a revolution of the same sort, has strongly saddened all the friends of the public good."[93] After this reminder of the Maupeou coup, in which the paper's position had been so clear, the *Gazette* settled in to await word from the French provinces, where both sides expected the issue to be decided.

At first, as the paper reported, there was less overt resistance to Lamoignon's measures than had been expected. After the first week,

92. Also in *CBR*, 3 May 1788. The story that d'Eprémesnil had obtained a copy of the edict by bribing a worker in the royal printshop is mentioned in a number of sources of the period, including Lescure, *Correspondance secrète*, 2:255.

93. *GL*, 16 May 1788. It is clear that this hostile attitude toward the coup emanated from Boyer in Paris and not from Luzac in Leiden because the same stories appeared in *CBR* although that paper's editor, Manzon, inserted his own footnotes sharply attacking the parlements: "How many times has this *sanctuary of the laws*, this *refuge of liberty*, already been profaned by atrocious injustices, by cowardly cooperation with arbitrary authority, as long as it only exercised its terrible effects on individuals without connections" (21 May 1788, editor's note to Paris, 11 May). From the beginning of June 1788 until the fall of Brienne in late August, the news coverage published in *CBR* ceased to duplicate what was printed in *GL* and in fact sharply contradicted it on the merits and prospects of the court reform scheme; after Necker's reappointment, the two papers' content began to run parallel again.

the Paris correspondent remarked, "one has every reason to believe . . . that the great revolution in the judicial order will be carried out peacefully and without much difficulty." The article went on to point out the advantages of the rationalized judicial system that Lamoignon meant to install, but it warned that the reforms could not legally be extended to areas whose special rights were embodied in their charters, "engagements, from which Royal Majesty itself can never release itself." [94] But this evaluation of the reform's chances was short-lived. Although the paper printed the texts of Lamoignon's edicts and his speeches justifying them, it carefully collected all evidence of opposition and undermined the government's claims that the lower courts were accepting the new arrangements.[95] At the beginning of June, the paper publicized the Assembly of the Clergy's protest against the reforms and its call for the Estates General, as well as the refusal of the country's lawyers to plead in the new courts.[96] As issue followed issue during June, the paper filled up with reports from Pau, Rennes, Toulouse, Lyons, and elsewhere indicating continued opposition to the government. As an editorial comment in the paper put it, the fundamental issue underlying this widespread opposition was the determination of provinces "that have only been united to the Crown of France by virtue of bilateral pacts, which contain conditions contrary to the new system of universality and uniformity," to defend their traditional rights, and there was no doubt of the paper's sympathy for this attitude.[97]

By the end of June, the paper was not only reporting the extent of resistance to the ministry but predicting that it would succeed; it said that everyone in Paris was convinced that the parlements would be recalled.[98] This observation was bound to have an influence on the events it purported to describe: such a prediction from a respected source like the *Gazette de Leyde* could only encourage the parlementaires and discourage the government's supporters, who no doubt remembered only too well what had happened to Maupeou's asso-

94. *GL*, 23 May 1788. This was precisely the issue raised in the first wave of protests against the reform (Chérest, *Chute*, 1:516, 536). This issue of the paper would have reached France about the time of the first violent protests in Pau, Grenoble, and Rennes.

95. *GL*, 30 May 1788.

96. *GL*, 3 June 1788. On the significance of the Assembly of the Clergy's resistance, see Michel Peronnet, "Les Assemblées du clergé de France sous le règne de Louis XVI (1775–1788)," *Annales historiques de la Révolution française*, 1962, no. 167:31.

97. *GL*, 17 June 1788.   98. *GL*, 1 July 1788.

ciates in 1774. Subsequent stories emphasized the cross-class nature of the opposition to Lamoignon's new courts, showing that it was not based only on the privileged classes. They also indicated that the government could hardly hope to govern without the support of the nation's elites and concluded that Lamoignon's plan would make the courts entirely subservient to the ministers, thus raising the old specter of ministerial despotism.[99] Several weeks before the ministers and other well-informed observers had concluded that the reform plan would have to be abandoned, the *Gazette de Leyde* had already proclaimed its failure.[100] The paper had done more than merely report on events in France during this crisis: by bringing together news of the opposition to the government from widely separated provinces, by collecting the official statements of a wide variety of corporate institutions and underlining the common theme that united them, and by doing all this in the guise of being an objective reporter of events with no direct involvement in them, the paper had undermined the government's reform plan in a way that the openly partisan pamphlets produced inside France could not. It is obvious from the fact that Brienne and Lamoignon tried to ban the *Gazette*'s distribution in France in July 1788 that they regarded the paper's role as dangerous. (As usual, Luzac called on his friends in the foreign ministry to get the ban lifted.)[101]

Even before the end of the crisis, Brienne and Lamoignon had been forced to take a major step that the *Gazette de Leyde* warmly welcomed, since it put the government in line with the policy the paper had been urging from the very beginning: on 5 July 1788 the ministry had announced that the king would convoke the Estates General. The paper's Paris sources had had advance notice of this decision, and the

99. *GL*, 4 July and 8 July 1788.

100. The British ambassador Dorset's letter of 2 July 1788 said that, although the French government would have to act quickly to defuse opposition to its plans, he was still confident they could be carried out. By 31 July the duke of Dorset had concluded, "There is every reason to expect from the present complexion of affairs, that Government will be obliged to give way" (Oscar Browning, ed., *Despatches from Paris, 1784–1790* [London, 1909–10], 2:72–73, 83).

101. *GL* was banned in Paris after the arrival of its issue of 22 July 1788, according to a letter of Thomas Jefferson in Julian P. Boyd, ed., *The Papers of Thomas Jefferson* (Princeton, 1950–), 13:467. Jefferson and other members of the diplomatic corps continued to receive their copies by private mail. By 27 August 1788, shortly after Necker's appointment, Caillard was able to report to Luzac that letters from himself to Rayneval, another reform-minded foreign ministry official, and from French ambassador Saint-Priest to the foreign minister, Montmorin, had led to intervention in Paris and a lifting of the ban (Caillard Correspondence, letter of 27 Aug. 1788, in Luzac Archives, carton 29).

paper urged the nation "to seize this *juste milieu* that, by avoiding extremes dangerous both to the liberty of peoples and to governments, will make the Sovereign Power more stable, thanks to the barrier that will separate it forever from despotism." [102] When the announcement of the impending assembly proved insufficient to quiet the provinces, the paper clearly indicated its preference for moderate measures. It contrasted the violence breaking out in Brittany with the more orderly measures being taken in Dauphiné, where "the spirits . . . are calmer; they proceed step by step and always in a legal manner." [103] Once again, the paper was not merely transcribing events but stepping in to evaluate and direct them. The basic issue on which the *Gazette de Leyde* was eventually to break with the French revolutionaries — the role of violence in carrying out political change — had already come to the fore. But there remained several months of frantic political maneuvering before the Estates General assembled and the Bastille fell.

The announcement that the Estates General would be convened was issued on 5 July 1788. It also invited the people of France to advise the government on how that assembly should be structured, and had in effect suspended the censorship of political publications. The reaction to the measures of 8 May 1788 had already unleashed a flood of pamphlets, which swelled to an even greater volume by the end of the year. But this indigenous political literature, produced on the spot, did not render the *Gazette de Leyde* and the other foreign-based newspapers irrelevant to French politics. Censorship remained in effect for periodicals, and nothing resembling a reliable political newspaper appeared inside France until after the deputies had assembled at Versailles. Furthermore, the pamphlet literature, although produced far more rapidly than books, inevitably lagged behind events and was liable to be outdated; pamphlets against Brienne were suddenly rendered obsolete on 25 August 1788 when Necker was called in to face the financial crisis. In spite of the delay imposed on foreign newspapers by extraterritorial publication, they kept up with the pace of events as well as the pamphlet press, and their periodical nature enabled them to adjust to unexpected occurrences. The *Gazette de Leyde* was certainly less outspoken than the voluminous pamphlet literature in the fall of 1788 and early 1789, but it remained a valuable source of information for French readers about events in their own country.

102. *GL*, 11 July 1788.   103. *GL*, 15 Aug. 1788.

The reappointment of Necker as controller general in August 1788 considerably changed the tone of the paper's reporting. With the Estates General now imminent — Necker initially hoped to call them as early as January 1789 — and a minister the paper had always praised in control, the *Gazette de Leyde* saw every reason to expect that France would escape safely from the perils of bankruptcy and disorder that had threatened her. The paper's correspondent was even willing to stretch the truth on behalf of the new ministry: he announced that the shares of the government bank, the Caisse d'escompte, were rising again, although other sources indicate the opposite.[104] For the first time in many months, the paper carried material obviously supplied directly by the French court, when it told readers that the queen had personally asked Necker to accept the ministry and that Monsieur, the king's brother, had given Necker "the most flattering welcome" and promised not to oppose him as he had in 1781. The royal family obviously wanted credit for Necker's appointment, and such items served Necker's purposes, too, by emphasizing the solidity of his support in Versailles.[105] Throughout the fall of 1788, the paper put Necker's actions in the best possible light. It was no doubt the minister himself who authorized publication of a remark to his intimates that "everything will go well, if everyone will just agree, if harmony prevails; the French will not be as obligated to me as they imagine."[106]

The *Gazette de Leyde*'s favorable attitude toward Necker did not mean that it had gone from being an opposition paper, in the British sense, to being a ministerial one. For one thing, the paper's stories were critical from the outset of Necker's refusal to take immediate action to deal with pressing problems.[107] For another, it supported Necker only because it assumed, somewhat too optimistically, that the famous banker genuinely intended to promote constitutional reform along the lines the *Gazette* favored. The author of the paper's Paris letters now identified himself with the program of the Dauphiné reformers, led by Mounier, whom he had come to admire because of their firm but legal resistance to the Lamoignon reforms in the summer of 1788.

The paper praised and reprinted numerous documents from the

---

104. *GL*, 2 Sept. 1788. The assertion in this article contradicts information in British ambassador Hailes's letter of 21 Aug. 1788. Browning, *Despatches*, 2:89–91.
105. *GL*, 5 Sept. 1788; *CBR*, 6 Sept. 1788.
106. *GL*, 31 Oct. 1788.   107. *GL*, 9 Sept. 1788.

Assembly of Romans and lauded the talents of "M. Mounier, its secretary," who was, of course, the actual author of most of them.[108] The
Dauphiné program for the creation of both local and national representative assemblies, with double representation of the Third Estate
and voting in common, seemed to the *Gazette* to be the best answer to
France's needs. The paper defended this program both against tradi-
tionalists who opposed any dilution of the powers of the privileged
orders — "enlightenment . . . has spread in the last hundred years
[and] has created too much difference between the century of Louis
XIII and that of Louis XVI for one to believe that the two first orders of
the state . . . will refuse to see the obvious" — and against reformers
who proposed too much leveling — "it is part of the essence of a
monarchy that there be gradations between the different classes of
civil society." [109]

In embracing Mounier's program, the *Gazette de Leyde* separated
itself from its traditional ally, the Parlement of Paris, which it had
always treated as a legislative assembly and to which it had long
looked as a mainstay of French liberty. The paper had maintained its
position of support throughout 1787, even though it had often criticized the parlement for its position on specific reforms, and it had
certainly not abandoned the judges during the ordeal of the summer of
1788. It was precisely at the moment when the parlement was recalled
that the paper separated itself. The judges incurred the paper's disfa-
vor for two reasons. In the first place, they came dangerously close to
condoning the violent riots against Brienne and Lamoignon that had
broken out after their dismissals; as the *Gazette*'s Paris correspondent
reported, rather than blame the rioters, the judges had opened an
investigation to see whether the authorities had used excessive force in
controlling the crowd. If there was one consistent theme in the *Gazette
de Leyde*'s coverage of politics in all countries, it was opposition to
popular violence, and no movement that encouraged such activities
could expect the paper's endorsement. Second, the Paris parlement
had ruled immediately after its recall that the upcoming Estates General had to be held according to the "forms of 1614." [110] The significance

108. *GL*, 17 Oct. 1788. On Mounier's role in the Dauphiné movement, see Jean Egret,
La Révolution des notables (Paris, 1950).

109. *GL*, 31 Oct. and 25 Nov. 1788.

110. *GL*, 3 Oct. 1788. The paper's correspondent drew attention to the significance of
the Parlement's *petite phrase* as quickly as anyone in France. Luzac's correspondent in
the French embassy in The Hague, Caillard, also drew the editor's attention to the issue
in a letter of 27 August 1788, even before the parlement had taken a stand on the matter
(Luzac Archives, carton 29).

of this famous *petite phrase* was not immediately clear either in Paris or in Leiden, but within two weeks the paper had noted that this arrangement would give the privileged orders a double veto over the Third Estate as well as a two-to-one majority in deputies, which it found unacceptable. Although French pamphleteers offered a wide range of counterproposals, the *Gazette*'s correspondent committed himself immediately and firmly to the Dauphiné model that was ultimately to prevail in June 1789.[111] Whether the paper was following French opinion or helping to lead it, its course on this issue clearly indicated that it had shifted its loyalty from an institution — the parlement — to an ideology and a program of action. However moderate its tone and its goals, the *Gazette de Leyde*, like the *patriote* movement as a whole, had shifted from the defense of existing rights to revolution.

It was clear to the paper's authors that this revolution had brought on the scene a new force in French politics. A November 1788 article summing up recent pamphlet literature on the best form for the Estates General noted the works of Mably, d'Antraigues, Pierre Lacretelle, and Target, pointing out that the latter two in particular rejected "the form of the 1614 Estates General . . . where the most industrious class, that is, the one most useful to the nation, was counted for nothing." The reporter cited the demands throughout the country of groups speaking for the Third Estate, whose right to fair representation, he asserted, derived from "God and Nature," and he concluded by suggesting that a mobilized Third Estate would actually help the Crown strengthen its authority against the "esprit de corps" of the privileged orders.[112] But on the whole, the *Gazette de Leyde* did not throw in its lot entirely with the newly militant Third Estate. Despite the excellence of its news coverage of events at Versailles and in traditional institutions like the Paris parlement, it gave almost no press coverage to the new political institutions created by the revolutionary movement, such as the political clubs. This is particularly surprising in view of former editor Cerisier's personal involvement with one of the

111. *GL*, 31 Oct. 1788.
112. *GL*, 21 Nov. 1788. The paper had often drawn attention to pamphlets issued by Target and Lacretelle, two reform-minded lawyers who were involved in a number of important political issues before the Revolution; Target later headed the National Assembly committee that drafted the constitution of 1791. According to the abbé Morellet, Target was a member of the Duport circle, which included many prominent leaders of the National Assembly in 1789; Lacretelle participated in weekly gatherings at Morellet's house, which included some of the moderate members of the Duport group and other friends of Morellet and favored a less sweeping set of reforms. This gives some clue as to the personal contacts of the *Gazette*'s own correspondent (André Morellet, *Mémoires inédites de l'abbé Morellet*, ed. P. Lemontey [Paris, 1821], 1:336 – 37).

most important of these associations, the *Société des amis des noirs* —
which the paper never mentioned — and the paper's interest in the
activities of prominent members of such groups as the Society of
Thirty and the circle of writers that met at the abbé Morellet's house
once a week.[113]

The *Gazette* did give some coverage to new revolutionary doctrines
through its comments on the pre-revolutionary pamphlet literature.
But even here the paper was fairly conservative in its approach. In the
two years before the meeting of the Estates General, it mentioned
about 60 such works (as opposed to the 139 documents from the parlements, other courts, and other traditional institutions it published
during the same period) and gave the full texts of only a few. Furthermore, many of the more radical works named were mentioned only in
the context of a condemnation by the Conseil d'état or the parlement,
or else they were referred to long after their impact on French opinion
had passed. This was the case, for example, with the paper's one
reference to Sieyès's *Qu'est-ce que le tiers état?* toward the end of
March 1789.[114] The *Gazette de Leyde* thus did not serve to advertise the
existence of pamphlets promoting a more radical revolutionary approach than the paper itself overtly espoused.

The one radical revolutionary whose words were broadcast
through the paper with some regularity was the great tribune, the
comte de Mirabeau. The reasons for the paper's particular interest in
him are not entirely clear, but he had an advantage in the fact that he
was not a new man like Sieyès. The frequent pamphlets of this rene-
gade aristocrat had often been mentioned in the paper earlier in the
1780s, and the European press as a whole had helped to build him up
into a rare phenomenon in the Old Regime, an outsider who had
become a genuine political force in his own right. The *Gazette de Leyde*
was more likely than most papers to pay him some heed by 1788,
because he had come to the aid of the beleaguered Dutch Patriots with
his pamphlet *Aux bataves* after the Prussian occupation. In return, the
paper gave favorable coverage to Mirabeau's campaign for election to
the Estates General in Provence[115] along with the text of his speech
denouncing the nobles of the province.

113. On Cerisier's membership in the *Société des amis des noirs*, see Jacques-Pierre
Brissot de Warville, *Mémoires de Brissot*, ed. C. Perroud (Paris, 1911), 2:74.
114. *GL*, 24 Mar. 1789. Caillard had tried to encourage Luzac to publicize Sieyès's
ideas earlier, but without success (letter to Luzac, n.d. but between Oct. 1788 and Feb.
1789, in Luzac Archives, carton 29).
115. *GL*, 20 Feb. 1789.

On the whole, however, the paper's sympathy was reserved for the followers of the firm but moderate revolutionary path Mounier seemed to have marked out. The paper's authors realized that the privileged orders were an obstacle, although they tried whenever possible to prevent the revolutionary movement from becoming explicitly antinoble. A significant article in January 1789 reminded readers that it was not the nobility as a whole that was obstructing reform: "This order, whose distinctive characteristic has always been generosity, includes a very large number of members who are convinced that its superiority over the other citizens should not be based on their abasement, but on the civil and military virtues that the nobility will always be better placed to display than what is called the people." The real troublemakers, the paper contended, were the clergy and a few special privileged groups, concentrated mostly in Paris. Even within the Paris parlement there was a strong minority in favor of reforms, although the majority kept it from expressing itself.[116] Subsequent events, especially in Brittany, quickly proved that this estimate had been too generous to the privileged orders, and the *Gazette de Leyde* had to express its disappointment, particularly in the conduct of the parlements, which it now found to be in opposition to "the national cause. And, if one did not know the mistakes that the *esprit de corps* can lead to, it would be difficult to understand how these same bodies, who only stood up to arbitrary power thanks to the support of the people, in which they used to glory, and who knew they could do nothing without the people, can declare so openly against them." [117]

This was not only the view of the paper's Paris correspondent. Luzac himself wrote in an editorial comment in February 1789, where he made his choice between institutions and principles, "We have proved some time ago, even at the risk of displeasing an all-powerful minister, our respect for the virtues of the French magistracy. But, being as much enemies to the spirit of faction and schism as we are friends of true patriotism, we support good principles, just actions, and generous proceedings, and neither offices nor persons." [118] Nevertheless, both the paper's Paris correspondence and its editorial comments continued to warn against a violent rupture between the elites and the people and against the adoption of militant tactics. Reflecting the views of people in Paris who sought to steer the nation's impa-

116. *GL*, 16 Jan. 1789.   117. *GL*, 3 Feb. 1789.   118. *GL*, 17 Feb. 1789.

tience for reforms into a narrow channel that would avoid confrontations, the paper condemned "the amour propre of those who believe that their prerogatives and honors are going to be disregarded," but also warned against "the precipitation, the stubbornness, the impatience, the reckless desire to overturn everything, to make everything over anew, and obtain everything all at once" that it detected among some of the Third Estate activists. Such conduct threatened to "cause irreparable harm to peoples, just at the unique moment when it seems possible to consolidate their happiness for good." [119]

Reporting on events in Brittany, where the deadlock in the provincial Estates between the privileged groups and the Third Estate foreshadowed the course of the national Estates General, the paper's correspondent complained that the Third Estate's decision to boycott that meeting unless its demands for doubling of its representation and voting by head were granted indicated that "these pretensions are pushed to an extreme." [120] When the paper's French correspondents detected signs of genuine unrest among the lower orders, they instantly condemned them, and when the drawing up of *cahiers* for the Estates General began to bring radical demands to the surface, the paper was equally hostile: it criticized those over-excited citizens "who believed that all ecclesiastical, political, and economic reforms should be carried out by the very first assembly of the nation." [121] The paper's program was summed up in an article covering the first elections for deputies that stated, "The way to obtain nothing in civil contestations is to demand everything, and the public good has never resulted from the complete victory of one party or another." [122] This was the view of the forces in the French government — exactly which ministers they spoke for is not clear — who influenced the paper's Paris coverage, but it was Luzac's view as well. Dismayed by the unexpected intransigence of some of the privileged groups, he nevertheless continued to look toward a compromise that would not drive them into open hostility. With the lesson of the failed Dutch Patriot movement fresh in his mind, it was understandable that he, even more than his increasingly excited French readers, should keep in

119. *GL*, 30 Jan. 1789.   120. *GL*, 3 Feb. 1789.
121. *GL*, 23 Dec. 1788 (condemnation of peasant revolts in Languedoc); 31 Mar. 1789 (criticism of *cahiers* demanding reform of the French church).
122. *GL*, 24 Mar. 1789.

mind the possibility that radicalism and intransigence could lead to a disaster.[123]

A clue to the way the paper hoped that events would develop lies in its coverage of the actual elections to the Estates General. Evidently the *Gazette de Leyde* was far from anticipating that in a matter of weeks the predominance of the privileged orders would be swept away without a trace. Despite its excellent system for obtaining news inside France, the paper made no effort to compile national election returns as they came in; it gave only a scattering of results, mostly for areas around Paris. But there was nothing random about the names it printed: they were overwhelmingly the names of nobles, especially members of the peerage, and bishops elected to represent the clergy. Of fifty-two deputies mentioned by name before the assembly of the Estates, only five were going to sit with the Third Estate. This was not because the paper had made the mistake of interpreting the elections as a ringing vote of confidence in France's traditional elites: it was quite well aware that there had been an electoral revolt within the clergy at the expense of the bishops and that, although some districts near Paris had returned "seigneurs and persons of distinction," the trend in most places was quite the other way. Its final overview of the elections gave a very mixed assessment: "In the number of the representatives, there are, no doubt, some men of great merit; but one cannot hide the fact that, in many places, they were not the ones who were preferred to their rivals." [124] This passage appeared in at least two of the major European papers covering French events and must therefore be attributed to the semiofficial news service that they shared. It reflected a view that a man like Luzac had no difficulty agreeing with; he could not, however, foresee that France's traditional elites would not provide the leadership for its new regime. Distrustful of the clergy,

---

123. In their articles on the Dutch Revolution, Luzac and Cerisier had constantly accused their opponents, the Stadhouderien party, of trying to incite the lower classes against the respectable bourgeois Patriots "by delivering the respectable bourgeoisie over to be pillaged and to run the risk of being massacred by the populace and by ferocious peasants" (*GL*, 4 Sept. 1787). The paper was thus run by men already thoroughly imbued with fear of social disorder long before the radical phases of the French Revolution.

124. *GL*, 7 Apr. , 31 Mar., and 24 Apr. 1789. The last quotation also appeared in *CBR*, 25 Apr. 1789, with an insertion that neatly characterizes the difference in style between the two papers: after the sentence disparaging the deputies actually chosen, *CBR*'s version continues, "No doubt the people have their reasons for choosing them and perhaps they thought that the Estates General would be a bath that would reinvigorate all the impotent ones and cleanse all the lepers."

the editors of the *Gazette de Leyde* looked to the liberal nobility to provide the leadership of the reforming movement they supported so earnestly. They willingly printed articles demonstrating how close the views of the nobility and the Third Estate really were and emphasized the role of the liberal nobles in the elections of deputies for Paris, which voted later than the rest of the kingdom.[125]

The actual assembling of the deputies in Versailles ought to have found the paper in a confident mood: this was the realization of dreams its principal editor had cherished for many years. But in fact the circumstances filled him with misgivings. Aside from his doubts about the wisdom of many of the elections and the wide variety of demands being raised, he was haunted by the fear of lower-class upheavals. At the time of the Paris elections, the paper's correspondent had noted the social tension in the capital and the efforts of "the porters, the charcoal makers, and other people of this category" to get their grievances heard.[126] The outbreak of the Reveillon riot, in which a working-class crowd assaulted a wealthy manufacturer's property, promptly confirmed the paper's worst fears; its *bulletiniste*'s lurid report of the incident used language that foreshadowed Edmund Burke's view of the Revolution: "The rioters, drunk on wine and liquor they had plundered from these buildings, pushed their excesses to the most outrageous extent." [127] This social fear was widely shared in France itself, but it struck a responsive chord in the *Gazette*'s Dutch editor, who had always viewed the lower classes in his own country as a potential reservoir of antibourgeois violence that could be easily manipulated by the Stadhouder; he was thus more than prepared to accept an alarmist view of the French situation as well.

With the Estates General actually assembled, the paper's main news-gathering task was a relatively simple one: the coverage of the proceedings in the three chambers. In this it succeeded brilliantly. The "news service" by which it was supplied provided a summary of proceedings that is more detailed than the transcript provided in the *Archives parlementaires* and other reports on which historians have often relied. Much of this *reportage* was not exclusive to the *Gazette de Leyde*, since it also appeared in the rival *Courier du Bas-Rhin*, but it was certainly more detailed than the coverage in any of the new papers

125. *GL*, 5 May 1789.   126. *GL*, 28 Apr. 1789.
127. *GL*, 8 May 1789; *CBR*, 9 May 1789.

that sprang up inside France for the express purpose of reporting on the Estates General. Recognizing that the traditional role of the foreign-based papers in French life was threatened by these new competitors, the *Gazette de Leyde* made repeated efforts to convince readers, first, that the new papers were unreliable since government pressure on them continued — thus it pointed out that the *Journal de Paris* had been authorized to report the deliberations but that it was still subject to censorship[128] — and second, that its version was more detailed and complete, as was in fact the case. Despite the advantage in timeliness it had to concede to its new Paris- and Versailles-based rivals, the *Gazette de Leyde* had by no means resigned itself to the loss of either its French market or its influence on events in the kingdom.

In its coverage of the proceedings on which France's future hinged, the *Gazette de Leyde* remained true to the course it had followed throughout the pre-revolutionary period. It continued to castigate extremists of all parties and to express its hopes that such well-intentioned men as Necker and deputies like Mounier in the Third Estate and Lally-Tollendal and Clermont-Tonnerre among the nobles could come together to work out a suitable solution to the crisis. As the outlines of the deadlock between the Third Estate and the privileged orders became clear, the paper handed out criticism to both parties. An article in early June urged "on the one hand, that one . . . know how to put limits on the dangerous *desire to change*, which is not always the desire to improve and which, even when the intention is good, is often deceived in the means to carry it out, and, on the other hand, that one . . . make a distinction between sound and healthy principles, and the stubbornness of trying to pass off as fundamental rights what was originally simply an abuse . . . incompatible with the present state of the government and the people." [129]

When Sieyès persuaded the Third Estate to "cut the cable" on 10 June and declare itself the National Assembly, the paper did blame the nobles for making this radical step inevitable. Its criticism of the noble opponents of vote by head had already been strong enough to lead its targets, like d'Eprémesnil, to complain openly in the sessions of their

128. *GL*, 5 June 1789. Officially, the deliberations of the Estates General were to have been held in secret — an obviously unenforceable plan, given the extent of public interest, the large number of deputies involved, and the precedent already established during the meetings of the Assembly of Notables in 1787 and 1788 — but publication of reports on the proceedings was officially authorized on 19 May 1789.

129. *GL*, 12 June 1789.

chamber.[130] But the paper was going along with the radical measures taken by the Third Estate primarily in the hope that its members would bring an end to the crisis by peaceful means; the editors still pinned their hopes firmly on the liberal nobles, who were making every effort to get their order to accept the Third Estate's demands. As the first defectors from the privileged orders arrived to claim seats in the National Assembly, the paper expressed cautious optimism: "The moment is very stormy. . . . Nevertheless it is becoming more and more probable that the national wish will be fulfilled and that the representatives of the most numerous, as well as the most essential, part of the French people . . . will triumph over their adversaries."[131] Confident that the assembly had "the general opinion"[132] behind it, the paper believed that the worst was over when the king, after the failure of his *coup de force* at the Royal Session of 23 June, yielded and ordered the privileged orders to join the assembly. "We have just escaped from a most disquieting situation," the paper reported.[133] In private, Luzac expressed the opinion that both the revolutionary party and its opponents were too intransigent. His own philosophy was one of principled moderation: "Truth is found at the center of errors, equally distant from one side of the circle and the other; but the spirit of party rarely recognizes this point, so visible but so small." The fact that "your popular enthusiasts find our reports too favorable to the opposing party, and the chief of that party, the agitator d'Epr[émesnil] denounces us as enemies of the aristocracy" gave him some satisfaction: his paper was evidently not allied with either extreme. Luzac's own hopes continued to rest primarily with Necker, because, despite his shortcomings, Necker had "the determination, so rare in a minister, to act for the national welfare."[134]

This momentary expression of optimism gave way almost immediately to new concerns sparked by the continuing disturbing reports coming in from France. The *Gazette de Leyde* quickly realized that the parliamentary revolution had not ended the struggle. Although the increasing involvement of the people in expressing support for the assembly was a good way of intimidating potential counterrevolutionaries, it led to such outbreaks of violence as the stoning of the

130. *GL*, 19 June 1789; 7 July 1789.   131. *GL*, 26 June 1789; not in *CBR*.
132. *GL*, 30 June 1789.   133. *GL*, 3 July 1789; not in *CBR*.
134. Luzac to Johan Valckenaer, 7 July 1789, in Leiden University Library, ms. BPL 1030. Luzac's personal admiration for Necker led him to take the uncharacteristic step of drafting a fan letter to the minister in late 1788 (Luzac Archives, carton 28).

archbishop of Paris. The paper also noted the tendency of the Paris garrison to side with demonstrators and not to uphold law and order.[135] An article just after the reunion of the three orders warned, "The events which we have witnessed these last few days have given further proof of how close the greatest evil is to the greatest good and how easily the restoration of national liberty can lead to anarchy, if the people do not have enough virtue to limit their desires." After giving reassuring news about popular demonstrations of enthusiasm for Necker and the king and queen, the article continued by asserting that the intentions of the king's brother, the comte d'Artois, and of the majority of the nobles who had resisted unification had not been evil. It also gave advance justification for the summoning of additional troops to Paris. Clearly this article, based partly on the views of the counterrevolutionary circle in Versailles, reflected a cautious reporter's unwillingness to see traditional authority entirely destroyed.[136]

The *Gazette de Leyde* proved exceptionally well informed about the plans for a counterrevolutionary coup that culminated in Necker's dismissal, although the paper's editor did not approve of such a project. His main concern continued to be to support the moderate reformers in the newly unified assembly; although the paper reported the movement of troops toward the capital, it gave clearer attention to the threat of the mob. "Now that the reunion of the orders and the harmony that appears to be establishing itself in the National Assembly give us the most reassuring hope, we must wish that the people, especially those of the capital, will not trouble the work of their representatives, the confidence of their king, and the perspective of the common happiness."[137]

On the day that this article appeared in Leiden, the Paris crowd was storming the Bastille. It was a scene that chilled the hearts of men like Cerisier and Luzac, but the provocation that had brought it about— the dismissal of Necker and the clear threat to the National Assembly — forced them to give at least grudging approval to this one eruption of popular violence. The paper was reluctant to publish the initial rumors of bloodshed and violence in Paris, preferring to wait for more reliable reports.[138] The next issue gave a vivid account of the first great revolutionary *journée*, but it was hardly the heroic recital the revolu-

---

135. *GL*, 3 July 1789; not in *CBR*.   136. *GL*, 10 July 1789; *CBR*, 11 July 1789.
137. *GL*, 14 July 1789; *CBR*, 15 July 1789.   138. *GL*, 21 July 1789.

tionaries themselves were to provide. According to the *Gazette*'s reporter, when news of Necker's dismissal reached Paris, "the populace, eager to take advantage of public calamities either by abusing the
pretext of liberty or by serving as the instrument of despotism in giving
itself over to pillage . . . spread terror and panic everywhere." The
bourgeoisie thus had no choice but to arm itself in defense against the
lower classes, and the storming of the Bastille was made to appear as a
defense of social order, rather than a reaction to a counterrevolutionary menace. Having recounted the repercussions in Versailles —
Necker's recall and the yielding of the last diehards among the privileged orders — the paper cautiously concluded, "It is thus that good
results from the midst of the most extreme evils." [139] Luzac's personal
view was a little less alarmist than the one published in the paper, but
not much. "If the nation triumphs," he wrote to his cousin Johan
Valckenaer in Paris, "as I like to hope in view of the patriotic spirit and
the unanimity that appears to guide it, I pray that, first, it will exploit
this triumph with moderation and wisdom, and second, that this
moderation will not prevent it from banishing from the vicinity of the
throne those vermin whose perfidious counsels have exposed the
kingdom to turmoil and the most complete disintegration." [140]

But subsequent reports in the *Gazette* emphasized the violence that
had accompanied this extraordinary episode rather than the possible
benefits it might bring. Distance from the events did nothing to make
the paper happier about them. In fact, the details of the deaths of De
Launey, Foulon (from whom the paper printed a letter, received just
after his death, denying any complicity in the counterrevolutionary
plot that led to Necker's dismissal), and Berthier, only served to underline for the paper how perilous France's state remained. "It is time
for the friends of true liberty to realize this truth, that unbridled license
often overturns it at the moment when it could be established, the
arbitrary power of the multitude being far more dangerous to it than
that of despotism itself," the paper warned. [141] While the *Gazette de
Leyde* had worked hard for the reform and regeneration of France for

---

139. *GL*, 24 July 1789. *CBR* of 25 July 1789 gave the same account but included an
additional comment: "This *journée* has more than a passing resemblance to the time of
the Sixteen and the barbarous executions they ordered. Posterity may be inclined to
excuse the Parisians, however; they fought today only for their liberty."

140. Luzac to Valckenaer, 21 July 1789; Luzac had just learned of Necker's recall.
Leiden University Library, ms. BPL 1030.

141. *GL*, 31 July 1789; *CBR*, 1 Aug. 1789.

several decades before the Revolution, it was not prepared to accept the form in which the end of the Old Regime finally arrived. Far from representing to the paper the triumph of liberty after so many years, the storming of the Bastille was the sign that France had failed to find that small but visible point to which Luzac had referred. By the fall of 1789, when its hero Mounier fled the country, the paper was convinced that no good could come of the National Assembly. In 1792, even before the final overthrow of the monarchy, Luzac wrote that the French Revolution seemed to prove "that true liberty is not made for the human race," although he himself refused to completely embrace this gloomy view.[142]

With the fall of the Bastille, the last restrictions on political journals inside France also crumbled. The *Gazette de Leyde* and other foreign-based papers lost their unique position as the only publicly tolerated periodicals offering an uncensored account of French domestic politics. They did not completely lose their French audience; some of the early Jacobin clubs, for example, continued to subscribe to the *Gazette* despite its distinctly hostile view of the Revolution.[143] And the *Gazette* continued to have an influence in other countries, where it did not suffer from arriving later than the Paris papers. The *Gazette de Leyde* and the system of news reporting it represented had been a vital, if unacknowledged, part of the politics of the French Old Regime. With the events of the summer of 1789, its role in French domestic politics was transformed. Even though the paper continued to appear under Luzac's editorship until 1798 and survived under the thumb of the Dutch revolutionaries and later of the French authorities in Holland until 1811, it was no longer the same paper it had been in the days of the French monarchy. Long the voice of political insiders within France who could not legally publish their views there, it was on its way to becoming the organ of outsiders, the émigrés and royalists who had no place in the new revolutionary order of things. Like the many reforming groups within France's old institutions for which it had served as

142. *GL*, 29 June 1792. The article made a contrast between the violent French Revolution and the peaceful process by which the Polish Diet was writing a new constitution for that country.

143. In his recent study of the Jacobin clubs in the early years of the French Revolution, Michael Kennedy found that at least four of these associations subscribed to the *Gazette de Leyde* at some point between 1789 and 1791. But this was far fewer than the number that subscribed to most of the significant Paris papers (*The Jacobin Clubs in the French Revolution* [Princeton, 1982], appendix E).

an essential outlet, the paper had contributed to undermining the absolutist institutions of the Bourbon monarchy, but it had destroyed its own raison d'être in the process.

As this detailed analysis of the *Gazette de Leyde*'s coverage of French domestic politics from 1774 to the Revolution has shown, this officially tolerated newspaper gave publicity to a wide variety of reports that official French publications scrupulously blacked out. In a curious analogy with the twentieth-century arrangement by which the French government maintained strict control over radio and television broadcasting within the country, while tolerating and indeed actually owning parts of stations based in neighboring countries that operated in defiance of the government's own rules,[144] the *Gazette de Leyde*, although certainly independently owned, actually received much of its apparently controversial information with the blessing of the French authorities, whose approval was needed for the paper's distribution within the country. This was true in spite of the fact that the *Gazette de Leyde*'s contents, even before the final stages of the pre-revolutionary crisis, effectively undermined the theoretically absolute institutions of the Old Regime. The paper frequently criticized ministerial policies and cast doubt on their chances for success, as in its ambivalent reaction to Turgot's grain policy, its publication of criticisms against Calonne's financial dealings, and its campaign against the Lamoignon edicts. It undermined the identification, carefully maintained in the official press, between the king's will and the ministers' policies; by rarely mentioning the king, it spared him any direct criticism but also reduced him to the status of a figurehead. Above all, by summarizing the major speeches in the Paris parlement and, on occasion, in such bodies as the Estates of Brittany and the Assembly of the Clergy, the paper gave these groups the appearance of legislative assemblies, similar to the English parliament whose proceedings always made up one of the largest portions of the paper. If the essence of representative government is the public discussion of laws, then the *Gazette de Leyde* made it appear that France under Louis XVI was already far advanced on the path toward such a system. France's parlements, Estates, and the Assembly of the Clergy were not representative institutions in the sense that these words acquired after 1789. Given effective publicity

---

144. The French government's connections with Radio Luxembourg and Radio Monte Carlo are described briefly in Ruth Thomas, *Broadcasting and Democracy in France* (Philadelphia, 1976), 102.

for their proceedings, however, these bodies could and, to some extent, did begin to fill some of the functions of representative assemblies. They insisted on their right to take up all pressing public issues. Aware that an audience was watching them, they began to play to that audience, consciously seeking its applause and support. The *Gazette de Leyde* played a major role in this process by serving as the vehicle for publicity, especially in the case of the Parlement of Paris.

In his well-known article on the role of the parlements in the last years of the Old Regime, William Doyle has argued that the monarchy always had the power at hand to tame these bodies if it wanted to and that it tolerated their noisy assertions of authority as window dressing. Ministers of the period, Doyle says, "knew that if the public believed in the power of parlementaire resistance it must also believe that the power of the government was not unlimited and that the French monarchy was not a despotism. Not only was this good for credit; it also kept the king happy. In a curious way, therefore, the government needed the opposition of the parlements." [145] It is true, of course, that in both 1771 and 1788 the government succeeded in dispersing the members of the parlements, although in both instances, the government eventually felt compelled to recall them. The case of the *Gazette de Leyde* shows that the situation of the press was similar to that of the parlements: the government could, if it chose, ban these publications or limit their flow of information, but it eventually found the price of such measures too high to be worthwhile. The analogy does not, however, strengthen Doyle's argument that the opposition of the parlements and the appearance of quasi-representative mechanisms in French politics at the end of the *ancien régime* were essentially meaningless. An examination of the *Gazette de Leyde*'s political role suggests that by tolerating institutions that made it appear that France was not an absolute monarchy, the government had in fact limited its own options. Its tacit bargain with both the parlements and the press was a Faustian one: having allowed the French people to become accustomed to the idea that they were protected by courts that would remonstrate in favor of their rights and by a press that would give them an immediate account of significant political events, even before the final outcome was clear, the government could not easily revert to autocratic forms. It took Robespierre to create a government ma-

---

145. "The Parlements of France and the Breakdown of the Old Regime," *French Historical Studies* 6 (1970): 454.

chinery forceful and single-minded enough to accomplish such a task, and he understood that the systematic annihilation of an independent press was an integral part of that process. Short of adopting such drastic measures, pre-revolutionary governments had to acknowledge the influence of the press and conduct themselves accordingly, even if they never conceded to it any legal rights.

The circulation of political information not only served to create an informal political constitution in France quite different from the absolutist model, but it served also to bring a new group into the political process: the public. The principle of political secrecy was a logical consequence of the doctrine of absolutism and the assertion that the king's will could neither be swayed nor constrained by any outside human agency. The publication of news about the government's actions, whether or not it was critical of the government, implicitly admitted the need for royal policies to have sanction from some other source — specifically that vague but nonetheless important fount of legitimacy, the people. To be sure, the sort of reportage that appeared in the *Gazette de Leyde* was far from representing the outlook of public opinion in any modern sense. Indeed, the newspaper did not claim to speak for the people, as the later revolutionary journals in France did. Luzac's goal was to serve as an "impartial narrator," an instant historian of events. But the notion that the reading public deserved an immediate account of what was happening represented an important concession to the public's right to know. Having allowed this kind of reporting to become institutionalized, the rulers of France would have had a very hard time completely suppressing it. The existence of the *Gazette de Leyde,* relatively controlled though it was, meant that the principle of public participation in politics had won some tangible acceptance in France long before the Revolution. As the revolutionary publicist Pierre Manuel remarked, looking back after 1789, "A people that wants to educate itself is not content with the *Gazette de France.*"[146]

The toleration of a publication like the *Gazette de Leyde* necessarily altered the conduct of actors within the French political system. It forced ministers and even the king himself to work at cultivating their public image, and the material published in the *Gazette de Leyde* clearly reflected the varying success with which different ministers did so.

146. *La Police de Paris dévoilée* (Paris, 1791), 1:201.

Thus even the paper's support for Turgot's reforming efforts could not disguise his failure at generating favorable publicity for them; Necker's obsession with publicity, which considerably predated his famous *Compte rendu*, led him perhaps to err on the other side, by encouraging or tolerating such a profusion of praise that the encomiums lost their credibility. Beyond personal publicity, however, the existence of the *Gazette de Leyde* encouraged and promoted a new form of behavior that, under the ground rules of absolutism, should not have existed. It allowed the introduction of an ideological element into French political discourse, primarily in the form of reprinted *remontrances* and texts of speeches from the Paris parlement. As long as the parlement dealt with the government in secret, its members had no reason to frame their positions in ideological terms: they could bargain, compromise, and promote their own selfish concerns as they saw fit. Once they began to play to a public audience, however, they were bound to behave differently. Even if, as has often been charged, selfish private motives still guided their conduct, the magistrates had to cloak them in a language of public purpose, in general and ideological terms, and this ideological criticism of absolute monarchy had effects even if its authors were not inwardly committed to all its implications. Once bound by their public statements, the magistrates also found their own freedom of action reduced: they could not easily abandon the positions they had publicly promised to uphold. The very existence of foreign-based French-language newspapers reporting on French politics exerted a pressure in the direction of ideological confrontation and foreshadowed the political systems that grew out of the Revolution.

This is not to ignore the important differences between the *Gazette de Leyde* and the revolutionary newspapers that came into existence after 1789. The later papers featured ideologically motivated calls to action; their purpose was not to describe the political world but to change it. The *Gazette* never claimed to be the voice of the public. Although it publicized dissent against the conduct of the French government, the dissent it reported came almost entirely from privileged groups with some definite political status under the Old Regime. The paper acknowledged a public right to know about politics but not a public right, open equally to all citizens, to be heard; the people who had a right to have their opinions voiced were largely nobles and representatives of traditional corporate institutions. For all its modern-sounding appeals to "patriotism," the sort of polity the authors of the *Gazette de Leyde* had in mind was based solidly on deference to the leadership of traditional elites; even after the doubling of the Third Estate had been conceded in December 1788, the paper's well-informed sources continued to assume that enlightened nobles would dominate French political life. Even as the *Gazette de Leyde* faithfully recorded the disintegration of the old order, it remained a part of that order. But its existence and the information that it transmitted indicate that we need to revise our image of the Old Regime: by no means as closed to political publicity as has often been thought, the old monarchy showed that, although it would not openly recognize political publicity as a right, it would in practice tolerate a fairly large degree of freedom of information rather than exert the force necessary to choke it off.

Chapter Four

The *Gazette de Leyde:*
The Opposition Press and
French Politics, 1750 – 1757

CARROLL JOYNES

The aggressive reporting found in the *Gazette de Leyde* during Louis XVI's reign had its origins in the 1750s. At midcentury, amid the unfolding of an intense religious and political controversy, we see early indications of the problematic nature of its reporting on France, as well as its tendency to take the parlementary side on a wide range of issues. A case study of the newspaper during this turbulent era reveals the contours of its later coverage with remarkable clarity.

In the spring of 1752 the biweekly *Gazette de Leyde* abruptly focused its attention on a series of troubling incidents in Paris involving the refusal of last rites to suspected Jansenists.[1] This doctrinal quarrel,

This chapter was researched and written at the Regenstein Library of the University of Chicago and the Newberry Library. Many thanks go to their able and hospitable staffs. I also received generous support from Lang College of the New School for Social Research in New York. Dale Van Kley provided valuable suggestions on earlier drafts, for which I am grateful. Special appreciation goes to Jack R. Censer for insightful criticism of various versions of this essay. His generous and constructive efforts as an editor helped make the task of revision a rewarding one.

1. There is no comprehensive history of the affair over the refusal of sacraments. Jacques Parguez, *La Bulle Unigenitus et le jansénisme politique* (Paris, 1936), reproduces a number of important documents, but it does not provide a reliable narrative. A brief but intelligent account appears in the more recent work by Jean Egret, *Louis XV et l'opposi-*

along with the growing hostilities between France and England, overshadowed all other stories until the latter part of the decade.[2] Although the coverage of the war differed little from the coverage accorded earlier European conflicts, the *Gazette*'s treatment of the
refusal-of-sacraments crisis marked the beginning of a significant
transformation in political journalism. Before this upheaval, the *Gazette*'s readers had been treated to a predictable and rather monotonous diet of military, court, and commercial news, leavened from time
to time with aristocratic gossip and accounts of diplomatic intrigue.
Reports from the major cities in Europe were characteristically terse,
densely packed narrative summaries that rarely extended to a full
column. As a rule, they contained little analysis or editorial comment.

By contrast, the first reports of incidents of the refusal of sacraments that appeared in the spring of 1752 were noticeably more detailed and analytic in their treatment of events, and they were sympathetic to the parlementary magistrates' spirited defense of suspected
Jansenists. At first, the accounts were relatively brief, but as the crisis
deepened and nearly all the important corporate bodies joined in the
fray, the narrative accounts became more detailed and complex,
sometimes taking up as many as four of the eight available pages. The
editorial commitment to cover this controversy seems only to have
increased as the years passed.

An examination of how an international newspaper like the *Gazette
de Leyde* understood the protracted controversy over the Jansenist
heresy and the refusal of sacraments and presented it to the reading
public enables us to trace some important developments in political
journalism under the Old Regime. More specifically, it allows us to see
how journalists reacted to, defined, and helped shape public perceptions of a major religious and political crisis. In both their narrative
treatment and the character of the documentary coverage they regu-

---

tion parlementaire, 1715–1774 (Paris, 1970), especially 50 – 89. In *The Jansenists and the
Expulsion of the Jesuits from France, 1757–1765* (New Haven, 1975) and *The Damiens
Affair and the Unraveling of the Ancien Régime, 1750–1770* (Princeton, 1984), Dale Van
Kley deals with the refusal-of-sacraments controversy as part of the broader crisis facing
the monarchy.

2. The refusal-of-sacraments crisis began in early 1749 and came to an unofficial end
in late 1756, at which point parlementary control over the administration of sacraments
was tacitly acknowledged by the Crown and the episcopacy. In the *Gazette de Leyde*,
there was almost no mention of incidents of refusal before April 1752 and very little after
July 1756. See the Appendix for information about the *Gazette*'s coverage of the religious
and political crisis during this period.

larly provided, they tried to generate public interest and mold public opinion. The *Gazette* often referred to this controversy as the "focus of all the public's attention," something about which the public (both in France and abroad) needed to stay informed as the "most pressing issue of the times."[3] By 1755–56, there were clear indications in the *Gazette* that "public opinion" had come to hold an important place in what one historian has called the "politics of contestation."[4] Understanding this conflict through the eyes of an organ like the *Gazette de Leyde* enables us to begin tracing both the evolution of the political press in the eighteenth century and the broader political culture of which it was a part.

Given the seriousness and duration of this particular controversy, it is not surprising that it served as the catalyst for a journalistic revolution. Far more than a doctrinal dispute, the refusal-of-sacraments quarrel ultimately gained the attention not only of the clergy but also of the parlements and the entire judicial hierarchy, the Sorbonne, and the princes and peers. Journalists who became involved helped to shape nascent public opinion by reporting and commenting on a complex and increasingly broad set of issues, including the Crown's religious, judicial, administrative, and fiscal policies, and ultimately on the nature of royal authority itself.

The vocabulary and arguments employed to discuss these issues underwent an equally notable transformation. At the center of the phenomenon was the tradition of parlementary constitutionalism. This array of judicial and legislative precedents invoked by the sovereign courts allegedly imposed restraints on the Crown's right to interfere in the courts' activities and thus bolstered the courts' claim to a significant measure of judicial and legislative independence from royal interference. To understand how parlementary constitutionalism became so intimately linked with Jansenism, however, we have to turn back to the seventeenth century and briefly examine the origins of this perplexing and tenacious religious movement.

Jansenism's eighteenth-century incarnation was quite different in certain respects from the version elaborated by founder Cornelius

3. See the *Gazette de Leyde* (hereafter cited as *GL*), 5 May, 18 May, 20 May, and 26 May 1752.
4. See the essay in this volume by Keith Michael Baker for a discussion of the emergence of public opinion, a development that was concurrent with the shift in the 1750s toward what he calls the "politics of contestation."

Jansen in the 1640s, but it remained at its core an austere, psychologi-
cally demanding form of Christianity.[5] This was true even after alleged
"Jansenists" increased their political involvement after the death of
Louis XIV.[6] Nevertheless, Jansenism's entanglement in political affairs, which arose largely because of its efforts to stave off persecution,
had profound ecclesiological and political consequences. These consequences, rather than its doctrinal and theological evolution, are the
focus of this section of my study.

Jansenism was a part of the complex reaction of besieged Catholics
to the Protestant Reformation. Throughout the seventeenth and eighteenth centuries, Jansenism maintained its harsh, predestinarian vision of the Christian message, focusing on the sinfulness and corruption of man and society. The movement, which had no institutional or
corporate existence, demanded strict penitential discipline from the
spiritual athletes who embraced it. Given its theological outlook, it is
hardly surprising that many Jansenists sought the cloistered life of
ascetic contemplation as a refuge from earthly temptations. Its emphasis was on achieving an interior renewal, perceptible only to oneself,
that would render the mind and the soul truly worthy of receiving the
sacraments. Individual conscience thus played a key role in determining a person's spiritual standing in the eyes of God. This intensely
personal and reflective path to salvation also clearly deemphasized
the role of clerical intermediaries, a characteristic of Jansenist theology
that could hardly endear it to the ecclesiastical hierarchy.

Both in France and in Rome, this morally unforgiving and theologi-
cally combative sect raised fears about the religious stability of France
and the unity of the Catholic faith. The Jansenists' emphasis on individual conscience, their principles of efficacious grace and gratuitous
predestination, and their tendency to proceed toward salvation without the mediating efforts of the clergy aroused the opposition of the
Vatican, the French episcopacy, and the Crown.

5. The most important general works on Jansenism in France are Augustin Gazier,
Histoire générale du mouvement janséniste depuis ses origines jusqu'à nos jours, 2 vols.
(Paris, 1923); Charles Augustin Sainte-Beuve, *Port-Royal*, ed. Maxime Leroy (Paris,
1952); Antoine Adam, *Du mysticisme à la révolte: Les Jansénistes du XVIIIᵉ siècle* (Paris,
1968); and Alexander Sedgwick, *Jansenism in Seventeenth-Century France: Voices from the
Wilderness* (Charlottesville, Va., 1977).
    6. The two important works on the politicization of the Jansenist movement at the
end of the seventeenth and the beginning of the eighteenth centuries are Robert
Kreiser, *Miracles, Convulsions, and Ecclesiastical Politics in Early Eighteenth-Century Paris*
(Princeton, 1978); and René Taveneaux, *Le Jansénisme et politique* (Paris, 1969), especially 122 – 63.

In 1656 a papal-episcopal campaign to impose doctrinal uniformity began in earnest. It culminated in September 1713 with the arrival in France of the papal bull *Unigenitus,* which condemned 101 allegedly Jansenist propositions drawn from a popular and influential biblical commentary.[7] In the half-century before the appearance of this papal bull, the Jansenists responded to steadily increasing persecution by forming defensive alliances in order to combat both the episcopacy and the Crown.[8] They also began to shift their attention to more lay-oriented, collegial activities and to temper their doctrinal stance.

Between 1650 and 1713, the parlementary magistrates became the Jansenists' most prominent supporters, a development explained in part by the large number of conversions among the magistrates. Even more important was the parlement's long-standing commitment to defend the French church and the French monarchy from papal interference and to protect the secular authorities' right to ensure that church affairs were conducted in accordance with the accepted body of Gallican canons.[9] The magistrates, whose dislike of papal meddling had erupted during the sixteenth-century wars of religion, devised an impressive arsenal of legal weaponry with which to impose their views on the clergy. As a quasi-autonomous judicial body, the parlement was capable of hobbling the execution of royal justice with a profusion of official protests and delays, delegations, and even judicial strikes. Bolstered in addition by its well-publicized self-portrait as a *corps d'état* with constitutional authority equal to or greater than that possessed by the Crown, the parlement was able to make expansive claims about the barrier it represented against growing royal and episcopal despotism.[10]

Louis XIV had little success in his efforts to quash Jansenism in the last decades of the seventeenth century. The ill-fated attempt to impose *Unigenitus* as a means of putting the troublesome theological

7. The condemned work was Pasquier Quesnel, *Le Nouveau Testament en français, avec des réflexions morales sur chaque verset, pour en rendre la lecture plus utile et la méditation plus aisée.* First published clandestinely in 1668 and then expanded and reissued in 1692, Quesnel's volume was only the most popular of many such works published during this era.

8. A detailed description of the Jansenists' efforts to find adequate protection from persecution can be found in Kreiser, *Miracles, Convulsions, and Ecclesiastical Politics.*

9. The most provocative analysis of the ties among Jansenism, Gallicanism, and parlementary constitutionalism is Lucien Goldmann, *Le Dieu caché: Etude sur la vision tragique dans les "Pensées" de Pascal et dans le théâtre de Racine* (Paris, 1955). A more recent attempt to explain the connection can be found in Van Kley, *The Jansenists,* especially chap. 1.

10. See Van Kley, *The Damiens Affair,* especially chap. 5.

ideas of Jansen to rest only served to unleash a new controversy about the legality of the bull and its enforcement as a law of church and state. This battle dragged on for decades.[11]

A new chapter in the dispute began in early 1749 as the result of a decision by the recently appointed Parisian archbishop, Christophe de Beaumont, to rid France once and for all of the alleged heresy. Inured as the Jansenists were to the tactics of persecution employed by papal, episcopal, and royal authorities, they were caught off guard by the archbishop's strategy.[12] After the archbishop's inauguration he instructed the clergy under his jurisdiction to refuse sacraments and especially last rites to people suspected of Jansenist leanings. The litmus test of orthodoxy was a *billet de confession* signed by a confessing priest, which was to be presented before receiving the sacraments. The *billet* verified the parishioner's acceptance of the doctrinal authority of the papal bull *Unigenitus* (1713), but it was actually a test of the parishioner's acknowledgment of episcopal authority on doctrinal and ecclesiastical questions.

The controversy over the archbishop's inquisitorial policy escalated quickly, in large part because of the dogmatic and polarized positions of the clergy and the magistracy. In reaction to the episcopacy's tactic of demanding *billets de confession*, the magistrates made it clear that they would intervene in any case of refusal that was brought to their attention. In support of their actions, they had to work out an elaborate legal and constitutional argument to justify their bold interference in what were clearly the most sacred functions of the clergy.

The parlement was committed to ending both the persecution of alleged Jansenists and any sort of papal interference in French affairs. Not surprisingly, the doctrine of parlementary constitutionalism became the basis for opposition arguments during the 1750s, because it could easily incorporate antihierarchical, anti-absolutist arguments drawn from Augustinian theology, Gallican ecclesiology, canon law,

11. See Kreiser, *Miracles, Convulsions, and Ecclesiastical Politics;* Van Kley, *The Jansenists;* Parguez, *La Bulle Unigenitus.*

12. A dated but adequate biography of the controversial Parisian archbishop is Emile Regnault, *Christophe de Beaumont: Archevêque de Paris, 1703–1781,* 2 vols. (Paris, 1882). There has as yet been no attempt to explain why Christophe de Beaumont felt compelled to initiate another assault against the Jansenist "heresy," especially since relations had calmed down considerably during the preceding decade. The most detailed accounts of the period preceding the midcentury explosion are Georges Hardy, *Le Cardinal de Fleury et le mouvement janséniste* (Paris, 1925), and, more recently, Egret, *Louis XV et l'opposition parlementaire.*

and natural law. The resulting amalgam could in turn be corroborated with revisionist versions of French constitutional and political history.[13] These arguments were gradually integrated into the forms of opposition discourse employed by newspapers like the *Gazette* and presumably by some portion of their readers as well. By 1755, in fact, some of the polemical pamphlets reproduced in the *Gazette* made a direct connection between parlementary-Jansenist opposition and the increasingly open criticism of royal absolutism (both theoretical and practical) that was appearing in the clandestine press during the 1750s.[14]

The treatment of this controversy in the *Gazette de Leyde* spans the years between 1752 and 1756. It can be divided into three major stages that correspond both to developments in the controversy itself and to the evolving political position of the *Gazette's* editor. The first period extended from March 1752, when detailed accounts of incidents of refusal began to appear in the *Gazette*, until May 1753, when the Crown exiled the magistrates for fifteen months.[15] During the first stage, incidents of the refusal of sacraments were reported in great detail in Paris and in the provinces. An increasingly wide spectrum of the populace became involved in the bitter confrontations that usually followed these episodes. By the spring of 1753 the circle of participants included most of the clergy, many of the parlementary magistrates in Paris and the provinces as well as magistrates in lower tribunals like the *bailliages*, *sénéchaussées*, and *présidiaux*, and, increasingly, the princes and peers, the universities, and the Crown. In response to this deepening crisis, the *Gazette* steadily expanded its coverage. By January 1753 the paper was providing extensive, up-to-date reports of developments in nearly every issue.

13. See the important but largely forgotten study by Georges Frêches, *D'Aguesseau: Chancelier gallican* (Paris, 1939). Frêches traces the role of Gallicanism, the ecclesiological doctrine of Richerism, and parlementary constitutionalism in the political writings and programs of Henri-François d'Aguesseau. Also see Taveneaux, *Le Jansénisme et politique;* Victor Martin, *Le Gallicanisme politique et le clergé de France* (Paris, 1929); Van Kley, *The Damiens Affair;* Carroll Joynes, "Jansenists and Ideologues: Parlementary Opposition in the Parlement of Paris, 1750–1774" (Ph.D. diss., University of Chicago, 1981).
14. For example, *Lettre de Chevalier de ——— à M. ——— à un de ses amis à Paris, à l'occasion de l'Assemblée du Clergé* (1755) and *Lettre de M*** à un gentilhomme de Savoie, au sujet des disputes de religion dont la France est agitée* (1755).
15. It is not clear why editorial attention was focused on the controversy in March and not several months earlier, when one of the most famous incidents of persecution and parlementary reaction occurred in the parish of Saint-Etienne-du-Mont in Paris.

The second period covered the months of the magistrates' exile.[16] As the political and constitutional issues raised by the refusal of sacraments began to rival the religious and ecclesiastical ones in importance, the reporting provided by the *Gazette* responded accordingly. The newspaper also chronicled the geographical shift of activity away from Paris and into the provinces. It paid close attention to developments in provincial centers where the local clergy and parlements confronted one another in a spirit as polarized and intractable as the one that had prevailed in Paris before the exile. The *Gazette* also reported in detail the active involvement of the public, which had access in papers like the *Gazette* to the full range of official and clandestine documents produced by the participants. During this second stage, the *Gazette* increased substantially the amount of supporting documentation it reproduced in its columns.

The third and final period commenced with the recall of the parlements in September 1754, an event the Crown (and the *Gazette*) hoped would mark the end of the crisis.[17] The royal "Declaration of Silence" imposed as a condition for the return of the magistrates an interdiction on the discussion of all topics related to the dispute.[18] The problem, however, was not to be so easily solved. Upon the magistrates' return from vacation in early November, reports of incidents of refusal began to flow into Paris from all over France, and the parlements quickly resumed their role as champions of the persecuted appellants of *Unigenitus*. A full year of religious strife ensued, culminating in the Crown's desperate attempt to eclipse the parlement by superimposing a new, more cooperative and obedient sovereign tribunal, which would have jurisdiction over cases involving not only the refusal of sacraments but any other troublesome issue on the Crown's agenda.[19] The series of confrontations began in November 1755. The *Gazette* provided extensive coverage of these events, but in early 1756 the

16. The period of the magistrates' exile is treated in A. Grellet-Dumazeau, *Les Exilés de Bourges (1753–1754), d'après des documents inédits et le journal anecdotique du président de Meinières* (Paris, 1892); and Bernard de la Combe, *La Résistance janséniste et parlementaire au temps de Louis XV: L'Abbé Nigon de Berty, 1702–1772* (Paris, 1949).

17. The *Gazette* greatly expanded its documentary coverage in the last years of the controversy — especially 1755 and 1756. Reports in the *Gazette* during the summer of 1754 speculated at length about the date and the conditions of the magistrates' return from exile and the consequences their return would have for the refusal of sacraments. See, for example, *GL*, 24 Mar., 28 May, 9 Aug., 13 Aug., and 16 Aug. 1754.

18. For the text of the "Declaration of Silence," see *GL*, 13 Sept. 1754.

19. See Egret, *Louis XV et l'opposition parlementaire*, 65–76.

growing conflict between England and France began to compete for column space and gradually became the dominant focus.

The controversy was resolved somewhat anticlimactically during the summer of 1756. The Parlement of Paris, proceeding confidently with a well-honed set of political skills and a firm base of public support, carefully orchestrated an attack on the royal administration. The Achilles' heel of the monarchy had long been its fiscal policy, which the magistrates recognized since they had to register all royal fiscal edicts. The parlement picked the moment when hostilities with England began to take center stage — when the Crown was most in need of the court's cooperation — to force a settlement. Louis XV had called a special session of parlement to approve a series of tax increases designed to raise revenues to pay for the war, and the parlement refused to cooperate unless he dropped his plan to establish the rival tribunal. The magistrates' strategy was a complete success. In the months and years that followed, they proceeded to capitalize on their politically ascendant position by embarking upon what historian Jean Egret has called the "procès administratif," in which the parlement challenged the Crown on a wide range of fiscal and administrative policies.[20]

The *Gazette*'s coverage of these events signaled the appearance of a new kind of reporting — detailed, analytic, and unabashedly partisan — a prodrome of the kind of journalism that matured fully during the Revolution. The reports appearing in the *Gazette* were focused and comprehensive, and the paper's editorial commitment was sustained over a period of years, diminishing only slightly when the parlement began its broader attack on the royal administration in late 1756. During the span of the refusal-of-sacraments crisis, the *Gazette* provided at least some coverage in 80 percent of the nearly five hundred issues that appeared.[21] The editorial emphasis given to the quarrel (up to one-half of available column space) suggests that editor Etienne Luzac thought it one of the single most important political controversies in Europe during the 1750s, not only for the French but for subscribers throughout Europe.

We know relatively little about the *Gazette*'s sources during the 1750s, but it is evident from the reliable, well-informed coverage they furnished that they had well-established contacts, especially within

20. Ibid., 106–43.   21. See Appendix.

the parlement.[22] Their in-depth accounts of the confrontations between the clergy and the judiciary appeared in the Leiden newspaper
twice each week (if indeed there was news to print), providing some of
the most up-to-date, comprehensive information available in Paris.
Through their network of correspondents, the editors had access to
nearly all the relevant documents in the dispute, which they made
available to their readers along with nuanced coverage of fast-break-
ing developments. Some of the documents they reproduced were
already available to the public through bookstores and *colporteurs,* but
in some cases the editors received advance copies, which they immediately incorporated into their coverage. The *Gazette de Leyde*'s documentary history consisted of a variety of official documents: parlementary judgments, orders, decrees, speeches, briefs, minutes, and
excerpts from other official sources.[23] Most important, however, were
the *remontrances:* during the 1750s they came to be directed not so
much at the Crown as to an educated reading public; they were less
often expressions of corporate grievance than skillfully written polemical manifestos designed to initiate and guide public discussion of
controversial issues. The *Gazette* would frequently serialize the entire
text of these parlementary documents, footnotes and all.[24]

These official documents were often supplemented with excerpts
from, or notices about, important polemical works that emerged from
the clandestine press. What is most striking about both the official and
clandestine publications is their level of complexity. The audience was
evidently expected to be familiar with, among other things, French
and English constitutional history, Gallican ecclesiology, and canon
law. There were no simplified explanations for the uninitiated, no

22. One source was the Jansenist barrister Louis Adrien LePaige, a canon law spe-
cialist who worked in the Parlement of Paris and then during the 1750s for the prince de
Conti. He served as a conduit of information from the parlement to the *Gazette* beginning with the exile in 1753. This is evident from his letters, which, along with his entire
library, are housed in the Bibliothèque de Port-Royal in Paris (see especially vols. 561
and 562). The *Gazette*'s other sources during this period remain unknown. The work of
Jeremy D. Popkin is very helpful for later decades, especially in its suggestion that the
Crown itself was responsible for channeling much of the information directly to the
opposition press (see Popkin's essay in this volume).

23. The amount of documentary evidence provided in the *Gazette* increased significantly after the exile and remained great until the end of the crisis in 1756.

24. This was the case with several of the *remontrances* of the Parlement of Paris, the
celebrated *remontrances* of the Parlement of Rouen in 1756, and to a lesser extent those of
the parlements in Toulouse, Aix-en-Provence, and Rennes (for example, see *GL*, 28 June
1756).

summaries or recapitulations for latecomers. The *Gazette de Leyde* served informally as the newspaper of record during this period, and it assumed readers could handle this type of material.

The *Gazette* reproduced comparatively fewer documents from the clergy and the Crown. Royal *arrêts de conseil, déclarations,* and edicts appeared regularly, but they were nearly always furnished as part of the necessary background or context for a parlementary ruling or decision that the *Gazette* wanted to underscore. The same can be said about the clergy's *remontrances,* declarations, and pastorals.

The *Gazette* coverage was quite partisan, presumably reflecting the views of its Protestant editor. His interest in the complex quarrel had less to do with the theological movement of Jansenism than with the parlement, which he saw as the most powerful opponent of absolutist kingship in the French state and France's last remaining vestige of representative government. The combined efforts of the Catholic Crown and episcopacy to crush a small group of religiously unacceptable members of French society was the kind of cause that the Dutch paper could easily embrace. By the end of the controversy, the newspaper was portraying the sovereign courts of France as the last bastion against episcopal, ministerial, and royal despotism, an interpretation to which it adhered until 1788. But even though the *Gazette* openly supported the parlement on a wide range of issues, it was not entirely blind to the overzealous behavior of the magistrates in their campaign to check the Crown and the episcopacy and to regenerate what they believed was the true version of France's ancient constitution.[25]

One final characteristic of the *Gazette*'s new brand of journalism was its style of writing. As its coverage of the crisis increased, its tone became increasingly animated. The reports communicated the urgency and seriousness of the situation, which contrasted starkly with the effect of the spare, almost clinical prose employed in previous decades (and even in the 1750s when dealing with the rest of Europe). The extent to which this new journalistic style was a function of a real engagement in the issues by the correspondents and the editor of the paper is hard to evaluate. But such an interpretation is fully in keeping with the frequent remarks of political diarists and commentators like

25. Although the *Gazette de Leyde* endorsed the political stand of the parlement and its opposition to both episcopal and royal authority, there were a number of instances when the paper criticized the magistrates for being overly militant and too precipitous in their response to crises.

the marquis René-Louis de Voyer d'Argenson and Edmond-Jean-François Barbier to the effect that the refusal-of-sacraments controversy was the focus of all public attention and that it dominated French domestic affairs at midcentury.[26]

March 1752 to May 1753

The struggle between the episcopal authorities and the parlementary magistrates over the refusal of sacraments was already well under way by the time the *Gazette de Leyde* began to give it sustained coverage in April 1752. The *Gazette*'s twice-weekly accounts of the controversy furnished readers with detailed accounts of actual incidents of refusal, of popular protests in favor of the victims or the clergy, and of the corporate combatants' bitter public confrontations, calculated political maneuvers, and endless legal wrangling.[27] The *Gazette*'s reports also revealed the ways in which the crisis was coming to dominate Parisian public affairs and the extent to which it had generated a dangerously polarized atmosphere.[28]

The incidents of refusal of sacraments recounted with such frequency and in such detail by the *Gazette* usually had strong structural similarities, and they read like morality plays. The drama would customarily begin when a priest, acting on orders from the archbishop of Paris, would refuse last rites to a parishioner who lacked a *billet de confession*. The magistrates would be alerted, and they would assemble within a few hours. There would follow the forcible arrest, interrogation, and imprisonment of the offending priest, a process that could keep the magistrates in session for anywhere from five to fourteen hours. On several occasions, the parlementary assembly did not break up until two or three in the morning.[29] The magistrates usually tried to force the clergy to administer sacraments, sometimes with

26. Barbier, *Chronique de la Régence et du règne de Louis XV (1718–1763), ou Journal de Barbier* (Paris, 1866), 7:207; E.-J.-B. Rathery, ed., *Journal et mémoire du marquis d'Argenson (René-Louis de Voyer, Marquis)* (Paris, 1867), 9:318.
27. The editorial policy of the *Gazette* was to provide at least a brief summary of all reported incidents relating to the controversy and to update the most important ones frequently. Selected incidents would be described in great detail, often with supplementary documentation.
28. For an account of events during the first years of the refusal of sacraments (1749–51), see Egret, *Louis XV et l'opposition parlementaire*; and Parguez, *La Bulle Unigenitus*. A more recent and specialized treatment of events in this tempestuous decade is Van Kley, *The Damiens Affair*.
29. See, for example, *GL*, 2 May and 30 June 1752.

success. The episcopacy would then lodge a complaint with the Crown about the interference of the secular judiciary in matters of theological doctrine. Traditionally, the appeal to the Crown was thought of as a last resort, but in the incidents between 1752 and the magistrates' exile in May 1753, the speed and frequency with which the clergy appealed to Versailles for assistance increased significantly.

The denouement of these episodes often came when the parlement delivered formal *remontrances* to the Crown, usually accompanied by a threat to cease all other judicial activity until the crisis was resolved. Louis XV and his ministers deeply resented the arrogance and the intransigent attitude of the magistrates but, according to the *Gazette*, failed to understand the seriousness and complexity of the problem. Faced with two powerful bodies that refused to negotiate with each other and a situation that only seemed to worsen with each passing month, the Crown simply floundered.[30]

The tone of urgency in the *Gazette*'s reports suggests that the editors believed this unfolding drama merited its readers' serious attention. The crisis was at its core a religious one, and the ominous analogies between this attempt to enforce orthodoxy and similar disastrous attempts in the wake of the Protestant Reformation were not lost on the *Gazette*'s columnists.[31] Other news accounts emphasized the depth of the crisis. For example, in May 1752 an incident occurred in the diocese of Langres "that so disturbed the people that the hysteria threatened to spread to the whole kingdom and to envelop France in religious and civil strife that would prove difficult to curb."[32] A few months later, the *Gazette* reproduced a formal address given by parlementary first president Maupeou to Louis XV in which he warned that "schism is beginning to spread. It has started to appear in every corner of the kingdom, . . . and it is the worst wound that the Church could suffer."[33]

These remarks were not unwarranted. The controversy soon spilled over into all areas of religious, social, and political life and by the autumn of 1752 came to command most of the Crown's time and

---

30. The portrayal of the Crown and ministers in the *Gazette* is predictably ambiguous. Because permission to distribute the paper in France came from the Crown, there was a limit to the amount of open criticism the editors could print. Although the reporters regularly underscored the apparent sincerity with which the Crown pursued a solution, they nonetheless found ways to suggest that it was seriously lacking in the requisite talent and skills.

31. See, for example, *GL*, 1 June 1753.   32. *GL*, 23 May 1752.

33. *GL*, 28 July 1752.

energy. On 26 May 1752 the *Gazette* reported that "this divisive conflict
is the focus of everyone's attention. It divides not only the capital but
the entire kingdom. All of Paris is watching and listening."

The *Gazette* furnished its readers with a colorful and illuminating
portrait of the religious animosities and the penetration of the crisis
into both the social and the political structure of France. Its columns
regularly provided detailed, poignant renderings of incidents in
which people desiring last rites endured severe crises of conscience.
They wanted to be obedient to the Church but could not bring themselves to acknowledge the legitimacy of *Unigenitus*. The issue divided
families, *quartiers*, and parishes and affected men and women of every
order, Estate, and corps. Documented cases of refusal recounted in the
Gazette involved servants, artisans, lawyers, magistrates, priests,
canons, bishops, and even a few members of the nobility. No one was
safe from the inquisitorial campaign.[34]

These public incidents separating people who accepted *Unigenitus*
from people who did not became increasingly widespread. The incidents had disruptive consequences for the communities in which they
took place. In a small parish in Orléans, for example, the curé Boutard
brought down the wrath of the parlement for his persecutions of
suspected Jansenists. A parlementary *arrêt* charged him with delivering "scandalous sermons in which he called some of his parishioners
'innovators, heretics, Jansenists, Quesnelists, schismatics, and party
men'; addressing them by name; telling the assembled that they
should be avoided like the plague; then publicly threatening to refuse
them sacraments; declining to hold a church procession until they left
the premises; exciting his flock into aiding and abetting him in banning the suspects from the parish church, saying that he would be the
first to drench his hands in their blood." The populace, in turn, became so agitated that "they stoned the alleged Jansenists while berat-
ing them for being heretics and Calvinists and then tossed them into
the swamp."[35] A similar incident had occurred a week earlier in Brittany. There, a parish priest's public refusal of sacraments set off a riot,
and royal troops were required to restore order.[36]

In other incidents, parish churches were closed down for weeks or
even months, bishops clashed with neighboring bishops over the doc-

34. The largest number of victims were Jansenist clergy. Only occasionally were
members of the nobility or the bourgeoisie mentioned. See *GL*, 28 Feb. 1755.
35. *GL*, 20 Feb. 1753.   36. *GL*, 9 Feb. 1753.

trinal interpretations of visiting clergy in their dioceses,[37] the Parlement of Paris conducted mass interrogations of priests who favored the archbishop's program, and even the Faculty of Theology at the Sorbonne and several religious orders were wracked by internal dissension over the enforcement of the controversial papal bull. One small convent, the Order of Saint Agatha, was even disbanded by the archbishop of Paris.[38]

If the *Gazette* portrayed the episcopacy as the villain and the parlementary magistrates as the heroes, the Crown emerged as fundamentally well intentioned but inept. A key component of its role was the mediation of disputes among the corporate bodies constituting the state, but in the 1750s it proved unable to comprehend the gravity and pervasiveness of the refusal-of-sacraments crisis and incapable of negotiating even a provisional peace among the growing body of combatants.

The Crown usually initiated its efforts with moderate measures — issuing *arrêts de conseil* to quash inflammatory publications, meeting with representatives of both sides, and even establishing a bipartisan, blue ribbon commission (whose activity the *Gazette* followed with great optimism).[39] When these strategies failed, which they invariably did, the Crown resorted to more draconian and judicially irregular measures. Louis XV forbade the parlement to mention the papal bull *Unigenitus* in any published judicial briefs or decisions, summarily annulled parlementary judicial proceedings in cases involving *billets de confession*, regularly evoked cases to the royal Conseil d'état for final judgment, and issued *lettres de cachet* to an expanding circle of alleged offenders. According to the *Gazette*, these acts of royal repression escalated rapidly in 1752 and 1753. It is important to note, however, that monarchical actions were by no means directed entirely at the magistracy. The archbishop and his followers sometimes received harsh treatment as well. By early 1755, the Crown had twice resorted to exile as a solution, once with the magistrates in his sovereign court and once with the archbishop of Paris. The *Gazette* often remarked on the inordinate amount of time and energy the monarch spent on this crisis and how desperate members of his ministry were to find a solution. It is obvious that the royal stock of strategies had been depleted rapidly, leading to the use of more extreme measures. And it was these mea-

37. *GL*, 2 Mar. 1753.   38. *GL*, 26 Jan. 1753.   39. *GL*, 26 May 1752.

sures, in the end, that helped transform a relatively circumscribed crisis into a national and even an international one.

During the six months prior to the magistrates' exile, the parlementary magistrates mobilized themselves as a corporate body and cultivated an appealing public image as part of their broader strategy of opposition to the episcopacy and the Crown. Parlementary strategists knew that it was important to present an image of confidence and solidarity, as much to the public to whom they were appealing for support as to their adversaries. Rumored arguments about the limits of the parlement's right to interfere in a matter of church doctrine and discipline were occasionally mentioned in the *Gazette*'s columns, but they were never discussed in detail, apparently because the parlement effectively enforced the confidentiality of its internal deliberations. What emerged were statements of accord and solidarity, with little trace of the internal divisions that had to be overcome. The *Gazette*'s correspondents usually presented whatever dissension they had noticed as a footnote to the parlementaires' acknowledged ability to present a powerful and appealing public image and thus to successfully mobilize public interest and support.

Evidence of this self-conscious attempt to implement a public relations strategy appeared quite early in the controversy. Parlementary propagandists using the *Gazette* as a forum tried to cast their net as widely as possible in their appeal to the public, going beyond religious issues to royal fiscal and administrative policy. For example, the Paris correspondent mentioned that "this body, which regards itself as the 'father of the people,' has heard the populace cry out about the price of grain and has taken this to heart. The [magistrates] are making detailed inquiries to determine which greedy persons have removed grain from the capital and sold it to foreign markets. If caught, no one, no matter how illustrious, will be spared."[40]

More subtle and ultimately more important than the magistrates' attempts to cast themselves as the people's benefactors were their behind-the-scenes efforts to ensure that the controversy receive attention not only in newspapers like the *Gazette de Leyde* but also in as many other written forms as possible. On 6 February 1753 the *Gazette* reported that "the public was buried in writings on this controversy."

40. *GL,* 7 Aug. 1753.

The daily meetings of the parlement and the actions that followed provided ample subject matter for pamphleteers.[41] And in case Parisian readers missed the most important of these informal commentaries, the *Gazette* frequently published texts of the judicial decisions brought against allegedly subversive publications — decisions issued by either the clergy, the Conseil d'état, or the parlement itself, which conveniently served as lists of recommended books.

The effect of the dissemination of official documents was probably even more corrosive than the effect of the deluge of clandestinely published pamphlets and books. The *Gazette* itself reproduced hundreds of official documents that had been drafted with an eye to the general reading public. *Remontrances*, declarations, decisions, decrees, judicial minutes, and briefs frequently appeared in the *Gazette*'s columns. If they were not actually reproduced, they were described in detail.

A single issue of the *Gazette* might include two or three items in the large body of documentation produced by the parlementary propagandists. In these items, there were frequent efforts to present a more radical, revised version of parlementary constitutionalism. It had been a longstanding tradition among the magistrates to give their role in judicial, legislative, and administrative affairs an independent complexion: their description of their position had received its first major revision during the insurrection known as the Fronde a century earlier. During the refusal-of-sacraments dispute, the tendency to revise the historical and constitutional record suddenly accelerated again. An especially vivid instance occurred during the summer of 1752 when readers got an early glimpse of the magistrates' famous "doctrine des classes" or "union des classes." Completely rejecting the notion that the parlements were separate tribunals established by the sovereign to dispense justice in his name, parlementary propagandists argued that all the parlements composed a single corporate entity whose roots could be traced to early medieval assemblies and whose authority was therefore separate from that enjoyed by the Crown. This authority could, in turn, be employed on behalf of the nation when the monarch failed to take appropriate action. This idea would achieve its full

41. The enormous increase in the number of publications dealing with religious (and related political issues) is documented in the *Catalogue de l'histoire de France,* 16 vols. (Paris, 1855), especially vol. 7.

articulation three years later in the famous *remontrances* of 27 November 1755.[42]

Because the *Gazette* embraced the parlement's constitutional position, it provided an ideal forum for presenting both the arguments themselves and the extensive documentation furnished by parlementary propagandists. In the documents reprinted in the *Gazette*, the parlement was portrayed as the people's champion against religious persecution, the protector of the threatened Gallican church against prelates with suspiciously strong ties to the papal See, and the defender of the rights of France.[43]

The episcopacy, on the other hand, drew little but criticism from the *Gazette*. The paper presented the archbishop as arbitrary and intransigent. His decision to use all available means to excise a virulent heresy from the body of the Church was portrayed as a willfully despotic and destructive effort that threatened both religious and political stability. The same editorial opinion was expressed about the king when he supported the efforts of the episcopacy. On these occasions, Louis XV appeared heavy-handed and dismayingly literal in his interpretation of divine-right royal absolutism. The frequency and suddenness with which he resorted to *lettres de cachet*, evoked contested cases to his council, confiscated parlementary documents, and relied on arrest, imprisonment, and exile showed that he neither fully understood nor appreciated the gravity of the problem. And it was organs like the *Gazette* that helped inform and shape the opposition's views.

As 1752 yielded to 1753, the *Gazette de Leyde* focused increasingly on this conflict and its divisive effects. Its coverage particularly revealed the growing abyss between the point of view of the parlement and those of the clergy and Crown. The *Gazette* presented the magistrates' efforts to protect appellants from episcopal persecution as part of a broader patriotic struggle against the "arbitrary" tactics of their opponents. Hence the newspaper recorded sympathetically the magistrates' call for the princes and peers to meet with them in a plenary

42. Historians in the past have argued that this constitutional argument first appeared in 1755, but it is clear that the idea was taking shape as early as the summer of 1752 (see *GL*, 30 May 1752).

43. The best historical accounts of the constitutional issues involved in the parlementary arguments are Elie Carcassonne, *Montesquieu et le problème de la constitution française* (Paris, 1926), especially chap. 6; and Roger Bickart, *Les Parlements et la notion de souveraineté nationale au XVIIIᵉ siècle* (Paris, 1932).

assembly and their public request for a "concile nationale," both of which would focus on ways to solve the refusal-of-sacraments crisis.[44]

By contrast, the *Gazette* presented the episcopacy as dedicated to enforcing *Unigenitus* at any cost. And the Crown was depicted as desperate to find a solution to an intractable problem but hindered in its efforts by its own confusion and uncertainty. As the *Gazette*'s correspondent pointed out in January 1753, when the parlement illegally published the outline of its forthcoming *grandes remontrances*, "If the king wanted to crush the parlement with all of his authority, he could certainly do so," but for a variety of reasons he did not. It was already becoming clear that the very definition of royal sovereign authority was at stake and that the king had already made a grave tactical error. Instead of working out a settlement between the parlement and the clergy in private deliberations, Louis XV permitted the confrontations, negotiations, and ensuing debate to take place in the public forum where his own authority became the object of scrutiny for a growing body of interested royal subjects, a body described in the *Gazette* as always hungry for news of developments in this crisis.

May 1753 to August 1754

The exile of the magistrates on 9 May 1753 was, by all accounts, a very dramatic and troubling event, the effects of which were precisely the opposite of what the Crown had hoped.[45] Late the evening before, armed guards delivered *lettres de cachet* to 250 magistrates, instructing them to leave Paris within twenty-four hours for Bourges, Poitiers, or Auvergne. The *Gazette*'s correspondent described in detail the large crowd that gathered at the gates of the Palais de Justice, hoping to find out more about the rumored exile and displaying sympathy for the magistrates, whom they considered judicial heroes martyred in the struggle against clerical and royal despotism. "All of Paris is aghast at the disgrace of so many people whom the public has always regarded as the defenders of their rights," the *Gazette* remarked. "It is impossible to describe the concern with which everyone is trying to determine

44. *GL,* 6 July 1753.
45. An account of the exile can be found in *GL,* 18 Mar. 1753, and the two preceding issues.

what this shocking event will lead to, especially inasmuch as the same attitude exists within all the other parlements in the kingdom."[46]

The clash between the king and his magistrates over the *remontrances* of 9 April 1753 and the fifteen-month exile that ensued comprise the second stage of the prolonged conflict over the refusal of sacraments. This period is important both because of political developments and because of the evolution in the kind of coverage furnished by the *Gazette*. During this period the *Gazette* chronicled the steadily deteriorating relations among the combatants and furnished subscribers with reports of the increasingly divisive political atmosphere that was gripping Paris.

Far from providing a solution for a beleaguered monarchy, the exile developed quickly into a stalemate. By August of the following year it had grown into a painful and embarrassing failure for Louis XV. His attempt to respond forcefully to the parlement's challenge to royal sovereignty met with well-organized, effective countermeasures. In the anxious months that followed, the "solutions" implemented periodically by the Crown served only to aggravate the situation. To make matters worse, the coverage provided by the *Gazette* chronicled these stunning strategic failures in humiliating detail. The parlementary strategists used the Crown's clumsy efforts to their own advantage, rallying public opinion to their side. The Parlement of Paris and the provincial parlements were able to survive the efforts of the Crown to enforce obedience and returned triumphantly in August 1754 with their privileges intact and their public reputation enhanced.

While the monarchy's earnest attempts failed dramatically, they did help to put in relief many of the political and religious problems that had been taking shape since 1750. Even though public outrage was expressed over the punishment of the magistrates, contemporary accounts of the episode also convey a sense of exhilaration and relief that the crisis had finally come to a head after months of provocative maneuvering.

The political consequences of the exile erupted immediately, as long-festering religious divisions fueled vicious attacks and counterattacks. The episcopacy, believing it had defeated the magistracy, stepped up its efforts to crush all opposition to *Unigenitus*. The *Gazette* reported that two priests from one parish had been banished from the

46. *GL,* 22 May 1753.

kingdom for life and "more than three hundred other appellants would [soon] meet the same fate if they did not renounce their opposition to the papal bull *Unigenitus* . . . , the Bastille's population grows daily, and it is rumored that the king has been given a list of all the clergy suspected of being opposed to *Unigenitus*."[47]

The exiled magistrates responded in kind. In a remarkable demonstration of solidarity, the remaining tribunals as well as the various corps of court personnel went on strike, refusing to handle anything but cases concerning the refusal of sacraments. Reliable channels of communication were established among the exiled magistrates, the other provincial parlements, and the complex hierarchy of lower tribunals. In this way, the parlement was able to provide its supporters with protection against persecution and to put steady pressure on the Crown to bring them back to Paris. Parlementary strategists reinforced these countermeasures with a sophisticated propaganda campaign designed to galvanize public opposition both to the Crown and to the episcopacy. Consequently, the exiled magistrates were able to maintain their influential role both in the refusal-of-sacraments controversy and in the broadening political and constitutional crisis.

Before turning to an examination of the *Gazette*'s coverage of the exile and its aftermath, two major political events need to be mentioned, both of which had a serious impact on the way the crisis developed. Both were treated in detail by the *Gazette* and other Dutch newspapers. The first was the Crown's heavy-handed attempt to transform the rump parlement that remained in Paris after the exile into a loyal and cooperative court of final appeal—the Chambre royale. The *Gazette* openly speculated that the Crown would permanently replace the exiled parlement with this new tribunal if cooperation were not forthcoming from the recalcitrant magistrates.[48] But the Crown chose to ignore, or simply miscalculated, the extent to which the magistrates commanded respect and loyalty from the other parlements and from the lower courts within their vast jurisdiction; thus they were able to sabotage any attempts by the Crown to eclipse the Parlement of Paris.

---

47. *GL,* 25 May 1753.
48. This royal maneuver was first reported in *GL* on 2 Oct. 1753 and received detailed coverage for several months. The dismantling of the substitute sovereign court was one of the conditions insisted upon by the magistrates in the negotiations that took place for their return to Paris.

The Crown felt the pressure almost immediately, and the *Gazette* covered the increase in tension as part of its focus on the growing problems in France. The administration of justice was essentially brought to a halt in Paris; lawyers and all other court personnel acted in solidarity with the magistrates, ensuring that even if the Crown did try to erect new tribunals, there would be no cooperation and the latter's jurisdiction would not be recognized. According to the detailed reports in the *Gazette*, the Châtelet immediately announced its refusal to hear any cases other than those relating to the refusal of sacraments until the parlement was recalled.[49] In support, the lower courts like the *bailliages*, the *sénéchaussées*, and the *présidiaux* refused to register the royal edict establishing the new surrogate tribunal. All subsequent royal attempts to elicit cooperation met with the same reception. "Even though the new tribunal attempted to bring these lower courts to heel by calling the head of each to Paris, it met only dogged resistance; the representatives firmly refused to take responsibility for the decisions made by members of their respective tribunals."[50]

The exile rather naturally gave birth to the second major development: the focus of political activity and consequently of the news shifted from Paris to various provincial centers. Evidence of this shift began to appear in the *Gazette* during the late autumn of 1753. By December the paper was providing regular coverage of activities in Rennes, Rouen, Orléans, Troyes, Montpellier, and Toulouse, but under the Paris dateline. In late 1754 and early 1755 centers like Rouen had their own correspondents issuing independent reports, but only as long as the particular incident of refusal of sacraments they were covering remained unresolved. The reports bearing provincial datelines were nearly always similar to the earlier reports emanating from Paris in their degree of detail and quantity of supplementary documentation.

The *Gazette* significantly expanded its coverage in response to political developments. Although the character of the reporting remained roughly the same, the newspaper came out much more openly in support of the parlement than it had before, even to the point of adopting the adversarial, constitutional rhetoric of the parlementary opposition. Reporters consistently portrayed the exiled magistrates as courageous, steadfast opponents of clerical and royal despotism, the

49. *GL*, 9 Oct. 1754.   50. *GL*, 14 Dec. 1753.

defenders of the ancient constitution, and the only body capable of keeping France from descending into religious and civil war.[51] By contrast, they saddled the episcopacy with responsibility for the crisis and described the lower clergy as simply carrying out the draconian directives of their ecclesiastical superiors. They charged that the Crown was becoming more and more deeply entangled in the affair, regularly misreading the complex events, overreacting, making dogmatic and unreasonable demands, and failing to implement any kind of clear and consistent policy. The *Gazette* periodically suggested that the king's myopic perceptions of the crisis posed a grave danger to the stability of the state and lamented that "the evil everyone wants uprooted seems to be getting worse each day—the means employed to cure the malady seem by some sort of contrariness to make it all the more incurable."[52]

The *Gazette* was sensitive to the seriousness of the exile and to the public interest in the debates that accompanied the crisis. It noted that nearly any kind of publication dealing with the controversy was picked up by the reading public the moment it appeared, thus contributing to the general crisis. "It is impossible to describe the impatience with which the public awaits some kind of resolution to the frightful affair over the parlement."[53] And six months later: "The public takes the greatest interest in the fate of this respected corps; last week when hawkers selling pamphlets and books cried, 'Decree of the parlement, here!' no one even gave them time to say which decree or from which parlement, and people paid two or three times the price, thinking it was issued by the Parlement of Paris. In fact, it was only from the Parlement of Toulouse . . . , and had been approved for publication by the Conseil d'état."[54]

The *Gazette* recommended that its subscribers read a new work on Jansenism, the refusal of sacraments, and Gallican ecclesiology entitled *Apologie de tous les jugements rendus contre le schisme.* . . .[55] The paper noted that the book was in such demand that after only one week the two-volume set increased in price from 11 to 18 livres. Similar incidents were reported regarding the illegally distributed *remon-*

51. For example, see *GL*, 27 July, 26 Oct., and 14 Nov. 1753.
52. *GL*, 28 Dec. 1753.
53. *GL*, 19 June 1753.
54. *GL*, 1 Feb. 1754.
55. (Amsterdam, 1752–53.) This study was written by the abbé Claude Mey, a canon lawyer in the Parlement of Paris and member of the *parti janséniste,* and was referred to as a "seminal work" in the *Gazette* when it appeared (see *GL*, 28 July 1752).

trances of the Parlement of Rouen, which received enthusiastic advance press from the *Gazette*. Manuscript copies that appeared in Paris a few days before publication sold briskly at 16 livres.[56] The newspaper also reminded subscribers that although a variety of *remontrances* and other important documents were excerpted or reprinted in its columns, copies could also be obtained easily from bookstores or *colporteurs*, not just in France but all over Europe.[57]

From an editorial point of view, the persecutions surrounding the enforcement of *Unigenitus* and the political imbroglio that followed were the most important story in France for months on end; they also made good copy. The *Gazette*'s editor did everything possible to provide prompt, lively, comprehensive coverage of developments, while communicating to readers how very serious the situation had become. By mid-July, the *Gazette* estimated, more than ten thousand people had left Paris as a result of the exile, including members of the magistrates' families and households, a large body of judicial personnel, and a substantial number of individuals who followed the magistrates in the hope that their cases might be adjudicated.[58] And in the provinces, the situation had become particularly nasty. In Rouen, for example, a priest was alleged to have announced to his parishioners "that to extirpate the Jansenists it would be necessary to have another St. Bartholomew's Day [massacre]."[59]

By the autumn of 1753 the situation had deteriorated even further, and editorial attention shifted dramatically to the crisis in the provinces. In mid-October 1753 a report came from Rouen that a large group of armed and masked demonstrators had gathered at three o'clock in the morning in front of the Jesuit residence and carried out a mock interment of the bull *Unigenitus*. They then quietly dispersed.[60] This episode took place only a few weeks after more than 6,200 royal troops had been moved to Rouen and installed around the episcopal palace in order to prevent violence over the bishop's enforcement of the controversial papal decree.[61] A similar military buildup in Pontoise (where many of the exiled magistrates were residing) was reported on 2 November 1753: "Nobody leaves or enters without permission of the formidable royal guard at the gates. The commander has orders not to

56. *GL*, 3 Aug. 1752.   57. *GL*, 26 Apr. 1754.   58. *GL*, 20 July 1753.
59. *GL*, 1 June 1753.   60. *GL*, 23 Oct. 1753.   61. *GL*, 4 Sept. 1753.

let certain people leave. This situation does not bode well. . . . Here in Paris licentiousness spreads and grows by the day."

In response to the deepening crisis, the coverage provided by the *Gazette* not only expanded, it also became increasingly analytic. The picture drawn by the *Gazette* during these months was one in which the opposing sides operated according to fundamentally different first principles. Their definitions of legitimate judicial authority (and hence the definition of sovereign authority itself) were so divergent that there was little room for meaningful dialogue.

A good example of this ideological rupture can be found in a detailed judicial brief reprinted in the *Gazette* in which the attorney general of the Parlement of Toulouse attacked two allegedly libelous anti-parlementary writings that had recently appeared for sale in Paris. "With the most incredible excess and licentiousness," the attorney general argued, one of the authors complained that he could not "believe that His Majesty would permit a case [of the refusal of sacraments] to be heard by a group of judges who showed themselves so impassioned, so prejudiced, and so guilty of calumny, deceit, rebellion, and the sacrilegious usurpation [of authority]. Permit me," said the attorney general, "to leave aside the ignorance, bad faith, false maxims, and ridiculous conclusions [that appear in these works] and to draw attention only to the section in which the parlement is so unjustly accused of challenging the right of the sovereign to act as judge in cases he decides to hear personally." This was, of course, the main point of contention among the magistrates, the Crown, and the clergy. The parlementaires argued that their opposition to *Unigenitus* and to royal policy in general was based upon and justified by their elaborately worked out interpretation of France's constitution. The libelist, on the other hand, claimed that the parlement had so distorted the constitution that kingship had become a "vain title, [a] mere phantom of sovereign authority. . . . A monarch here is nothing more than an idol. It is not permitted for him to speak, to see, to hear, or to act except through the agency of his parlement. Our masters are in trusteeship, and the parlements are their eternal guardians . . . the prince has the title and the parlements the exercise [of authority]." And to support this vicious attack, maintained the attorney general, the author "has dared to corrupt, falsify, and distort the texts that he has before him, either by using words in ways that belie the most common and accepted usage or by boldly assembling pieces of unrelated evidence."[62]

The *Gazette*'s treatment of royal policy also helps to corroborate the existence of this widening ideological abyss and the newspaper's perception of the stalemate that had developed. Late in July the paper reported that the king had been approached by a parlementary delegation about a new, more restrained set of *remontrances*, but "no audience was granted them and probably will not be, since His Majesty wants, above all, to be obeyed as sovereign."[63] Two weeks later, the *Gazette* noted that the king "as sovereign persists in demanding from the [parlement] unlimited obedience" before any substantial progress can be made.[64]

In the middle of a grave religious and political controversy, the *Gazette* was openly raising issues concerning the nature of sovereign authority as topics for public debate. The extent to which the newspaper believed it was simply reporting what was actually taking place — that public discussions of this sort were becoming commonplace — indicates that a transformation in accepted forms of political practice was occurring, which posed a threat to the stability of the state. The impending crisis was noted by the paper on several occasions: on 5 June 1753, for example, it remarked that some new means must be found to adjudicate the differences between the clergy and the parlement, that the Crown had run out of ideas, and that as a result "things are becoming more serious each day."

Although the coverage provided by the *Gazette* in the wake of the exile of the parlementary magistrates followed the same basic guidelines as in the first stage of the crisis, it is significant for a number of reasons. First, reporting on the controversy increased substantially as the result of the intensification of the crisis and the consequent editorial judgment that the reading public should be kept well informed. There was also, of course, a body of readers with a sustained interest in the controversy and its implications. Second, the *Gazette* became more openly partisan in its coverage, sounding at times almost like the parlementary propaganda it reprinted in its columns. Third, it became more analytic in its reporting. Important issues were raised and examined, supplemented by partial or complete texts of original docu-

62. *GL*, 3 July 1753.   63. *GL*, 31 July 1753.   64. *GL*, 10 Aug. 1753.

ments, both official and clandestine. Finally, the crisis had now become a national one and, from this point on, was treated as such.

September 1754 to July 1756

The last stage of the controversy extends from the magistrates' triumphant return from exile in September 1754 to the summer of 1756, the point at which the *Gazette's* reporting of incidents of refusal dropped off sharply. During the first twelve months, the parlementary magistrates achieved their short-term goals of ensuring protection for persecuted appellants of *Unigenitus* and making major advances toward neutralizing the effects of the refusal-of-sacraments campaign. Then, from the autumn of 1755 until mid-1756, the parlement once more openly confronted the Crown, this time in response to the latter's renewed attempt to establish a competing tribunal with sovereign judicial authority. The magistrates' successful counterattack enabled them to enhance further their already substantial authority and to embark upon an even more ambitious attempt to overhaul the Crown's fiscal and administrative policies. The magistrates' success in bringing the administration of sacraments under their control provided them with a base from which to launch the next stage of the parlementary attack on the practice of royal absolutism and its theoretical underpinnings.

With the return of the parlement, the *Gazette* expressed great optimism that the dispute had finally been brought to an end. The lull lasted only a few weeks, however, before the animosities existing among the parties to the dispute became more pronounced than ever. The Crown's clumsy attempt to secure peace by imposing a formal declaration of silence on all matters related to the papal bull *Unigenitus, billets de confession,* and the refusal of sacraments served only to aggravate the situation. It was perhaps not surprising that the Crown would issue such a decree, but it was striking that it chose to make the parlementary magistrates responsible for enforcing the decree. The *Gazette* made no comment, openly ignoring the fact that the very group exiled for more than a year for its part in a bitter controversy had become judge in its own cause and was endowed with the authority to persecute its old episcopal enemies. In fact, the magistrates made it their first order of business to register a formal protest over the wording of the Declaration of Silence. They did not register the king's declaration until November and urged all the provincial parlements to follow the same strategy for as long as possible. As a result of this organized resistance, the Declaration of Silence did not become law in France until April 1755.

Despite its initial expression of optimism, the *Gazette* was soon forced to shift back to the story of persecution, confrontation, and impasse that had become so commonplace during the preceding years. If anything, the divisions it described were stronger than ever. By Christmas the reports were once again full of news of the parlement's vigorous prosecution of cases of the refusal of sacraments; they thoroughly covered the pertinent judicial *arrêts*, *arrêtés*, and other official documents, all of which had been strictly forbidden by the Declaration of Silence. On 4 March 1755 the *Gazette* reported that the "angry fire of division between the clergy and the parlement burns with even greater fury than ever." Clinging to its earlier hope, however, the paper mentioned a week later "that incidents relating to *Unigenitus* have begun to die down noticeably since the Declaration of Silence, . . . there are almost no reports coming in of new incidents of persecution."[65] However, the news reported in the *Gazette*'s columns during the preceding few months told a quite different story.

The *Gazette*'s treatment of the controversy was as deeply engaged as ever. Despite its tone of cautious optimism, the paper presented overwhelming evidence of the seriousness of the crisis. For the first twelve months after the magistrates' return from exile, the *Gazette* continued its extensive coverage of individual incidents of the refusal of sacraments. But it also reported other activities of the clergy, including episcopal efforts to block the proposed imposition of the *vingtième* tax on the clergy, the "reactionary" and "self-serving" episcopal agenda in the Assembly of the Clergy, and the efforts of the Sorbonne to exclude appellants of *Unigenitus* from its faculty and student body. Even more important, it attempted to underscore the divisions believed to exist within the body of the clergy itself, especially between the privileged and powerful episcopacy and the disaffected lower clergy.[66]

65. *GL*, 7 Mar. 1755.
66. Many instances of quarreling within the ranks of the clergy are recounted in *GL* during the 1750s; for an example, see *GL*, 8 Oct. 1754.

Even though the crisis was now competing for space with the escalating conflict between France and England, the *Gazette* continued to provide richly detailed accounts of the day-to-day clashes between the parlement and the clergy. By December of 1754, widespread reports of priests demanding *billets de confession* and refusing sacraments suggested that the stakes were getting higher on both sides. The magistrates finally persuaded Louis XV to exile the archbishop of Paris to his estate in Conflans for flagrantly disobeying the Declaration of Silence.[67] The *Gazette* remarked a few weeks later that this had had little effect; the archbishop continued to ignore the Declaration of Silence, and his supporters were not in the least intimidated. They visited him in exile and were allegedly "paid generously" for their loyalty.[68] The archbishop's intransigent refusal to cooperate resulted in an even more extreme exile to a distant monastery in Champeaux.

He was not the only bishop to suffer this harsh treatment. A few days before the new year, the *Gazette* reported that the bishop of Orléans had also been exiled by the Crown, along with three other bishops, one of whom allegedly embarked "voluntarily" so as not to give the Crown the opportunity.[69] Finally, the bishop of Nantes, who had openly defied the royal Declaration of Silence by ordering his diocesan clergy to demand *billets de confession* from every parishioner, provoked the parlement to confiscate and sell all of his belongings (both from the episcopal palace and from his family chateau). In addition, he was fined a total of 18,000 livres for three separate offenses: refusal of sacraments, disturbance of the peace, and contempt of court. His behavior had so flagrantly defied the Declaration of Silence, said the *Gazette*, that the Crown upheld the decision.[70]

The *Gazette* included in its portrayal some of the troubling effects of the controversy on French parishes. In one incident, the paper reported that all the priests in the small town of Nevillac, fearing episcopal persecution, had vanished from the parish several weeks earlier. "There are no masses being held, no communions; baptisms now take place in people's homes, and burials are not carried out properly." The embittered residents finally convoked a public meeting outside their boarded-up church "to demand the death of all Jansenist clergy in the

67. For a description of Archbishop Christophe de Beaumont's exile to Conflans, see *GL*, 20 Dec. 1754, and for his additional exile to Champeaux, see *GL*, 4 Mar. 1755.
68. This unsubstantiated allegation appeared in *GL*, 3 Jan. 1755.
69. *GL*, 17 Dec. and 27 Dec. 1754.   70. *GL*, 31 Jan. 1755.

parish."[71] The *Gazette* showed increasing interest in the effect of events like this on public opinion. On 7 January 1755 it reported that "the archbishop of Paris's behavior was serving more and more to alienate Parisians. A day rarely passes when one does not hear derogatory remarks or see pasquinades attacking the archbishop."

Like the *Gazette*'s view of the gravity of the crisis, its attitude toward the combatants did not change significantly once the parlement returned from exile. The parlement continued to enjoy an almost unqualified endorsement. On 28 January 1755, the *Gazette* lauded the parlement, "a body that . . . neglects no opportunity and works with unparalleled energy to extirpate the scandal that has caused all of these ecclesiastical disturbances, but that is always restrained by sentiments of honor and probity." On 3 June of the same year, the *Gazette* expressed hope that the archbishop of Paris would henceforth try to be less rigid and observe carefully "the wise conduct of the parlement, from which all of us can learn." By contrast, the paper cast the clergy as a greater villain than before, largely because of the episcopacy's resolute refusal to compromise. The Crown, with its erratic policy and extreme measures, continued to be regarded as dogged but inept.

The conflict entered a new and more openly hostile stage in October 1755 as a consequence of the dispute over the Grand Conseil. This was the last major test of strength between the Crown and the parlement during the 1750s. Even the *Gazette* was finally provoked into openly criticizing the monarchy for its role in a second awkward attempt to establish a more cooperative surrogate for the parlement. Armed with special *lettres patentes* (the full text of which appeared in the *Gazette*), Louis XV endowed an existing tribunal, the Grand Conseil, with authority essentially identical to that of the parlement. This amounted to a test of his right as sovereign to oversee the administration of justice and to reform the judicial structure according to the needs of his subjects. When the parlement emerged victorious the following summer, the magistrates took it as a propitious sign to begin an aggressive, well-publicized campaign to reform the royal administration on a much broader front.

This battle between the Crown and the parlement marked a significant turning point in the general character of the *Gazette*'s coverage, one that alerted readers to the seriousness of the constitutional issues

71. *GL*, 11 Oct. 1754.

being debated. The Crown had abruptly altered course, leaving behind its role of mediator and embarking on an aggressive attempt at
institutional reform. With their judicial authority so clearly under
attack, the magistrates retaliated by launching a campaign to inform
the public of the threat inherent in this royal revamping, a threat that
they argued endangered the ancient constitution itself. The situation
deteriorated, and by 2 March 1756 the *Gazette* could only lament that
"our political institutions are now completely adrift. The quarrel between the Grand Conseil and the parlement has led to incidents that
completely dominate the public's attention."

To the magistrates, the idea of an obedient, hand-picked tribunal
composed of paid civil servants (*commis*), rather than people who had
purchased their offices (*officiers*), was a direct attack on their prerogatives and their property, and thus an attack on the fundamental laws
as well. In a report that appeared the following April, the *Gazette* made
it clear that the magistrates were not the only party in France alarmed
by the change in royal behavior. "We were astonished by the huge
number of *remontrances* that appeared during the previous year, coming from all parts of the kingdom. In addition to all the ones dealing
explicitly with the Grand Conseil, we can detect a set of concerns that
centered on a single, fundamental issue — evocations — whose sole
purpose seems to be to diminish the authority of the sovereign tribunals and to vest it in commissions."[72] By midsummer, in the aftermath
of royal orders to the parlement to turn over all documents in a case it
was in the midst of trying, the *Gazette*'s tone became quite impassioned. "It is the depository of the laws that is now being pursued right
into the inner sanctum [of justice]; the very foundations of government are being overturned and sacrificed to the pernicious plans of an
arbitrary government."[73]

The extreme character of the Crown's efforts to eclipse the parlement elicited an equally extreme response from the magistrates. The
Gazette de Leyde endorsed this response implicitly by serializing the
remontrances. Moreover, in the beginning of the sixteen-part series,
the *Gazette* openly adopted the position of the parlement, remarking
that "if ever a work deserved to be distributed to the public, this is it."
It also alerted readers to the fact that the *remontrances* were being
made available to the public before they had even been presented to

72. See *GL*, 13 Apr. and 14 May 1756.   73. *GL*, 16 June and 14 May 1756.

the king.[74] In this way, the paper suggested the active, scrutinizing role that society ought to play in the political arena.

The argument contained in the *remontrances* was a skillful blend of polemical argument and elaborate historical revisionism, a combination the parlementary propagandists had mastered. France's ancient constitution, they argued, had been under attack by the monarchy for centuries, but only recently had the situation become critical. The Crown's attempts to expand and strengthen its sovereign authority had been realized at the expense of constitutionally established intermediary bodies like the parlement and the provincial Estates. These bodies had checked absolute royal authority and ensured that France would not devolve into a despotism. But now, in its attempts to circumvent the parlement, the Crown was endangering the constitution itself. If it were allowed to continue unchecked in this manner, "it would spell the end not only for the parlement but also for the citizens, the judicial order, the rights of princes and peers, the *police générale*, the constitution of the kingdom, and the sanctity of the fundamental laws."[75] The magistrates thus provided an elaborate reinterpretation of French constitutional history from the parlementary perspective, which supported their efforts to reassert the parlement's "rightful" participation in a wide range of legislative, judicial, and administrative affairs. To substantiate this claim, they tried to demonstrate that the parlement had evolved from the earliest plenary assemblies of the princes, peers, and barons under the Merovingian and Carolingian dynasties. The monarchy and the parlement, they argued, had existed together for thirteen hundred years, the parlement always having been "the same tribunal, exercising the same functions in the state, . . . [serving as] the true court of France, . . . one branch of the essential form of government."[76]

The *Gazette* presented this political declaration as the manifesto of a nationwide movement by the sovereign courts, describing (and in some cases reproducing) similar *remontrances* produced by other parlements.[77] Its treatment revealed that the Parlement of Paris was united with the other parlements and coordinating the activities of the

74. The famous *remontrances* of 27 Nov. 1755 are serialized in *GL* beginning with 25 Mar. 1756.
75. *GL*, 6 Apr. 1756.   76. *GL*, 9 Apr. 1756.
77. Examples of other parlementary *remontrances* issued in support of the Parlement of Paris and reprinted in the *Gazette* are Bordeaux: *GL*, 6 Apr. 1756; Rouen: *GL*, 5 Mar. 1756; Toulouse: *GL*, 16 Mar. 1756.

vast network of lower courts as well. And, in fact, the only justice administered in the kingdom for several months was carried out under the supervision of the Parlement of Paris. Lawyers, prosecuting attorneys, and court functionaries refused to work with the Grand Conseil, and litigants, in turn, shied away from having their cases tried there.

Just as important to the success of the parlementary counterattack was a remarkable outpouring of polemical literature: books, pamphlets, collections of judicial and constitutional documents, histories, and even satirical poems. Most of the serious pieces were either excerpted in the *Gazette* or else flagged for its subscribers. The constitutional issue sparked parlementary propagandists to produce particularly bold treatises, some of which took up a full page or even two or three pages of the eight available in the *Gazette*. All these publications encouraged the parlement to hold firm and exhorted the public to give the magistrates their support.

The resolution to the crisis was achieved during the summer of 1756. The war with England was not going well, and the Crown desperately needed new tax revenue to pay for this expensive undertaking, which meant obtaining the consent of the magistrates, who had to register any new tax edicts. The parlement knew it had the Crown in a corner. The *Gazette*'s correspondent characterized the resulting clash as "a kind of war going on within the kingdom."[78] The parlement succeeded in making the king back down on the issue of the Grand Conseil, and this victory marked a turning point for the magistrates and their public following. They had battled the clergy and the Crown for several years and had at least provisionally brought the archbishop of Paris and his campaign under control. Now, with the help of the provincial parlements and lower courts, they were prepared to challenge an array of royal fiscal and administrative policies.

Conclusion

The refusal-of-sacraments crisis and the political confrontations that followed upon it provide an opportunity to examine an important turning point in the development of political journalism in Old Regime France. In addition, the manner in which the *Gazette de Leyde* interpreted this bitter quarrel tells us some important things about the

78. *GL*, 20 Aug. 1756.

evolution of political culture during the last decades before the Revolution.

In the course of the 1750s, the political press changed in a number of ways. In contrast to the dry, rather antiseptic chronicles of diplomatic maneuvering and aristocratic intrigue that characterized the paper in earlier decades, the *Gazette* provided vivid and often insightful coverage of an intensifying brawl in the political arena: public confrontations, imprisonments, exiles, banishments, midnight meetings, and bizarre public processions. It gave its readers access to a view of politics that they had not heretofore experienced. Coverage of what the editor evidently considered the most important political development in Europe (next to the war with England) was delivered in an animated and engaged journalistic style. It was detailed, quite comprehensive, and generally reliable. Editorial policy was clear. If an important development occurred in this controversy, room was made for it in the *Gazette*, even if this meant omitting news from other capitals.

Even though the *Gazette* supported the parlementary magistrates in their fight against royal and episcopal efforts to enforce obedience to the bull *Unigenitus*, the paper managed to keep its partisan views from becoming too blatant. It was, in part at least, simply being prudent; the *Gazette* had no desire to aggravate the royal censors unnecessarily and make distribution any more of a problem than it already was. More important, however, the *Gazette* had learned to get its editorial point of view across in subtler ways. In its accounts of the crisis, it selected documents and juxtaposed them in suggestive ways. In effect, the documents were allowed to speak for themselves, which made it possible to avoid criticizing the monarchy openly. As the crisis deepened, the parlement and its supporters became more explicit in their attacks, but the *Gazette* always maintained enough distance to protect its credibility as an international newspaper with high editorial standards.

The preceding examination of the press shows that an emphasis on contestation was hardly new to the *Gazette de Leyde* in the 1780s. It also indicates some important things about political practice and the emergence of a widely disseminated discourse of opposition after mid-century. Parlementary constitutionalism — a well-established judicial and historical tradition that provided the parlement with a generous measure of autonomous authority — was the primary weapon in the campaign against enforcement of *Unigenitus*. By integrating anti-absolutist and antihierarchical Gallican arguments into the secular tradition of parlementary constitutionalism, the magistrates' propagandists emerged with an enhanced vehicle for opposing royal and clerical authorities. More specifically, they were able to generate an alternative, "constitutional" model of monarchical authority, using sources and traditions with which educated French people were familiar. This model was widely disseminated in official and clandestine publications, helping the magistrates to gather public support for their ongoing assault on the "despotic" and "arbitrary" behavior of the Crown and the episcopacy.

These arguments were consciously directed to a reading public that wanted to be well informed. Parlementary *remontrances* written during this period were carefully designed to appeal to a wide audience. The success of this effort is attested to by their extensive dissemination.[79] It was certainly to the parlement's advantage if these documents, which were designed to spark public debate on important political and constitutional issues, appeared in as many places as possible.

It was the *Gazette de Leyde* and other Dutch newspapers that served as additional vehicles for the publication of these kinds of documents as well as for a growing body of clandestinely published polemical literature. The foreign press helped make it possible for the reading public to examine issues in detail and with a wealth of documentation. The very act of providing detailed, sophisticated coverage for months and years on end assumes the existence of the public as a political participant that needed to be informed. Either consciously or unconsciously, the *Gazette*'s editor was encouraging the development of public opinion.

Neither the clergy nor the Crown realized that the battle was no longer restricted to Versailles and the chambers of the Palais de Justice; it was also being fought at the public level with a new contingent of participants. In other words, the whole character of political confrontation and negotiation was beginning to change. It is hardly surprising that the two keystones of the absolutist edifice, the clergy and the monarchy, were unable to see what was happening. And even if the king and his ministers sensed at times that something was very wrong — that royal authority was being attacked in new ways — they repeatedly demonstrated that they were incapable of halting the distri-

79. See, for example, the discussion in GL, 5 Mar. 1756.

bution of illegal publications or controlling the content of papers like the *Gazette de Leyde* and the *Gazette d'Utrecht*.[80] It was these illegal publications and foreign newspapers that helped create and inform French public opinion. And they have helped us see more clearly the outlines of French political culture at midcentury — a culture that involved many more people and was considerably more sophisticated, diverse, and complex than we have heretofore been led to believe.

80. An examination of the *Gazette d'Utrecht* during the same period further corroborates the changes in press coverage and the political culture at large seen in the *Gazette de Leyde*. Indeed, the *Gazette d'Utrecht* shared many of the characteristics of the *Gazette de Leyde*, and the reporting on the refusal-of-sacraments controversy in particular was very similar. The two papers provided the same kind of detailed coverage of day-to-day events and reprinted many of the same official and clandestinely published documents, including especially the parlementary *remontrances*. We will not have a full picture of the extent of the press revolution that began at midcentury until further work is undertaken on the Dutch press as a whole.

Appendix: The *Gazette de Leyde* and the Debate on the Refusal of Sacraments

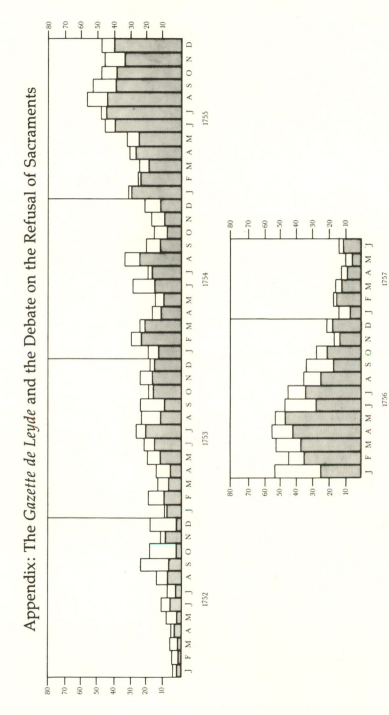

The white blocks indicate the percentage of column space per month devoted to the coverage of religious and political disturbances throughout France; the shaded blocks reflect similar coverage for Paris and environs.

Chapter Five

English Politics in
the *Courrier d'Avignon*
JACK R. CENSER

Even as the Old Regime was collapsing, its political press continued to focus on events in foreign lands. Newspapers published within France kept their attention almost exclusively on foreign developments. In the eighteenth century, all but a handful of papers for the French audience originated across the border,[1] and some of these foreign publications, like the *Gazette de Leyde,* concentrated on the difficulties of the Bourbon monarchy.[2] But the Leiden paper also printed material

This relatively small project has a long history. I have incurred debts to so many people that I cannot publicly thank them all. Most helpful has been Jane Turner Censer, who labored over many drafts. And although I have not accepted all of Jeremy D. Popkin's suggestions, his assistance has greatly improved this article and my understanding of the press in general. Others who read drafts and gave useful advice were Lenard Berlanstein, Jon Dewald, Marianne Elliott, Cissie Fairchilds, Robert Forster, Steve Kaplan, Emmet Kennedy, Robert Kreiser, Sara Maza, Pat O'Brien, Don Reid, George V. Taylor, and James C. Turner. The views expressed by Lynn Hunt and Keith Michael Baker helped shape a large portion of the revisions. Finally, I received helpful questions from audiences who heard versions of this paper at the 1983 meetings of the Society for French Historical Studies and the Irvine Seminar in Social History and Theory and at seminars at Cornell and Syracuse Universities.

1. Jean Sgard, ed., *La Bibliographie de la presse classique (1600–1789)* (Geneva, 1984) contains the most complete list to date of periodicals of all types. See also Gilles Feyel, "La *Gazette* à travers ses réimpressions en province, 1631–1752" (Thèse de IIIe cycle, Université de droit, d'économie, et de sciences sociales [Paris 2], 1981).

2. See in particular the articles in this volume by Carroll Joynes and Jeremy D. Popkin. Other exceptional periods, particularly wars, would increase reporting on

emanating from around the Western world, and other foreign papers reported little more on France than the papers inside the realm did. Consequently, the coverage of foreign news must be understood in order to evaluate properly the eighteenth-century newspaper.

Despite the significance of this genre of reporting, historians of the press have seldom studied it. A search of the literature revealed only a handful of attempts to examine the ways French-language papers covered foreign events. One author looked at reports in the mid-seventeenth century.[3] Another examined reporting in 1778, in an essay that proved more descriptive than analytic.[4] A third, in a chapter from an unpublished dissertation of the early 1940s, provided interesting insights based on a broad but very superficial scanning of the press of the 1780s.[5]

To increase our understanding of this genre of reporting, this article analyzes how the biweekly *Courrier d'Avignon,* whose circulation of three thousand led most journals of the time, reported its most covered subject — English politics during the American Revolution.[6] The sur-

France, although concentration on her armies made the news more international than domestic. A brilliant description of another exceptional period of reporting may be found in Pierre Rétat, ed., *L'Attentat de Damiens: Discours sur l'événement au XVIIIᵉ siècle* (Paris, 1979).

3. Howard M. Solomon, *Public Welfare, Science, and Propaganda in Seventeenth-Century France: The Innovations of Théophraste Renaudot* (Princeton, 1978), 123–61, and "The *Gazette* and Antistatist Propaganda: The Medium of Print in the First Half of the Seventeenth Century," *Canadian Journal of History* 9 (1974): 1–17.

4. Michel Baridon, "L'Angleterre dans la crise (1ᵉʳ mai–31 août 1778)," in *L'Année 1778 à travers la presse traitée par ordinateur,* ed. Paule Jansen et al. (Paris, 1982), 43–73.

5. Richard M. Leighton, "The Tradition of the English Constitution in France on the Eve of the Revolution" (Ph.D. diss., Cornell University, 1941), 521–90. Less related to the subject of this essay but still on foreign reporting are the following: Claude Labrosse, "Stratégie et discours, les nouvelles de Pologne dans quelques périodiques français de décembre 1734," *Etudes sur la presse au XVIIIᵉ siècle* 3 (1978): 5–17; Peter Ascoli, "The French Press and the American Revolution: The Battle of Saratoga," in *Proceedings of the 5th Annual Meeting of the Western Society for French History,* ed. Joyce Duncan Falk (Santa Barbara, Calif., 1977), 46–55; Jean-Louis Lecercle, "L'Amérique et la guerre d'indépendence," in *L'Année 1778,* 17–42; Jean-Claude Bonnet, "Les Problèmes alimentaires dans la presse de 1768," in *L'Année 1768 à travers la presse traitée par ordinateur,* ed. Jean Varloot and Paule Jansen (Paris, 1981), 101–48, "La Presse et le problème alimentaire," in *Le Journalisme d'ancien régime,* ed. Pierre Rétat (Lyons, 1982), 271–78, and "Les Problèmes alimentaires dans la presse de 1778," in *L'Année 1778,* 159–82. Many other studies touch briefly or tangentially on the way the French-language press treated foreign news. Perhaps the best insights on this subject may be gathered by reading the old but still excellent work by Eugène Hatin, *Les Gazettes de Hollande et la presse clandestine aux XVIIᵉ et XVIIIᵉ siècles* (Paris, 1865).

6. René Moulinas, *L'Imprimerie, la librairie, et la presse à Avignon au XVIIIᵉ siècle* (Grenoble, 1974), 348–54.

vey commences with the report in 1773 of the outbreak of hostilities
and concludes with the signing of the peace treaty in 1783.

The Milieu of Production

Explaining the *Courrier d'Avignon*'s coverage of England during the
upheaval in the colonies requires a brief summary of the relevant
portions of the paper's history. Founded in 1733, the *Courrier* generally
appeared biweekly in a four-page edition with occasional supplements until its demise in 1794. Its price (18 livres per year by mail)
ensured that most clients were well-to-do, whether noble or common.
Although the paper was published in papal territory, it found the great
majority of its customers in southern France. Avignon's proximity to
the Midi provided an immense advantage in delivery time over other
foreign journals, all of which issued from more distant places such as
Holland. The publisher sold mostly to the French, and it was the
French government that really dictated the terms of the paper's operation. Frequent French invasions had convinced the papacy that this
territory remained in its hands only as long as it followed Bourbon
policies. Surrounded by French lands and unprotected by any local
government, the *Courrier* bowed to directives from its neighbor.

This interaction with the French administration led to considerable
turnover among the personnel, in the era of the American Revolution
and at other times as well. In 1768, during one of the many disputes
between Rome and Paris over Gallicanism, the French had underscored their point by occupying Avignon. The Bourbon monarchy,
which usually allowed only one domestic news journal, the *Gazette de
France*, outlawed the *Courrier d'Avignon*. The founder of the *Courrier*,
François Morénas, had lost the ownership to the Girouds, an Avignon
publishing family; but from 1750 until the French invasion, Morénas
had edited the paper for them. When the new government abolished
the paper, it was Morénas who applied for the right to issue a periodical from Monaco, another enclave within France. He entitled it the
Courrier de Monaco and became publisher as well as editor. In late 1774,
when the French evacuated Avignon, Morénas had just died. Even
though anonymous successors tried to maintain the *Courrier de Monaco* and were successful for six months, Bourbon officials had always
perceived Monaco as a temporary arrangement and insisted that the
Courrier resume in Avignon. By then, the head of the Giroud family
had apparently lost interest in the *Courrier*, and Joachim le Blanc, an

important French official working in Avignon, received the privilege to publish in 1775. At his death in 1782, his wife assumed control, which she exercised through the Revolution. Le Blanc first hired one abbé Roubaud to edit the periodical, and then in the spring of 1776, he turned to Jean-Baptiste Artaud, who continued until 1784. Sabin Tournal, who would achieve fame in the Revolution, edited the *Courrier* after 1784.[7]

Contemporaries regarded the *Courrier de Monaco* and the *Courrier d'Avignon* as one, in part because the father of both papers was François Morénas and because little time elapsed between the demise of one and the establishment of the other. For this and other reasons, I merged the two newspapers together to follow their coverage of France's main antagonist over the entire revolutionary decade.[8] For the sake of convenience, I shall refer to both papers as the *Courrier d'Avignon*.

This outline of the *Courrier*'s development further suggests that any explanation for the reporting on England must consider the influence of the audience, the French authorities, and the publishers and editors of the paper, as well as the availability of news. Establishing these categories proves easier than finding documentary evidence for them: the journalists left no diaries to record why they filed the reports they did, and the editors remained equally silent. Nonetheless, a variety of clues suggests that the editors' selection of news was the best compromise they could make among conflicting pressures.

The position of the French authorities gave them great potential power over the *Courrier d'Avignon*, which they had amplified in two general ways. Since the seventeenth century, French authorities had supplied a flood of information in support of their own policies. In addition, they had initiated special campaigns to structure the news on particular subjects. One example of this practice was the effort by Gravier de Vergennes, foreign minister from 1774 to 1787, to promote the alliance of France with America. He forbade any negative reports on the situation in the colonies throughout their struggle for independence.[9]

Nonetheless, this dominance had always possessed limits, and

---

7. Ibid., 300–345.   8. Ibid., 323–29.
9. On efforts to control the press, see Joseph Klaits, *Printed Propaganda Under Louis XIV: Absolute Monarchy and Public Opinion* (Princeton, 1976), 58–85; Moulinas, *L'Imprimerie*, 372–79; and Bernard Faÿ, *The Revolutionary Spirit in France and America*, trans. Ramon Guthrie (New York, 1927), 54–56, 87–91. On propaganda, consult the Popkin

after midcentury it diminished further, especially for foreign reporting. Because French officials assigned no censor to Avignon, they put themselves in a position where they could only respond to objectionable news by suppressing the paper or demanding the withdrawal of a story. Once the *Courrier* had developed a significant clientele in France, embarrassment would necessarily accompany the restriction of the paper. The administration's interest in appealing to public opinion tied its hands.[10] Furthermore, a series of ministerial changes probably mitigated the government's direction of reporting. After Cardinal Fleury's death in 1743, rivalries among ministers and between ministers and the court grew precipitously. The independence of foreign papers such as the *Courrier d'Avignon* could only profit from this disorganization. The entrance of new administrators, imbued with the liberal ideology of the eighteenth century, encouraged journalistic autonomy still more, especially in the area of foreign reporting. Such men were willing on principle to allow foreign powers to present their versions of the news to French readers. Lamoignon de Malesherbes, the most important director of the censorship during the Old Regime, made this argument in internal memos. Since another principle of such men was that power deteriorated when unenforceable rules were promulgated, their general policy was to concentrate on what they could control and ignore the rest. Thus, they directed their efforts toward sanitizing remarks about French politics (particularly the monarch) and ensuring that sufficient propriety existed in references to French dignitaries and people allied to the government.[11]

---

essay in this volume, pp. 81–86; Faÿ, *The Revolutionary Spirit*, 55–61, 87–94; François Moureau, "Les *Mémoires secrets* de Bachaumont, le *Courier du Bas-Rhin* et les 'bulletinistes' parisiens," in *L'Année 1768*, 58–79.

10. For the government's long-term interest in appealing to public opinion, see Klaits, *Printed Propaganda;* Thomas Kaiser, "The Abbé de Saint-Pierre, Public Opinion, and the Reconstitution of the French Monarchy," *Journal of Modern History* 55 (1983): 618–43; and the essay by Keith Michael Baker in this volume.

11. The limits of controlling the press have yet to be delineated despite numerous studies on books, in particular Nicole Hermann-Mascard, *La Censure des livres à Paris à la fin de l'ancien régime (1750–1789)* (Paris, 1968). An understanding of the relationship between government and the periodical may begin, however, by matching various monographic accounts. I am hopeful that some historian will master this complex but exceedingly important subject in the near future. Among the most useful studies currently available are Jean Balcou, *Fréron contre les philosophes* (Geneva and Paris, 1975); M. Grosclaude, *Malesherbes, témoin et interprète de son temps* (Paris, 1962), 63–80 and 101–87; Raymond F. Birn, *Pierre Rousseau and the Philosophes of Bouillon* (Geneva, 1964); Frances Acomb, *Mallet du Pan (1749–1800): A Career in Political Journalism* (Durham,

For the most part, the French bureaucracy's power remained more potential than actual. On an everyday basis, the government supplied its version of current events through numerous channels and implicitly encouraged the use of this version by its geographical and political dominance over Avignon. But the threat posed by the Bourbons was greatly limited by their failure to install a censor; by the divisions in their administration; by the inclination of some administrators to allow the flow of information from foreign powers; and by the desire to concentrate controls on news about France instead of other countries. In the absence of active enforcement a simple advertisement of governmental views could not intimidate. Specific propaganda campaigns like the one of Vergennes for an American alliance had to be obeyed because they temporarily reversed governmental weakness and indecision. But such strenuous attempts occurred so seldom that they did not indicate an overall pattern.

The audience also exerted some pressures. Although no precise delineation of the *Courrier d'Avignon*'s subscribers is possible, they were probably similar to other elite readers. By the second half of the eighteenth century, Enlightenment notions had permeated the well educated within and outside the government sufficiently to create a degree of ideological consensus. As several scholars have shown, the most influential ideas included a commitment to comprehensive knowledge and a general sentiment that the established form of government and society required reform.[12]

N.C., 1973); and Denise Aimé Azam, "Le Ministère des affaires étrangères et la presse à la fin de l'ancien régime," *Cahiers de la presse,* July 1938: 428 – 38. For more information on Malesherbes's attitudes, see Bibliothèque nationale, Fonds français, Anisson-Duperron Collection 22134, nos. 228 – 30, and his *Mémoires sur la librairie et sur la liberté de la presse* (Paris, 1809).

More research is required to ascertain papal policy toward newspapers published in its territories but essentially aimed at a larger audience. The fragmentary evidence available (Moulinas, *L'Imprimerie,* 372 – 79) suggests that overall it was congruent with the French: occasional interventions but generally freedom for foreign reporting. Of course, the Avignon authorities possessed a particularly strong economic motive for allowing news: by keeping the *Courrier* interesting, they could attract livres into their enclave.

12. For information on elite opinion, see Robert Darnton, *The Business of Enlightenment* (Cambridge, Mass., 1979), 246 – 323; William Doyle, *The Origins of the French Revolution* (New York, 1980), 78 – 95. In *Culture et société urbaine dans la France de l'ouest au XVIIIe siècle* (Paris, 1978), Jean Quéniart has suggested interesting nuances within the elites; since such differences were mainly a question of degree, the basic agreement outlined here is not fundamentally disrupted.

Geographical factors and divisions within elite opinion somewhat diluted the audience's influence. The *Courrier* prospered because it lacked competition, so that even if readers disagreed with its stance, they could not easily threaten and thus manipulate the newspaper by canceling their subscriptions. Since the elite held widely varying viewpoints on the question of English politics, even if writers had wished to respond to their readership, they would have found it difficult.[13]

The availability of information also influenced the Avignon journalists. In their search for news, the editors made use of a wide range of reports from informed individuals scattered over the globe. In addition, they heavily relied upon other newspaper accounts, which were likewise borrowed or based on knowledgeable correspondents.[14] Most informants held beliefs that fell within the continuum of opinions of the elite in their area. To gain knowledge, they needed ties to the political actors. A certain number stood with the government, and some of them were even on its payroll. The connections of these informants meant that the European political elite, in general, and governments, in particular, could insinuate their notions of the news into the papers and indirectly set limits for the coverage available.[15]

All these influences had to be mediated through those who actually published the *Courrier d'Avignon*. Everything we know about these people suggests that generating profits was their basic purpose. René Moulinas has shown clearly that all the *Courrier*'s publishers valued the paper primarily for its money-making potential. They hired many different editors, all of whom seemed willing to sacrifice their own views for the profitability of the paper.[16] François Morénas, the paper's long-term editor and occasional publisher, provides the best example. Born the son of a wigmaker in Avignon in 1702, Morénas

13. For French views of English politics, see Leighton, "The Tradition of the English Constitution"; Frances Acomb, *Anglophobia in France, 1763–1789* (Durham, N.C., 1950); Gabriel Bonno, *La Constitution britannique devant l'opinion française de Montesquieu à Bonaparte* (1931; New York, 1971); and Josephine Grieder, *Anglomania in France, 1740–1789* (Geneva, 1985).
14. Moulinas, *L'Imprimerie*, 364–72.
15. See note 11 and Hatin, *Gazettes de Hollande*, 172–74. For the efforts of other national governments to influence news, see Jerzy Łojek, *Polska inspiracja prasowa w Holandii i Niemczech w czasach Stanislawa Augusta* (Warsaw, 1969) (English summary in *East Central Europe* 1 [1974]: 54–64). See also Darline Gay Levy, *The Ideas and Careers of Simon-Nicolas-Henri Linguet: A Study in Eighteenth-Century French Politics* (Urbana, Ill., 1980), 172–224.
16. Moulinas, *L'Imprimerie*, 278–345.

attended a Jesuit school and spent some time in the Cordelier order during the early 1720s. On 19 April 1727 he married; two months later his wife bore him a son. His wife died the following November, and fifteen days later Morénas married again. Reinforcing these hints of domestic instability is the financial assistance supplied by his brother in 1729 to prevent François from being imprisoned for debt. By the time Morénas next appeared in the public records in 1733, he had established the *Courrier d'Avignon*. By all accounts, his motive was to improve his financial position. The *Courrier* was only the first of at least eight periodicals that Morénas attempted, but none of them brought significant income. In addition, he wrote at least ten books and countless pamphlets, mostly histories and geographies intended to satisfy the demand for compilations of data. The content of these works suggests that, like the *Courrier d'Avignon*, they were supposed to provide not an outlet for personal expression but a livelihood for Morénas and his family.[17]

Morénas's activities suggest that the people responsible for the *Courrier* were concerned about the periodical's viability. They catered to the government in order to avoid difficulties. To ensure a profit, they also heeded the demands of their audience, even in the face of contradictory governmental pressure. In particular, they may have published the reports of credible sources in response to their subscribers' demand for reliability.

The method of selecting the news allowed the editors a way to accommodate the array of pressures they faced. For foreign news, they relied on reports that represented the majority viewpoint of the political elite in the nation of provenance. For example, the articles on Spain generally presented the beliefs that were currently dominant among groups active in the Spanish political process. This editorial policy contrasted with the one followed in the period before 1750. In the 1730s and 1740s, when a more united and less open-minded ministry could better discipline the press, the Avignon paper tilted its coverage to reflect French interests. It skewed the news to elevate the allies of France, denigrate its enemies, and ensure the inclusion of

17. Ibid., 295–300, and Raymond Moulinas, "Morénas," in *Dictionnaire des journalistes, 1600–1789,* ed. Jean Sgard (Grenoble, 1976), 284–85. See also Jack R. Censer, "Eighteenth-Century Journalism in France and Its Recruits: A Selective Survey," in *Consortium on Revolutionary Europe: Proceedings 1984,* ed. Harold T. Parker, Sally Parker, and William Reddy (Athens, Ga., 1986), 165–79.

praise for French influence. Instead of featuring the indigenous opinions of a foreign city, the early *Courrier* adhered to a French vision.[18]

The post-1750 approach to reporting the news must have satisfied, at least to some extent, the various masters of the *Courrier d'Avignon*. The liberal elements in the French government who believed that elite foreign opinions should be allowed expression in France would have offered no objection. Even administrators favoring control of foreign points of view would have been pleased to see the *Courrier* adhering to a particular standard of coverage, thus reducing the possibility that the paper would print reports indiscriminately. The coverage provided was relatively reliable and often unrelated to the views of the French government — characteristics strongly favored by elite audiences. Relying on the views of dominant groups also had the practical advantage of assuring the *Courrier* staff of constant sources of information. And finally, such reportage even allowed the journalists a measure of intellectual self-respect. Journalists of the eighteenth century claimed to be impartial conveyers of the truth. Because the journalists were giving a primacy to language over behavior that conflicts with mid-twentieth-century beliefs, recent historians have found it difficult to pinpoint the meaning of this journalistic impartiality.[19] Nonetheless, many others have, consciously or not, found the truth about societies in the way they envisioned themselves, and the *Courrier*'s editors need not be exceptional. The system of decision making at the *Courrier* — with its emphasis on a realistic accommodation to the pressures of the government, subscribers, and sources — may help to explain the high standard that these journalists proclaimed for themselves.

The Content of the *Courrier*

In part because of the editorial process for selecting news, English politics appeared in the *Courrier d'Avignon* not as a unity but as a kaleidoscope of varying images among which the reader might

18. See, for example, the reporting on Holland in the *Courrier d'Avignon* (hereafter cited as *CA*), 26 Jan. 1746 and 24 Sept. 1748.

19. Most studies have found the roots of the objectivity of journalists only in the early nineteenth century. See the following studies: Dan Schiller, *Objectivity and the News: The Public and the Rise of Commercial Journalism* (Philadelphia, 1981); Michael Schudson, *Discovering the News: A Social History of American Newspapers* (New York, 1978).

choose. The format of the *Courrier* complicated the narrative. Like almost all French-language periodicals, the *Courrier d'Avignon* was divided into sections that contained reports from different regions. Each edition commonly included five to ten reports, almost always from Europe or North America and generally containing the news deemed important to their city of origin. Consequently, the Paris section described not only the most recent occurrences in the French capital but also what its political elites held were areas of concern. A reader could follow significant battles or events in Turkey or America in the Paris section; the heading only guaranteed that the news would be significant to that area. Each report was written in the first person plural, making the reporter appear to represent the local citizenry.

London naturally served as the main depot for information on English politics. Although early in the Revolution America had provided the second most detailed coverage, it was replaced by Paris, Amsterdam, and other European cities as the war widened to include England's traditional foes. In short, the *Courrier d'Avignon*'s coverage of England consisted of a series of communications. News summaries, quotes from speeches and documents, and editorial comments (although not full-blown editorials) communicated the points of view of their sources.

The narrative style of the *Courrier* made the images communicated still more complex. The paper's pages were filled with a multitude of discrete descriptions, which almost invariably lacked an introduction or summary to place the material in context. The periodical provided no editorials or general interpretative articles to guide the reader, but only a pastiche of geographical perspectives and a multitude of facts.

Some linkages did exist among this wealth of data. Even though the journalists gave no indication that individual notices contributed to a series of news stories, information about one event was often reported in several different editions. Many relatively minor occurrences received serial coverage, and large issues — like the Gordon Riots in June 1780, the problems of the defeated Admiral Keppel in 1778 and 1779, and the fall of the North ministry in 1782 — received serious, sustained attention. Although such continuing reports remained the minority and could not really dominate the usual, unrelated news accounts, the relatively narrow focus of the *Courrier* fostered another kind of unity. In its coverage of England, the paper spilled the most ink about war and its domestic implications, diplomatic initiatives, the actions of the royal council, London politics, and the proceedings of Parliament. This focus, rather than a broader one that included provincial affairs and local occurrences, gave the paper a certain coherence.

Most editions of the Avignon paper conformed to this general outline. The copy of 2 May 1777 included a report of $1\frac{1}{4}$ columns with a London dateline of 12 April. Five stories, approximately one hundred words each, treated a variety of subjects: the delivery of a military plan of operations to the generals in America; the negotiations with German princes for troops; the advantages that domestic strife gave to foreign commerce; the effort by John Wilkes to win the office of chamberlain of London; and a terrible mine explosion in Scotland. An examination of each news item reveals how little effort the journalists made to situate these accounts in an explanatory framework. For example, the very first story began: "The operations plan for the campaign has just been sent to our generals. It is rumored that it specifies the use of powerful force to subdue the colonists." The article then noted that, although the opposition objected to this plan, the ministry countered with optimistic projections. Nowhere did it note the history of this confrontation between the ministry and its detractors or the fact that the subject had ever given rise to prior disagreement. In order not to exaggerate the disconnectedness of such reports, I examined the issues of the paper for the two weeks both preceding and following the edition of 2 May. The periodical twice previously and once subsequently reported, at least in general terms, the plan for the American campaign.[20] The negotiations for German troops also had been treated once before,[21] but the other three items had no companion pieces. Nevertheless, all the events except the mine disaster fell well within the *Courrier*'s normal areas of concern. The periodical's customary focus on war, London politics, and Parliament would have provided something of a background in which to integrate the new facts presented.

I tried to devise an approach that could deal with the paper's overwhelming complexity. Consequently, this article focuses on the way the *Courrier* presented the operation of the English political structure, a subject that almost every article on England considered either directly or implicitly. By organizing my study around this subject, I can

20. *CA*, 18 Apr., 22 Apr., and 16 May 1777.   21. *CA*, 18 Apr. 1777.

consider and evaluate a substantial amount of data. My approach may also reflect the audience's understanding of what it read. First, the readers faced the same complicated picture I did, and even when they could no longer recall specific events, it was likely they could still retain the image of government embedded in virtually every item. Second, the readers were well prepared to pay attention to the treatment of the English political system. Although the French elite knew about the influence of political events from across the Channel, they may have understood still better the general message delivered by the paper about the structure of English government. Since the philosophes and their opponents had for decades openly and emotionally debated the British constitution, French readers should have had little difficulty comprehending what the *Courrier* had to say on the question.[22]

From 1773 through 1783 a particular view of the structure of English politics remained implicit in the *Courrier's* coverage of England. From this perspective, King George III and the ministry composed the executive and oversaw and approved all actions actually taken. Responsible to Parliament, the executive received legitimacy from the legislature's adherence to its plans. Thus, the legislature exercised, at least in theory, the ability to block the actions of the monarch and his ministers. Furthermore, the theoretical tension between the executive and the legislature had a basis in reality: a minority in the House of Commons — which the *Courrier* usually deprecated — was critical of the ministers. The newspaper also reported on other political bodies, mainly municipalities, whose role appeared almost neutral since they impinged upon the legislative-executive relationship in conflicting ways. Finally, a complex relationship existed between the people of England (rarely broken down into constituent groups or classes) and their governing bodies. The king was sometimes presented as a patriarch watching over his flock. At most times, however, the king and the ministry existed to serve the people, who possessed the right to monitor them. In short, the *Courrier d'Avignon* explained English politics as

22. In addition to the works listed in note 13, see Joseph Dedieu, *Montesquieu et la tradition politique anglaise en France: Les Sources anglaises de l'Esprit des lois* (Paris, 1909); Gabriel Bonno, *La Culture et la civilisation britanniques devant l'opinion française de la paix d'Utrecht aux Lettres philosophiques (1713 – 1734)* (Philadelphia, 1948); and Georges Ascoli, *La Grande Bretagne devant l'opinion française au XVIIᵉ siécle* (Paris, 1930).

a confrontation between the monarch and his advisers on one side and Parliament and the people on the other. This confrontational model reflected more the common French understanding of the British system and the problems England was experiencing at the time than long-term developments, which since the late seventeenth century had promoted harmony over conflict.[23]

Such an overall picture does not fully explain the *Courrier*'s coverage during the eleven years surveyed. The paper actually gave a more complex and variegated account of English political structure. At times it emphasized one aspect more than another. For example, the paper might focus either on the relationship between the king and the ministers or on the interaction between Parliament and the executive. It also offered opinions — opinions that changed over time — about which parts of the structure ought to predominate. Because these varying viewpoints were each expressed in the first person by a correspondent who claimed to speak for the best interests of that society, such perspectives gained credibility and authority. The remainder of this section will explore these shifts in the *Courrier*'s coverage of England. They are best understood by first examining coverage reputedly of English provenance, since these reports provided the bulk of information on the sceptered isle.

The 1773 column from Great Britain generally limited its coverage of English politics to one report ranging from one-half to one page each week. Except for these reports, which came mainly from London and favored the king and the ministry, the *Courrier d'Avignon* printed almost nothing on the subject.

The journal did at times note the critics of the ministry and the Crown. It occasionally reported the activities of the opposition minority in the House of Commons and complaints by the fairly radical leadership of the City of London.[24] A report on the king's speech describing the state of the nation provided the most detailed coverage of the opposition during 1773. Commenting on the debates following this speech, the journalist cavalierly noted that such a clamor would not stop Parliament from acting for the good of England. He commented that a "spirit of party" emerged at such times and concluded that it fortunately would amount to nothing.[25]

23. Acomb, *Anglophobia*, 5.   24. For example, *CA*, 30 Apr. and 25 June 1773.
25. *CA*, 5 Jan. 1773.

Only occasionally that year did the English columns imply that Parliament and the populace had some stake in monitoring political affairs.[26] One aspect of this minimal coverage requires note because it recurs throughout the entire period from 1773 to 1783. The periodical's allusions to "the people" always referred to a unified English society with equal membership for everyone, without special consideration for social rank, geographical location, or the countless other distinctions that Europeans customarily expected.

Positive views of the executive, however, dominated the reporting during 1773, and the journal normally lavished great credit on the monarch and the ministers. In late 1773 the *Courrier* positively reviewed the English scene, concluding, "The ministry is very satisfied with the state of domestic affairs." The administration received few unfavorable notices, although one rare dispatch criticized both the king and his ministers. This item described Londoners' reaction to the cabinet's proposal to provide new governors to oversee the East India Company; they charged that the bill attacked private property and liberty and "gave more power to the Crown and destroyed without valid cause or legitimate procedure the most sacred rights of subjects."[27]

This remark was exceptional. Generally the *Courrier* was indifferent or hostile to Parliament, political opposition, and the people, commenting on them to remind readers that such political barriers restrained and conflicted with monarchical will. In effect, the *Courrier* preferred that the monarch and his subordinates should reign together virtually supreme. Of course, the people in the news throughout the revolutionary era did not always act according to the paper's ideals; their actions may have distorted the image the paper was trying to present. I have discounted that possibility because the leanings of the *Courrier* obviously undermined the representative quality of their actions. The *Courrier*'s reporting reflects, it would appear, not French preconceptions but the extraordinary acceptance in this period of the king's ministers led by Lord North. Complaints remained isolated, so the *Courrier*'s editors in their search for objectivity were able to find a consensus on the able leadership of the monarch and his subordinates.[28]

---

26. See, for example, *CA*, 27 July 1773.   27. *CA*, 7 Dec. and 25 June 1773.
28. Many books provide the basic chronology of English politics during the American Revolution. Among the best of these are: Charles R. Ritcheson, *British Politics and*

The year 1774 marked an important departure in the treatment of English politics. First, the *Courrier d'Avignon* began to concentrate more heavily on England and particularly on the conflict with her American colonies. Almost every issue contained such dispatches, mostly addressed from London but occasionally from the colonies. Second, the paper became more favorably disposed to the opposition than to the executive, a shift that would endure until mid-1778.

The news published from 1774 to mid-1778 under the London dateline generally did not lack support for the monarch. Even a simple description of the daily functions of the king added to his significance by indicating his activity and power. Occasional references about events at court also improved George III's image. For example, the *Courrier d'Avignon* noted, "Wednesday the king arrived at the queen's palace at Saint James, where the court was very brilliant and numerous. At the same time His Majesty received compliments on the queen's successful delivery."[29] Such descriptions of royal pomp must have struck a responsive chord in most readers. Finally, the coverage of the monarch's actual addresses to Parliament also aided his image. Although these speeches made clear the king's dependence on Parliament, he used them to assure the legislature of his solid bond with it and to express his assumption that it would support his projects.[30] With this kind of reporting, the *Courrier* revealed a monarch in charge of his country, the court, and Parliament.

Information from the *Courrier d'Avignon*'s London section did not offer as much support for the king's ministers. The range of their activities and decision making reported in the paper redounded to their credit, and their identification as monarchical appointees reflected favorably upon them. But rarely did the newspaper use positive adjectives to describe ministerial activities. Although, for example, it found Lord North's speech on the English constitution convincing,[31] such praise was rare.

Implicit attacks on the ministers obliterated whatever positive image had been fostered. The *Courrier d'Avignon* adopted a strong

the American Revolution (Norman, Okla., 1954); Ian Christie, *Wilkes, Wyvill, and Reform: The Parliamentary Reform Movement in British Politics* (London and New York, 1962), and *The End of North's Ministry, 1780–1782* (London and New York, 1958); Herbert Butterfield, *George III, Lord North, and the People* (New York, 1968). John Brewer has offered a major reinterpretation of the period in his *Party Ideology and Popular Politics at the Accession of George III* (Cambridge, 1976).
    29. *CA*, 25 Nov. 1777.   30. *CA*, 17 Nov. 1775.   31. *CA*, 14 May 1776.

antiwar stand, a position directly contradicting the executive's policy. Before the outbreak of hostilities, the paper had merely urged compromise with the Americans.[32] Once the Revolution erupted, the periodical pointed out English war atrocities. One article in effect labeled English actions a crime, describing a soldier who preferred to resign his commission rather than "adopt the horrible alternative of stifling his humane impulses and bathing his hands in the blood of his relatives, his comrades, and his compatriots."[33] The *Courrier d'Avignon* also concentrated on failures in battle. Even a review of an English military success was likely to point out the temporary and inconclusive nature of that victory.[34]

The newspaper also applauded the motives of the colonists and thus impugned the motives of the ministers who tried to suppress such noble people. In its view, the Americans possessed wisdom, moderation, and firmness.[35] Although such positions might also tarnish the monarch's image, the paper's direct criticism of ministers made them appear the principal target.[36]

The London reports in the *Courrier d'Avignon* openly accused the ministers of carrying out poor policies and immoral plans in violation of historic liberties: such misguided movements against freedom must come to grief. The journal attacked an array of ministerial efforts, including proposals for reorganizing the East India Company.[37] But its criticism focused mainly on their "tyrannical," "despotic," and "arbitrary" actions against the Americans.[38] Their efforts, which were designed to reduce the Americans to "slavery," would end in nothing and lead the nation to the loss of its "blood" and "treasure."[39] The newspaper linked the attack on Americans' freedom to a similar assault on the just liberties of Englishmen.[40] Another article assailed the ministry for failing to allow the king to receive the rightful complaints of the City of London in a suitably decorous manner: such errors might lead to a loss of confidence in the Crown and difficulty for the succession of the royal line.[41] Such a threat contained some criticism of George III, but the *Courrier,* at least on the surface, fired its salvos at the cabinet officers standing between it and the throne.

---

32. See, for example, *CA*, 21 Mar. 1775.   33. *CA*, 7 May 1776.
34. For example, see *CA*, 8 Nov. 1776.   35. *CA*, 4 July 1775.
36. For an exceptional criticism of the monarch, consult *CA*, 9 May 1777.
37. *CA*, 26 Dec. 1777.   38. *CA*, 28 July 1775.
39. *CA*, 14 Nov. 1775; 29 Nov. 1776.
40. *CA*, 24 Oct. 1775.   41. *CA*, 14 July 1775.

English dispatches rarely endeavored to explain this ministerial malevolence. When they did, their descriptions of motives further castigated the cabinet. On 27 March 1778 the report from England asked why so many detestable decisions had been made. It answered its own query: "Perhaps we would find it is pride arising from opulence that leads to the belief that one can subjugate all." It added that such venal souls scorned liberty, making a connection between wealth and political corruption that was common in English political assumptions of the day.[42]

Despite its fervent attacks on the cabinet, the *Courrier* eschewed strong support for the actual parliamentary opposition of the time, grouped generally around the duke of Rockingham and earl of Chatham. Nevertheless, the paper's recognition of the legislative critics of the ministry lent implicit credibility to the nay sayers. In fact, one item proclaimed that the reasoning of the opposition always seemed the most reliable.[43] On occasion, the newspaper lionized members of the opposition, including Chatham and Edmund Burke,[44] but overall it covered the activities of these parliamentarians infrequently. More often than not, it showed as much skepticism toward their beliefs as it did toward those of Lord North's coterie.[45] And it rarely mentioned the practical alternatives that the opposition proposed for the nation's problems.

The paper's lukewarm encouragement of an actual opposition paled beside its exuberant praise for the theoretical rights of the English people to oppose and thus control government. Its criticism of the ministers for damaging such rights implied their existence. Moreover, one report respectfully quoted the English radical John Wilkes, who argued that Englishmen were presently discontented because they ardently desired their rightful power to restrain the authorities. His assumption that the English should possess this power asserted its rightful existence.[46] A piece published on 3 October 1775 most strongly stated the case: laws not ratified by the public would become "odious and useless"; it was the spirit of the people that made the laws.

The writers of the *Courrier* believed that political rights issued from tradition. Defenders of the power of the public repeatedly harkened

---

42. See, in particular, the Whig ideology as defined in Brewer, *Party Ideology.*
43. *CA,* 5 Jan. 1776.   44. *CA,* 3 Nov. 1775.
45. *CA,* 24 Jan. 1777.   46. *CA,* 28 Mar. 1777.

back to English history to chronicle its development. Other writers simply referred to political rights as historic.[47]

According to the columns from London, Parliament remained the main route for Englishmen to realize their political liberties. In return for the people's allegiance, Parliament was to represent them directly. Legislative responsiveness, not virtual representation, was the principle enunciated.[48] Descriptions of interactions between constituents and members of Parliament reinforced such a viewpoint; an article on Edmund Burke exemplified such reporting. In notifying people in his home district that he had presented their petition against the war in America, Burke remarked that "the honor of receiving such instructions from a body as numerous and respectable as my constituents gives me all the pleasure of which I am capable in the actual state of England." Burke's indication of muted pleasure reflected not any depreciation of the principle of representation, but his depression over the war. He concluded with a hope that such moderate counsels of reason and truth would have a beneficial effect on the blind men who were prosecuting a bloody and ruinous war.[49] Such reports served as examples of a significant parliamentary role, the confrontation of the executive on behalf of the people.

On occasion, the newspaper suggested extraparliamentary actions it thought were appropriate for the English. One article reported a new club called the Association of London, which circulated the following announcement:

Deploring the fatal and dangerous crisis in which we find ourselves and seeing that all opposition in Parliament is ineffectual against the majority, which is tied to the ministry, . . . this association has resolved to beg the nobility of the kingdom, the representatives of the people, and all the friends of the glorious revolution and of the form of government then established to follow the example of their illustrious ancestors in times of public distress and calamities. Thus, we request them to assemble to deliberate with the townspeople on a general remonstrance to the king, a remonstrance that will present the state of the nation, the ruin of our commerce, the oppressiveness of our taxes, the perfidy of our foreign enemies, the opprobrium of civil war, the influence of venality and corruption, and the disruption that menaces our constitution and all that which is dear to us, as English and free men.[50]

Without any class consciousness, antimonarchical attitudes, or wish to depart from tradition, this statement urged Londoners to go beyond

47. For example, see *CA*, 28 Mar. 1777.   48. *CA*, 11 June 1776.
49. *CA*, 3 Nov. 1775.   50. *CA*, 28 Mar. 1777.

the legislature. Furthermore, when a few reports described mass demonstrations without comment, they gave implicit support to even
stronger actions.[51]

Nevertheless, the *Courrier*'s section on England omitted mention of
practical ways for the people or their representatives to implement
popular wishes. Just as the paper ignored the actual program of the
opposition in Parliament, it neglected to publicize other specific proposals. Plans for ending the war in America received little attention. A
few articles suggested the ouster of the current cabinet or vaguely
hinted that George III should be replaced, but in general, the newspaper reports did not go beyond proposing a system for complaints by
the public.[52]

From 1774 to 1778 the *Courrier*'s London-based reporting generally
suggested a relative decline in the fortunes of the executive in England
and an equivalent improvement among the opposition. The *Courrier*
provided scanty treatment of the executive branch, but it did praise
the monarch. Although it gave no real consideration to the possibility
of eliminating the ministry, its criticism of the ministers grew precipitously. Without actually encouraging Rockingham and Chatham's
followers in Parliament, the paper went far in advocating popular
authority, validating political rights by an appeal to the tradition of
English freedom and liberty. Yet the paper's failure to explore specific
means of action and its emphasis on working through Parliament
placed restrictions on its conception of the power of the people. The
continuance of the executive was never called into question. Nevertheless, the *Courrier* did report a shift of authority away from the
executive and toward the people and a parliament subordinate to their
will. In this period, a political system that might be called responsive
representation replaced the *Courrier d'Avignon*'s previous preference
for essentially monarchical government.

It is difficult to explain the newspaper's coverage of England for
this period because the editors deviated from their usual system for
selecting reports. Since the outbreak of hostilities had not yet damaged
North and his ministry, the reports did not actually follow majority
English opinion. It is possible that the editors abandoned their customary procedure to reflect the general French enthusiasm for America and the English supporters of America in Parliament and the popu-

51. *CA*, 1 Nov. 1775 and 2 Apr. 1776.   52. *CA*, 23 and 28 July 1775; 14 July 1775.

lace. Or Vergennes's policy favoring America may have contributed to the negative reporting on the British ministry. Yet these cannot be decisive reasons because, even though such French public and ministerial attitudes remained the same and even deepened, the *Courrier* covered British officials very positively beginning late in 1778. Perhaps the Avignon journal failed in its system of selection because a highly complicated political debate, greatly expanded by an unpopular war, had misled the normally astute editors. Perhaps they mistook the great flowering of opposition theory that existed in England until France's entry into the war for an acceptance of opposition in the political arena.[53]

The preeminence of the coverage originating from England continued after July 1778, but its tone altered to favor the executive over the opposition in theory and practice. This approach endured into the final months of 1780. Although the *Courrier*'s American reports did not shift, the number of reports from that quarter diminished so greatly that an analysis of their content proves unnecessary. As France and other continental nations entered the war against England, however, information on British politics began to appear in the columns issuing from those countries. Such coverage continued until 1783, increasing but remaining insignificant compared to that from England. It will be examined later.

The news items from England from mid-1778 to late 1780 continued to paint a positive picture of George III. The press persisted in praising explicitly and implicitly his performance as chief executive, his paternal relationship with Parliament and the people, and his position in a brilliant court.[54] It admiringly chronicled the king's activities as commander-in-chief of the military forces. One report noted that the royal example inspired the war effort of the entire nation.[55] This and similar encomiums reflected the *Courrier*'s new, favorable view of the war.

Not surprisingly, the changed outlook on the military conflict also improved the ministers' image. To be sure, the *Courrier*'s coverage still contained some criticism. One article delivered an extremely virulent blast at the war and the ministers. In the particularly sarcastic closing, it professed admiration for a system that had such far-flung

53. See note 28 and J. Steven Watson, *The Reign of George III, 1760–1815* (Oxford, 1960), 196–219.
54. *CA*, 17 Dec. 1779; 19 June 1778.   55. *CA*, 21 Sept. 1779.

LE COURRIER
DU MARDI 17 *Octobre* 1775.

De CONSTANTINOPLE *le* 20 *Août.*

LE défaut de Police dans cette Capitale continue à se faire sentir, & les plaintes qu'il occasionne, sont enfin parvenues à la Sublime Porte. La cherté des vivres, & la mauvaise qualité des alimens occasionnoient des murmures & des maladies. Le nouveau Grand-Visir est remonté jusqu'à la source de ces abus criminels ; & il l'a trouvée dans la protection vendue par l'Aga des Janissaires aux Marchands de comestibles, & en conséquence de laquelle ils se permettoient toute sorte de friponneries & de falsifications. L'Aga a été déposé, ainsi que le Topigi-Bachi ; & le Peuple, qui espere toujours quelque soulagement après la chûte des hommes en place, en Asie comme ailleurs, s'est livré à une joie d'autant plus vive, qu'il ne sait pas si elle doit être de longue durée, & si des nouveaux abus ne succéderont pas aux anciens. On voit souvent dans ce Gouvernement des gens déplacés, des têtes coupées ; & on diroit que ces opérations sont plus aisées à faire que de bons réglemens pour prévenir les abus qui les occasionnent ; il semble cependant que les Réglemens de Police devroient se multiplier dans les pays où de bonnes loix manquent.

De LEIPSICK *le* 4 *Septembre.*

Tous les jeunes Russes qui faisoient ici leurs études ont reçu ordre de la Cour de quitter sur le champ cette Université, ainsi que les Prêtres du Rit Grec qui faisoient le Service Divin pour eux dans une Chapelle particuliere. On fait sur cela deux conjectures ; les uns attribuent cette démarche à quelque motif de guerre ; d'autres prétendent que l'Impératrice de Russie ayant établi des Ecoles publiques dans ses Etats,

veut seulement que ses Sujets y soient instruits de préférence aux Universités étrangeres, & ce bruit paroit plus conforme à la vérité.

De LONDRES *le* 28 *Septembre.*

Le Gouvernement paroît déterminé à pousser la guerre contre l'Amérique avec la plus grande vigueur. Le plan actuel est d'envoyer une Armée de 18000 hommes dans la Nouvelle Angleterre ; une autre de 12000 agira en Virginie & dans les Provinces centrales ; & deux flottes seconderont les opérations des Troupes de terre, l'une commandée par l'Amiral *Shuldham*, & l'autre par l'Amiral *Byron*.

Une Lettre de Philadelphie nous apprend que le célebre Major *Rogers* y est arrivé d'Angleterre. Cet Officier s'étoit fort distingué en Amérique, où il a servi en qualité de Partisan, toute la guerre derniere. Aussi-tôt qu'on a su son arrivée, tous les Américains qui avoient servi dans les Chasseurs de *Rogers*, ont couru se ranger sous les drapeaux de leur ancien Chef. Avec ce renfort il a marché tout de suite dans l'intérieur du pays, où il a été joint par un nombre prodigieux d'Indiens qu'il a conduits à l'Armée Provinciale. Ses Soldats portent pour devise sur leurs bonnets, *Rogers & la Liberté.*

Le Lord Maire (M. *Wilkes*) a reçu une Lettre du Congrès général à Philadelphie, adressée à lui & à la Bourgeoisie de Londres. Malgré les menaces que la Cour a employées pour l'empêcher de communiquer cette Lettre, notre courageux Magistrat est décidé à la lire Vendredi prochain à l'Assemblée générale de la Ville.

La Milice du Comté de Surrey a reçu ordre de s'assembler ; les mêmes ordres vont être envoyés à toutes les Milices du Royaume. Tous les Régimens de Troupes réglées seront employés en Amérique.

Il s'est tenu hier une Assemblée très-nom-

London news in the *Courrier d'Avignon*, 17 October 1775.

repercussions: English corpses were already floating in the Ganges and the Hudson; soon would they grace African rivers.[56] But the ministers continued to accumulate implicit credit for their activities and their association with George III. And in general the *Courrier* covered the war and the ministers' role within it positively. Articles presented the war as invigorating and revivifying the English; they equated patriotism and support for the war.[57] Such reports commonly assessed the military situation sanguinely and viewed the actions of the cabinet as sagacious and crucial to success in the conflict.[58]

Although the cabinet received a more balanced treatment for its nonmilitary actions than it had in earlier reports from London, the negative remarks continued. One report focused on a problem that confronted tax collectors dealing with the poor during an economically depressed period, gibing that Lord North recruited officials who were ignorant of the English language and thus oblivious to the heart-wrenching appeals directed at them.[59] Another dispatch claimed that the ministers' prerogatives increased by diminishing the powers of the people.[60] The refrain that the cabinet sought its own financial gain continued, and articles added a new charge that the ministers subverted others with ill-gotten gains. According to the *Courrier* of 28 April 1780, cupidity and personal interest united the ruling clique and thus encouraged the corruption of the country.

Although such attacks simply maintained the earlier stance appearing under the English dateline, they were balanced by praise for cabinet members. One article lauded ministers for their courage.[61] Through editorial comments and careful attention to particular successes for the prime minister, the paper singled out Lord North for favorable attention, and one report was particularly sympathetic. After describing an attack by George Fox that condemned the entire North ministry, the periodical portrayed the conclusion of the debate:

This bloody diatribe was finished with nothing resolved.
   The minister constitutionally obliged to listen to all sorts of indignities, Lord N——H responded sensitively to the many reproaches. He is accused of having betrayed his country and having accumulated emoluments and offices. He offers to resign what the king has given him. Attacked for his love

56. *CA*, 19 Mar. 1779.   57. *CA*, 2 June 1778.
58. *CA*, 2 Oct. 1778; 10 Sept. 1779.
59. *CA*, 29 Jan. 1779.   60. *CA*, 20 Apr. 1779.   61. *CA*, 25 Apr. 1780.

for his family, he sheds tears at the memory of the death of the son that he has just lost; numerous legislators, thinking that a good father cannot be dishonest, defend him.[62]

To a society brimming with a new sentimentality, such phrases translated into a strong endorsement of North.

Although the *Courrier*'s treatment of the monarch and his ministers ameliorated, its coverage of the parliamentary opposition remained much the same — a mixture of criticism and praise. The newspaper gave these legislators credit for their accurate prediction of ministerial mismanagement,[63] but generally it tended to ignore them. Occasionally it attacked the opposition directly. One article, for example, followed news of achievements by Lord North with the assertion that the opposition party would never compliment him, preferring instead to wait for bad news as a pretext for its useless and eternal complaints.[64]

The largest decline in coverage came in the paper's treatment of the theoretical right of Englishmen to oppose their government. There was a report of a speech in Parliament by Charles Turner in which he argued that the people might shape their government as they pleased, creating either a monarchy or a democracy. The *Courrier* added that the multitude applauded wildly, for they hoped to regain their rights and defend their liberty and property.[65] But the usual favorable references to the power of the people and their parliamentary representatives disappeared. At most the paper implied the existence of a residual power by suggesting that the government should not push the people and legislature too far. Extraparliamentary efforts naturally met disapproval.[66] The single exception was the coverage of efforts by county associations (public pressure groups formed at this time) to convince Parliament to enact a program of representative democracy and reduce the budget and perquisites available to the king and the cabinet. Despite the fact that this movement garnered enormous support throughout England,[67] the *Courrier* considered it only a few times in 1780.

With few positive views of popular sovereignty and little praise of the parliamentary opposition, the focus of the *Courrier*'s English col-

62. *CA*, 13 July 1779.   63. *CA*, 28 Apr. 1780.   64. *CA*, 25 Jan. 1780.
65. *CA*, 2 May 1780.
66. For the importance of Parliament and people, see *CA*, 24 Aug. 1779; for hostility to extraparliamentary behavior, see 5 Mar. 1779 and 11 July 1780.
67. For an excellent account of this movement, consult Butterfield, *George III*.

umns from mid-1778 into late 1780 tilted back toward the executive. Criticisms of this branch, although still present, actually were fewer; and the treatment of the king and his ministers, which had diverged in previous years, tended to converge. The resurgence of the executive was not so great that readers could overlook the limits to royal authority, but these limits were restricted: the *Courrier* presented the English political system as a monarchy hampered only by a few low and somewhat inconsequential barriers.

Evidently, in the last years of the 1770s, the editor of the *Courrier,* Jean-Baptiste Artaud, resumed his paper's past method of providing English reports. His reliance on the monarchy and the ministry mirrored the majority viewpoint in England.[68] The direction of this coverage reveals the indifference of the French administration toward shaping foreign news. Even as the armed conflict between France and its ancient rival was intensifying, the *Courrier* was giving more favorable coverage to Lord North and George III.

In late 1780 an important shift appeared in the articles from London, which lasted until the announcement of a signed peace treaty on 28 November 1783. It negatively affected the image of the executive, including even the king, and boosted the stock of opposition.

In general, the *Courrier's* English section still treated George III respectfully. By continuing to print his addresses to Parliament without comment, it accepted and promulgated his vision of himself as the paternalistic leader of the country and the legislature.[69] By publicizing the king's domestic life and his presence at court events, as well as his decisions about the war, it implicitly acknowledged his significance. It also continued to bestow explicit credit. Lord Shelburne, then the king's chief minister, declared that since the state was monarchical, the first prerogative of its king, fully endorsed by the "constitution," was "to make war and peace without consultation." The newspaper strongly endorsed this view.[70]

Yet some cautiously couched criticism of the monarch crept into the English reports. Burke's justification of his proposal to limit court expenses received attention. In it, he implicitly charged George III with failure in his monarchical duties, by claiming that Louis XVI provided an excellent example of frugality.[71] Another piece registered

68. See note 28. 69. *CA,* 30 July 1782. 70. *CA,* 7 Jan. 1783.
71. *CA,* 6 Mar. 1781.

the paper's more obvious displeasure. A discussion of a speech given by the king on the chances for peace closed with the observation that he had not reassured them very much. Rather than speak of peace, which everyone desired, he had talked of honor.[72] Such a criticism reflected a changed perspective on the military conflict since, beginning in late 1780, the pages from London had again turned against the war.

This phase of the *Courrier d'Avignon*'s coverage added severe diatribes against the ministry to the mild attacks on George III. The paper saw the chief failing of the ministers in their role in the armed struggle, accusing them of persisting in the war against all reason, ruthlessly seeking to dominate all Europe, and misleading the nation about the chances for peace.[73] A new tone characterized the paper's coverage of the cabinet. It began to scrutinize the cabinet's activities far more closely, and its reports consistently revealed a group of men motivated by opportunism and necessity rather than political principle.[74] The *Courrier* reiterated its view that greed led the ministers to their evil deeds.[75] The fall of the North ministry in March 1782 (reported on 12 April) strongly reinforced this criticism, since it suggested the fate that might befall inadequate ministers.

This negative view of the king's advisers did not, however, completely banish the paper's implicit justification of them. Their role in decision making ensured their continued recognition by the press. During this period, the *Courrier* published one English column that specifically attested to the importance of the ministers: in 1783, during a period with no formally appointed ministry, the former treasurer of state Lord North remarked that without ministers the government floundered and "all departments suffered as one; most important negotiations were suspended; the breakdown of order in many places has already led to mutinies." The item ended with an optimistic assessment of the future, since a new cabinet had been formed.[76] Confidence in this governmental arm reflected favorably on the role of ministers.

Overall, however, the executive fared poorly. The parliamentary opposition did not do much better, even though the period from 1780 through 1783 saw several new governments with new people cast into

72. *CA*, 3 Aug. 1781.   73. *CA*, 12 June and 10 July 1781.
74. See the report in 5 Nov. 1782.   75. *CA*, 8 Jan. 1782.
76. *CA*, 4 Apr. 1783.

opposition roles. Articles often explained the motives of these men as strictly opportunistic, and they sometimes employed bitter invective. For example, the *Courrier* reported the opposition's strong protest against a peace treaty proposed by the ministry, noting, "While they wait for the explosion from the opposition to subside, the true patriots applaud the end of this ruinous war."[77]

Not all the reports in the English section derided the opposition. The *Courrier's* attention to administration critics increased in this period, implying at least a recognition of them. Moreover, the opposition enjoyed a very short period — actually its only period — of genuinely favorable coverage at the time of the fall of the North ministry. The issue of 12 April 1782 proclaimed that the ministry had fallen; "the project of peace with the Americans, imagined and sustained by the party of opposition, has fully succeeded, and there is now but a single voice in the nation to put an end to this unnatural and ruinous war." The party praised here, curiously enough, included many parliamentarians who, as the preceding paragraph revealed, the *Courrier* routinely castigated. The *Courrier's* commitment was still clearly to peace, not parliamentary opposition.

Nonetheless, beginning in late 1780, readers of the *Courrier d'Avignon's* reports from England would have observed a revitalized commitment to opposition by the people. Once again the articles advocated a responsive form of government. One piece quoted a speech by James Cowther, who argued that although a few leaders had stubbornly continued the war, the nation had now awakened and no longer wished to be misled; whatever its own wishes, the ministry ought to respond to these demands.[78]

The *Courrier* did not, however, primarily emphasize the rights of the public; rather the articles concentrated on Parliament as the exclusive administrator of such freedoms. On the rare occasions that reports alluded to direct, popular intervention, it was to disavow specifically such action.[79] Instead the columns stressed the rightful role of Parliament by repeatedly insisting that the legislative body was the people assembled.[80] A comment in the 6 December 1782 issue exemplified this attitude: "Parliament's return, scheduled for the 28th of this month, will doubtless open a new, very interesting scene. And the most im-

77. *CA*, 21 Aug. 1781; 18 Feb. 1783.   78. *CA*, 8 Jan. 1782.
79. *CA*, 9 May 1783.   80. *CA*, 19 Mar. 1782.

portant issues already secretly debated in the cabinet will be brought before this national assembly [Assemblée nationale]." And Parliament possessed considerable power, for it had garnered most of the credit for unseating the North ministry. By covering the gradual dissolution of Lord North's majority, which resulted in his dismissal, the *Courrier* implicitly argued that Parliament ultimately dominated the executive. The formal opposition gained glory by leading the attack, but in the final analysis, power rested with the legislature.[81] Clearly then, Parliament was to exercise the power of the people.

But the *Courrier* did not want the legislature to function as an opposition group. The articles proposed a parliament whose members acted only for the welfare of the nation, avoiding squabbles for power and ignoring organizational advantages in order to learn the people's will and accomplish the greater work of their society.[82] In short, while the paper acknowledged the power of Parliament, it never failed to reiterate its belief that the legislature should not usurp authority but serve the English people directly.

In brief, the *Courrier*'s reporting from late 1780 to almost the end of 1783 presented a fairly negative view of the English authorities. Some censure of George III appeared, but the ministers bore the brunt of criticism. Although the paper offered little support to the opposition party, it endorsed Parliament as a whole. Its reporting resembled the coverage from 1774 to 1778: becoming pessimistic about the executive, it turned toward the people and, this time, toward Parliament. England remained a society in conflict, but the people — as represented by Parliament — were dominant. In the final years of the American Revolution, the *Courrier* made clear its desire that the English political system be responsively representative.

This renewed emphasis on representation in the *Courrier* only followed the shift in attitudes within English public opinion. As the war became increasingly unpopular in England, more and more negative sentiment focused on the ministry. However, violent anti-Catholic riots in the capital and provincial efforts to gain popular control of Parliament encouraged much of political society to urge the opposition to confine itself to parliamentary action. The majority of the political actors wanted simply to reduce ministerial power, without

81. *CA*, 19 Mar. and 12 Apr. 1782.   82. Ibid.

opening the Pandora's box of large-scale societal involvement.[83] Those who selected this political middle road pushed the *Courrier* in the same direction.

In sum, during each phase from 1773 to 1783, the *Courrier d'Avignon* assumed that conflict was central to the English system. The ministers and the king composed the executive; they faced a hostile parliamentary opposition that the English section of the *Courrier* recognized but mistrusted. Within the conflict, Parliament and the united English people seriously restricted the executive's power.

The *Courrier*'s intermittent practice of treating the monarch and his advisers together should not obscure the fact that whenever it really mattered — whenever the king might receive serious damage — the paper tried to differentiate between the cabinet and royalty. Although it did not always make this distinction, in troubled times it praised the king while lambasting his ministers as incompetent and venal. The timing of this approach indicates that the paper considered only the ministry and not the king liable to harsh criticism.

Although the *Courrier*'s level of commitment to representative government also seemed to vacillate, the pattern of its alterations reveals a strong adherence to the belief that the English as a unified people could instruct Parliament, even though the basic structure of government might not be altered. Support for representation varied inversely with confidence in the ministry. Thus, the paper supported the power of an effective executive; it purveyed representation whenever the failings of government became apparent. In this way this ideology provided the basic fabric of politics within which the executive held power as long as good conditions prevailed.

These nuances in the *Courrier*'s attitude about the role of the ministers vis-à-vis the king and Parliament form essential parts of the London column's assessment of the English governing structure. Hostility to ministers and praise for the monarch complicated its vision of the role of the executive but did not substantially alter the paper's understanding of the conflict that characterized Britain's system. Placing the king out of range of criticism lessened confrontation, while debasing the cabinet's position increased the possibility of conflict. Each tend-

---

83. See especially Butterfield, *George III*; and Christie, *North's Ministry*.

ency neutralized the other. Moreover, the *Courrier*'s commitment to representation added an important dimension. By making a united populace the final arbiter in the struggle for power, the paper wanted the conflict inherent in English politics to be resolved not by a balance of forces but in favor of the populace and Parliament.

The views of England that originated in the reports with American and continental datelines reveal an essentially different notion of the English political structure. All the reports accepted the basic framework of English government. But the American coverage strongly encouraged conflict within the English system, while news from European cities virtually ignored this possibility.

Most of the reports that allegedly appeared from America between 1774 and 1778 clamored for English resistance and decried the executive. They brutally assaulted the motives and character of both the monarch and his advisers.[84] Only a single report sought to justify the king, and none admired the ministers.[85] The reports dramatically proclaimed a belief in popular sovereignty in England, reflecting the thinking of many Americans who wished to justify both their own behavior and radical activities in London that might benefit the rebellion.[86] Few limits on popular sovereignty were proposed — certainly not government by legislative representation, since Parliament was included among the oppressors.[87] The American columns also abounded with examples of practical applications of public activity. All in all, the coverage stemming from America propounded a heady ideology that was comparable to that of 1789 in France.

As American news about England tapered off in 1778, reports supposedly penned on the Continent began coverage with a different tone. There were some similarities, because these reports assailed George III and his advisers without reservation. According to the columns, the king and his ministers set out to dominate the seas to

84. For typical reporting from America, see *CA*, 8 Sept. 1775.
85. For the exceptional report on the monarch, see *CA*, 7 Jan. 1777.
86. For an understanding of how Americans viewed the British constitution, consult Caroline Robbins, *The Eighteenth-Century Commonwealthman* (Cambridge, Mass., 1959), especially 356 – 77 and 385 – 86; and Bernard Bailyn, *The Ideological Origins of the American Revolution* (Cambridge, Mass., 1967).
87. *CA*, 8 Sept. 1775. The American view of the role of Parliament contradicts the comprehensive portrait drawn earlier. But as this is the one place where this occurs in the *Courrier d'Avignon*, I decided to place Parliament as an opponent to the executive in the general description.

assure their economic and political preeminence. France and her allies had confronted the oppressor simply to preserve the freedom of the seas. Suffering great losses in war and much disruption at home, England was unable to realize her goals. No polite praise for an adversary muted this attack.[88] Nor did these reports view either Parliament or the opposition party positively. Unlike the American reports, the ones from Europe did not support public participation and opposition. Occasionally articles implicitly expressed a hope that internal forces might block the actions of the executive, but these sentiments remained rare.[89] The overall picture, which portrayed English politics as corrupt, domineering royalism, reflected the prevalent European opinion that England's bellicosity was a function of the greed and cynicism of George III and his ministers.[90] The reports' indifference to popular opposition doubtless also mirrored the suspicion toward the lower orders held by elites in highly structured European societies. The idea of reform was only acceptable if that reform were led by elites, as in America.

Such views contrast with each other and with the views in the English columns; they add nuances to the image projected from London and other British cities. But the opinions issuing from America and the European continent paled in magnitude beside the ones from England. Only reports from England appeared continuously from 1773 to 1783 in the *Courrier.* They dominated the Avignon periodical and provided the readers' basic images and interpretation of English politics.

Conclusions

How widespread was the message delivered by the *Courrier d'Avignon*? Of the many French-language news periodicals that existed from 1773 through 1783, only thirteen lasted the entire eleven years.[91] The government-controlled *Gazette de France* originated inside France, while the others published just outside the French borders. To corroborate my findings in the *Courrier,* I read extensively in three journals

88. For example, see Supplement to *CA,* 23 July 1779.
89. Ibid.   90. Acomb, *Anglophobia,* 51–68.
91. *Courrier d'Avignon, Courier du Bas-Rhin, Gazette universelle de Deux-Ponts, Gazette d'Amsterdam, Gazette de Berne, Gazette de Bruxelles, Gazette de Cologne, Gazette de France, Gazette de la Haye, Gazette de Leyde, Gazette d'Utrecht, Journal de Bouillon,* and *Journal de Genève.*

— the *Gazette de France,* the *Courier du Bas-Rhin,* and the *Gazette de Leyde.* I deliberately selected the first because of its association with the government; I chose the last two randomly. My goal was not to establish in detail these papers' point of view on English politics but to see if they emphasized the themes presented by the *Courrier d'Avignon.* To a large degree, they did. The one major exception was that none of the other newspapers shared the *Courrier d'Avignon's* bias against the parliamentary opposition. This difference, which is not profound, actually shows the papers' greater preference for representative government. By covering the opposition positively, they contributed more support for practical means of dissent. Otherwise, the vision of English politics proposed throughout the periodical press conformed to the one in the *Courrier d'Avignon.* Moreover, the papers all shared the *Courrier's* custom of reporting news from a correspondent on the scene, who was a member of English society, a device that added weight to the views presented.

With a broad spectrum of papers encouraging representative government for England, the coverage of foreign news could present to French readers ideas different from the official ideology of absolutism. Reports not only from England but from countries as diverse as Poland, Turkey, and America constantly bombarded elite audiences with beliefs about governing that were at variance with Bourbon proclamations. A rapid scan of a half-dozen papers over the second half of the eighteenth century suggests that the news from across the borders openly explored political alternatives addressed in other countries.[92]

This description of foreign news reporting reinforces and extends the interpretation of the political press advanced throughout this book. Other articles reveal that, when periodicals covered France, they showed a polity riven by conflict and a governmental structure that was hardly absolutist.[93] But many papers gave France only cursory attention; among this group, it was foreign news that introduced

---

92. *Gazette de France, Courier du Bas-Rhin, Gazette d'Utrecht, Gazette des Pays-Bas, Gazette de Leyde, Gazette de Cologne.*

Howard M. Solomon's argument in "The *Gazette* and Antistatist Propaganda" that the *Gazette* of the 1640s carried much detailed information on the English Revolution suggests that reporting on nonabsolutist developments had a continuous history from the seventeenth century. An examination of the *Gazette de France* of the first half of the eighteenth century reveals, however, that this paper had been thoroughly sanitized in its reporting about English challenges to the Crown. Hierarchy, even of republics, was treated respectfully, and in all cases reports of conflict remained minimal.

93. See in particular the essays by Carroll Joynes and Jeremy D. Popkin.

divergent political ideas and thus ensured that the eighteenth-century press provided varied fare.

The impact of foreign reporting — or any reporting — on society remains uncertain. Contemporaries failed to record how the papers they perused affected them. Nonetheless, because the readership consisted only of elites, reconstructing their relevant political beliefs allows us to speculate on how they might have responded to the notions in the periodicals. The following paragraphs assess the French reception of the message on England from 1773 to 1783 and, more generally, its reaction to the political diversity found in the foreign news.

Among the most important political views held by the educated of the eighteenth century was an opinion on the effectiveness and desirability of the British constitution. At midcentury Montesquieu had set out the lines of debate about the English political structure: he had argued that a version of the English system, which he saw as a combination of checks and balances, would produce the best and most efficient government for France. This formulation was adopted by the Anglophiles, who dominated public opinion from the 1750s until the War of American Independence. From the beginning, however, many people resisted the onslaught of positive sentiment toward England, the Anglophobes arguing that, in fact, no division of power existed in England. To illustrate the power of the king and his ministers, they stressed the existence of pocket boroughs and political corruption. Other people conceded the separation of authority but noted how much of society was omitted from representation. In 1778 the French alliance with America made these Anglophobes a majority. Indeed, the English effort to crush the colonies' bid for independence seemed to demonstrate weaknesses in its system of checks and balances. The war produced strong nationalistic impulses in France, making sympathy for the enemy seem traitorous. Yet, even before the antagonists had signed the peace treaty, Anglophilia resurfaced to become dominant once again. Its renewed popularity proved quite important in the first months of the Estates General, when many delegates proposed the English system as a guide for restructuring France. Ultimately the representatives of France selected another form of government, but the English model received serious consideration.[94]

94. Bonno, *La Constitution britannique,* especially 273–75.

The treatment of England in the *Courrier d'Avignon* and other newspapers helps to explain how Anglophilia became respectable again in the 1780s so that it could play a significant role in the Estates General. Doubtless, Anglophilia was revived and utilized to serve many needs. In the waning years of the Old Regime, elite critics of society utilized English politics to criticize the failings of Louis XVI's administration. But moderates in the Estates General employed British approaches, not to attack the monarchy but to save some sovereignty for it in the changed circumstances of 1789.[95] Surely such attitudes toward monarchy best explain the revival of Anglophilia. Nevertheless, certain aspects of the Old Regime press's coverage apparently protected the image of English politics well enough that such conceptions of government might be utilized.

As Anglophobia reached its height during the American Revolution, the coverage in the *Courrier* and other periodicals directly answered some of the major criticisms of the Anglophobes.[96] To counter those who believed that corruption had completely eroded the divisions between branches of government, the *Courrier* presented reports purportedly from a local correspondent (and therefore committed to the best interests of the English) who firmly believed in the reality of these divisions. By advocating that the people of England ought to hold the balance of power, this same reporter also refuted critics who argued that the British constitution ignored much of the populace. Since the correspondent had often recognized and criticized the power of the ministers, he was aware that the English people sometimes were not consulted. Nonetheless, because this reporter spoke in the first person and allied himself to England, he provided proof that a strong sentiment to ensure representation for everyone existed within his native land.

But the periodicals not only countered hatred of England, they may have also revitalized Anglophilia. Montesquieu had concentrated on the separation of powers in the English government, but the *Courrier* also pointed out that it was the people represented in Parliament who possessed the ultimate authority in the ensuing confrontation. This argument must have made the English constitution more palatable at the time of the French Revolution. Although the people promoting the

95. Ibid., 151–272.
96. For the Anglophobe arguments, see Acomb, *Anglophobia*, 19–68.

British system were attempting to preserve monarchical power, they accepted — and often welcomed — the reality that the nation had rebelled and the Estates General was acting as a representative body. No political philosophy could ignore that fact. Perhaps the press's emphasis on representation in England so influenced notions about political structure that delegates to the Estates General could propose the British constitution as a model for French government. Its coverage perpetuated Montesquieu's favorite system both by protecting it from being irrevocably tarnished and by altering it to achieve a new luster.

The different political possibilities presented throughout the newspapers' foreign reporting may also have influenced French readers. Charting their impact will become easier when scholars have examined other parts of foreign coverage. It would seem, however, that the elite had been trained to observe other societies closely. Old Regime education encouraged following classical examples, and travel literature since the seventeenth century had praised foreign nations. Indeed, the universalism of the Enlightenment encouraged a greater openness to alien experiences than had existed in the 1600s or would exist in the 1800s.[97] The educated of the mid-eighteenth century were sensitive to examples in the press, but they did not mindlessly adopt the foreign principles presented. Rather, the susceptibility of the French depended on their view of their own society. The satisfied inevitably regarded reports of other nations as interesting but not exemplary. But in those periods when sizable numbers of knowledgeable Frenchmen felt alienated from their own country, they may have been attracted to other political possibilities, some of which they found in the foreign reports.

97. Paul Hazard even made cultural relativism central to the origins of the Enlightenment in his classic book, *The European Mind* (Cleveland and New York, 1963), especially 3–28.

Chapter Six

Politics and Public Opinion
Under the Old Regime:
Some Reflections

KEITH MICHAEL BAKER

Recent historiographical debate over the nature and origins of the French Revolution has made one thing clear. We still understand relatively little of the dynamics of French political culture under the Old Regime and the processes by which revolutionary political practices were invented within the context of an absolute monarchy. To my mind, the great interest of the preceding essays is that they throw direct light on the first of these questions and prepare the way for a more sustained consideration of the second. Although they address a variety of aspects of the history of French journalism under the Old Regime, they suggest a common theme of fundamental importance: the nature and meaning of "public opinion" in pre-revolutionary political culture. In what follows, I shall try to explore some dimensions of this issue more fully.

Earlier versions of this article were presented to a seminar at the Ecole des hautes études en sciences sociales (Paris) and to a session of the 1984 annual meeting of the American Historical Association. I wish to thank the participants for their comments on those occasions. Aspects of the research for this paper were made possible by the textual database for American and French Research on the Treasury of the French Language at the University of Chicago (a joint project of the Centre national de recherche scientifique and the University of Chicago).

For such a purpose, the recently published *Histoire de l'édition française* offers a very suggestive starting point. In a fascinating contribution to that work, Roger Chartier and Daniel Roche have drawn attention to the significance of visual representations of the practice of
reading under the Old Regime.[1] In effect, they suggest the existence of
two principal ways in which that activity is portrayed. In the first,
reading is represented as an essentially personal and private act. The
reader is seen sequestered from the world, often as a woman moved
by her book to the experience of intense personal emotions or as a man
seeking consolation in solitude. The emphasis thus falls on the inti-
macy and privacy of the act of reading. In the second representation,
by contrast, reading appears not as a solitary but a communal activity.
The reader reads aloud to a less literate audience, typically as a father
to his family (children and domestics) or as a village notable to a
gathering of peasants. In these idealized social settings, patriarchal
and bucolic, the emphasis thus falls on the act of reading as it serves to
sustain traditional principles of order, hierarchy, and community.

If these are the two dominant representations of the act of reading
under the Old Regime, as Chartier and Roche suggest, then they are
no less significant for what they exclude than for what they present.
Conceived as either essentially personal or embedded in traditional
communal relationships, reading is construed as a fundamentally de-
politicized act, enclosed within a private, familial, or particularistic
space. It does not appear as a public rather than a private act, as
political rather than personal or familial, as an act of contestation
rather than an affirmation of traditional principles of moral and social
order. Do these representations suggest an effort to isolate reading
from political action, to suppress its public dimensions, to deny its
power to contest and subvert? Certainly, we look in vain among the
lavish illustrations of the *Histoire de l'édition française* for contemporary representations of the act of reading under the Old Regime that
might bear such connotations. Even where reading is presented as
occurring within a more or less public space — in the great libraries
that were gradually opened to the public or in the reading rooms that
became increasingly popular in the course of the century — the most
striking aspect of these illustrations is the extent to which it remains a

1. "Les Pratiques urbaines de l'imprimé, XVIIe–XVIIIe siècles," in *Histoire de l'édition française*, ed. Henri-Jean Martin and Roger Chartier, vol. 2, *Le Livre triomphant,
1660–1830* (Paris, 1984), 402–29.

Üe Perspectioe
de la Salle de la Société de Lecture établie à la Fosse à Nantes, levée et
dessinée d'après le Plan et Elevation Géometrale, au mois de Juillet 1763.

The reading room of the *société de lecture* of Nantes, 1763.

solitary, private act. The engraving of the reading room of the *société
de lecture* of Nantes in 1763, for example, portrays a space for public
reading: but that space is ordered and tranquil in the geometricality of
its design and organization; and each of the four readers appears
isolated within it, oblivious to the presence of the others, silently
engaged in a private search of the bookshelves or individual contemplation of the book before him.[2] Nothing is at risk in this peacefully
ordered space; nothing is allowed to suggest that reading might also be
a dangerous act, bound up with collective processes of political contestation.

Yet there are already representations of the act of reading under the
Old Regime that hint at its more dangerous political dimensions. Consider, for example, the activity on the quai des Augustins at the height

2. Ibid., 413.

Liberty of the press, 1797(?).

of the political crisis of the Regency in 1716, as portrayed in an engraving reprinted in the *Histoire générale de la presse française.*[3] There, on the street outside a bookshop, a manuscript newssheet is being read aloud to a group of listeners whose movements and facial expressions betray a passionate interest in its contents. By 1780, the approximate date of another representation of collective reading reprinted in the *Histoire générale de la presse française*, the newssheet has become a printed journal and the modest assembly of listeners, gathered together in what appears to be a public park, appears less fashionable. But their agitation of face and gesture has become more pronounced as they react to the news that the periodical press has brought them.[4]

This agitation is nothing, however, compared to the dramatic engraving from the revolutionary period that portrays "liberty of the

3. Claude Bellanger et al., eds., *Histoire générale de la presse française*, vol. 1, *Des origines à 1814* (Paris, 1969), plate facing 145.
4. Ibid., plate facing 240.

press." Here we see a tumultuous street scene populated by a mob of persons rushing pell-mell from a print-shop with broadsheets and brochures in hand. Their movements are disordered, their faces distorted as they clamor in response to what they have read.[5] We are left in no doubt regarding the dangerous power of the written word to subvert social order by entering into collective processes of political contestation. What has been suppressed and denied in the more tranquil representations of reading under the Old Regime considered by Chartier and Roche now appears in its full force.

The Politics of Contestation

That such processes of political contestation were already developing under the Old Regime now seems clear; important aspects of the pattern are well illustrated by the essays in the present volume. From the 1750s onward, a politics of contestation became an increasingly marked feature of French public life. Appropriately enough, it erupted first in the course of a conflict over religious matters: the quarrel over the refusal of sacraments to Jansenist dissenters discussed by Carroll Joynes in his contribution to this volume and explored more fully in several studies by Dale Van Kley.[6] Since the time of the Wars of Religion, as Hobbes and Bossuet had each emphasized in their very different ways, it had been the fundamental responsibility — and the principal justification — of absolute authority to contain the ideological potential of religious disputes to disturb political order. In the 1750s, however, the French monarchy found itself dramatically unable to perform this function. Every assertion of authority places that same authority at risk. Unable to impose peace upon the church hierarchy and the parlements (the contending parties in the bitter dispute over the civil rights of recalcitrant Jansenists), unable even to enforce their respect for the law of silence in this matter that it was driven in

---

5. Ibid., plate facing 352. Bellanger et al. give the date of this engraving as 1797. In *Histoire de l'édition française*, 2:607, it is reprinted with the date 1792, in illustration of the article on revolutionary reading practices by François Parent, "De nouvelles pratiques de lecture," ibid., 606–21.

6. *The Jansenists and the Expulsion of the Jesuits from France, 1757–1765* (New Haven, 1975), "Church, State, and the Ideological Origins of the French Revolution: The Debate over the General Assembly of the Clergy in 1765," *Journal of Modern History* 51 (1979): 629–66, and *The Damiens Affair and the Unraveling of the Ancien Régime, 1750–1770* (Princeton, 1984).

desperation to proclaim in 1754, the monarchy found the very nature of its own authority at issue in the new patterns of political contestation to which the quarrel over the refusal of sacraments gave rise. Absolute authority was at issue not only in the bold contentions to be found in the repeated *remontrances* presented by the parlementary magistrates to the king and in the stubborn refusal of the magistrates to abandon their position even in the face of exile. It was also at issue in the illegal and clandestine circulation of the parlementary *remontrances* and in the assiduity with which they were bought — in dramatic numbers — by members of the literate public. It was at issue in the proliferation of pamphlets that marked the rhythm of the dispute over the refusal of sacraments and extended its politicizing effects on French public life. It was at issue in the seditious murmurs — the *mauvais discours* — heard among the Parisian populace. And it was at issue (as the essays in this volume by Carroll Joynes and Jeremy D. Popkin suggest) in the space that a journal such as the *Gazette de Leyde* devoted to this dispute, in that journal's ability to enlarge the circle of readers following its course, in the editors' claim to announce the views of "the public" in such a contested manner.

Strictly speaking, of course, none of these political practices were consistent with the theory of royal absolutism. That theory depended on a view of the monarch as the only public person: the source and principle of unity in a particularistic society of orders and Estates. If politics is defined as the process by which competing claims and policies are transformed into authoritative definitions of the general good, then absolutist politics occurs, in ideal terms, only in the mind and person of the king. To save absolute authority from the taint of arbitrariness, the monarch must take counsel from others, and he may also seek advice at will; conversely, individuals and corporate bodies may make their own representations to the monarch, urging their particularistic claims and policies upon him. Authorized institutional channels existed under the Old Regime to maintain these practices of counsel and representation — the royal council, the parlements, the right of individual and corporate petition, etc. — and the king could create others should he feel the need to do so. There were also informal channels — the court, personal networks that could reach the king's ear, patterns of clientage and influence — that shaped royal decision making by means of personal intrigue. But there was no reason why the process of seeking counsel or offering representations should be made public beyond the particular (and particularistic) circles of actors directly involved, simply because there was no other public person to address apart from the king—no other person or entity or institutional process whose legitimate function it was to decide questions on behalf of the community as a whole. Hence the notion, frequently invoked, of government as the *secret du roi*. Hence the principle, fundamental to the politics of absolutism, that parlementary *remontrances* (since in theory they represented the counsel of the officers of a particular royal court before the throne) should never be made public or even circulated by one parlement among the others. Hence the illegality of open discussion, by unauthorized persons without explicit permission, of matters pertaining to governmental policy or public order. The politics of absolutism was not a public politics.

Yet first in the case of the disputes over the refusal of sacraments in the 1750s, then in the course of the institutional conflicts over the liberalization of the grain trade in the 1760s,[7] and finally in the context of a campaign against the fiscal practices and arbitrary procedures of the administrative monarchy that grew throughout the decades preceding the Maupeou coup,[8] French politics broke out of the absolutist mold. The reign of silence imposed by an absolute monarch could no longer contain debates and contestations that made increasingly explicit appeal to a world of public opinion beyond the traditional circle of institutional actors. Frustrated in its efforts to prevent open debate of religious politics in the 1750s, the royal government fought a rearguard campaign in the following decade to limit public discussion of financial administration. Obliged to solicit proposals for fiscal reform directly from the parlements and other courts in 1763, for example, the Crown took fright when the ensuing discussion spilled beyond its constituted channels. A royal declaration of 1764 insisted on the dangers of "memoirs and projects formed by persons without standing [*sans caractère*], who take the liberty of making [these works] public instead of submitting them to those persons destined by their position to judge them." To remedy such an "excess of license" the Crown prohibited the printing, sale, or hawking of any works or projects

7. See Steven L. Kaplan, *Bread, Politics, and Political Economy in the Reign of Louis XV*, 2 vols. (The Hague, 1976).

8. For a brief account of these developments, see Jean Egret, *Louis XV et l'opposition parlementaire, 1715–1774* (Paris, 1970).

"concerning the reform of our finances, or their past, present, or future administration." [9]

But these were "vain precautions," as one contemporary writer on administrative matters was subsequently to exclaim: "as if the greed of the foreign presses did not rush to publish everything and too often to distort everything." [10] The most immediate effect of the royal order was to provoke a dramatic response of the Parlement of Dijon (drafted in effect by Dupont de Nemours) denouncing the generality of the prohibition, insisting on the impossibility of stemming the tide of brochures by such means, and arguing for the importance of public discussion of administrative questions. [11] Despite its scope, the royal declaration of 1764 failed to contain the skirmishing of public political discussion that, by the time of the Maupeou coup, had expanded once again into a full-scale pamphlet war. "One writes; another will respond," reflected Mme d'Epinay in 1771, as she observed these developments. "Everyone will wish to examine the constitution of the state; heads will become heated. Theses are debated that one would never have dared imagine." [12] For observers of Mme d'Epinay's persuasion, such public contestations represented "an irremediable evil." By opening to public view the very "theology of administration," they

9. *Déclaration du roi, qui fait défenses d'imprimer, débiter, ou colporter aucuns écrits, ouvrages ou projets concernant la réforme ou administration des finances: Donnée à Versailles le 28 mars 1764.* For the earlier decision to request proposals for the reform of financial administration from the parlements, chambres de comptes, and cours des aides and to create a special commission to consider them, see *Lettres patentes du roi, portant établissement d'une commission pour l'exécution de la déclaration du 21 novembre 1763: Donnés à Versailles le 28 novembre 1763.* The context is described in Marcel Marion, *Histoire financière de France depuis 1715,* 6 vols. (Paris, 1914), 1:213–30; Egret, *Louis XV et l'opposition parlementaire,* 98–99; and James C. Riley, *The Seven Years War and the Old Regime in France: The Economic and Financial Toll* (Princeton, forthcoming, 1986).

10. Antoine François Prost de Royer, *Dictionnaire de jurisprudence et des arrêts, ou Nouvelle édition du Dictionnaire de Brillon, connu sous le titre de Dictionnaire des arrêts et jurisprudence universelle des parlemens de France et autres tribunaux. . . . ,* 7 vols. (Lyons, 1781–88), 2:838 (s.v. "Administration").

11. "The word *administration* is so broad a term that there are few questions that can be discussed without getting involved in matters that one could claim to be related to administration," the magistrates insisted. See *Très-Humbles et Très-Respectueuses Remontrances du parlement séant à Dijon au roi, au sujet de la déclaration du 28 mars 1764. . . .* (n.p., n.d.), 5. According to Dupont de Nemours, this protest drew extensively on ideas the physiocratic writer suggested for this purpose to one of the Dijon magistrates, the marquis de Malteste. See *The Autobiography of Du Pont de Nemours,* trans. and with an introduction by Elizabeth Fox-Genovese (Wilmington, Del., 1984), 266, 276.

12. Ferdinando Galiani, *Correspondance,* ed. Lucien Perey and Gaston Maugras, 2 vols. (Paris, 1881–82), 1:375.

threatened the essence of the state. Questions such as these could not be publicly discussed without risk that "the knowledge the peoples acquire must, a little sooner, a little later, produce revolutions."[13]

Unable to stifle these processes of political contestation, the government found itself under increasing pressure to participate in them. Jacob-Nicolas Moreau, the hired political pen whose campaigns in defense of monarchical authority eventually earned him the title of royal historiographer, was arguing by the end of the 1750s that, having lost public support to the parlements, the government was now obliged to appropriate the ideological strategies of the opposition for its own purposes.[14] In the course of subsequent decades, the preambles to important royal edicts grew longer and more explicit in their explanations and justifications of government policies; ministers proved adept in the strategic proliferation of pamphlets and anonymous brochures; apologists for absolute government sought to deploy the ideological resources of the monarchy in its own defense. Reluctantly, inconsistently, yet with an increasing sense of urgency as successive pre-revolutionary crises became more acute, agents of the monarchy found themselves presenting their briefs before the court of the public.

What was this "public" to which monarchical government and its critics competed to appeal? Clearly, its emergence was bound up with such complex sociological phenomena as long-term changes in literacy, the commercial expansion of the press, and the bureaucratic transformation of a particularistic social order into a more integrated national community.[15] But we should resist the temptation to understand the concept of "the public" simply in sociological terms, reduc-

---

13. Ibid.

14. [Jacob-Nicolas Moreau], "Principes de conduite avec les parlements," in Bibliothèque du Sénat (Paris), ms. 402, fols. 27–135. This memorandum was written in 1760; the date appears incorrectly as 1759 in my earlier account "On the Problem of the Ideological Origins of the French Revolution," in *Modern European Intellectual History: Reappraisals and New Perspectives*, ed. Dominick LaCapra and Steven L. Kaplan (Ithaca, N.Y., 1982), 214–16. On Moreau's career more generally, see Dieter Gembicki, *Histoire et politique à la fin de l'ancien régime: Jacob-Nicolas Moreau (1717–1803)* (Paris, 1979); Martin Mansergh, "The Revolution of 1771, or the Exile of the Parlement of Paris" (D. Phil. thesis, Oxford University, 1973).

15. The indispensable analysis by Jürgen Habermas, *Strukturwandel der Öffentlichkeit* (Neuwied, 1962), has recently been translated into French as *L'Espace public: Archéologie de la publicité comme dimension constitutive de la société bourgeoise*, trans. Marc B. de Launay (Paris, 1978). Important aspects of this complex social process are also considered by François Furet and Jacques Ozouf, *Reading and Writing: Literacy in France from Calvin to Jules Ferry* (Cambridge, 1982); Elizabeth Eisenstein, *The Printing Press as an*

ing it to a putative social referent among specific groups or classes. Beyond the fact that it assumed access to the printed word, the social composition of "the public" remained relatively ill defined in the last decades of the Old Regime, until clarification was forced by the political processes set in train by the calling of the Estates General. It took form as a political or ideological construct rather than as a discrete sociological function. "The public" emerged in eighteenth-century political discourse as a conceptual entity — the "tribunal of the public," or ultimate court of appeal. As such, it was an abstract category of authority, invoked by actors in a new kind of politics to secure the legitimacy of claims that could no longer be made binding in the terms (and within the traditional institutional circuit) of an absolutist political order. The result was an implicit new system of authority in which the government and its opponents competed to appeal to "the public" and to claim the judgment of that tribunal in their own behalf.[16]

The fundamental importance of this concept of "the public" as a political tribunal has been emphasized by Jürgen Habermas. In his analysis, however, the concept emerged in the mid-eighteenth century primarily to mediate the tension between the state and civil society: it served as the device by which bourgeois society sought to limit and transform the power of the absolute state.[17] In contrast, I wish to emphasize the extent to which the concept of "the public" took on meaning in France in the context of a crisis of absolute authority (neglected by Habermas, who underestimated the potential for political opposition under the Old Regime) as the Crown and its opponents within the traditional political system appealed to a principle of legitimacy beyond that system in order to press their competing claims. There is a revealing parallel to be drawn here between the mid-eighteenth-century appeal to "the public" in French domestic affairs and the similar appeal (at the very beginning of the century) to "the pub-

---

Agent of Social Change: Communications and Cultural Transformations in Early-Modern Europe, 2 vols. (Cambridge, 1979); Daniel Roche, *Le Siècle des lumières en province: Académies et académiciens provinciaux, 1680–1789*, 2 vols. (Paris and The Hague, 1978). See also Martin and Chartier, *Histoire de l'édition française*, and Bellanger, *Histoire de la presse française*.

16. For a similar emphasis on the importance of "the public" as an abstract rhetorical construct within a new kind of politics, see Rocco L. Capraro, *Typographic Politics: The Impact of Printing on the Political Life of Eighteenth-Century England* (Ph.D. diss., Washington University, 1984), especially chap. 13. I am grateful to Dr. Capraro for bringing his very interesting work to my attention.

17. Habermas, *L'Espace public*, especially 38–126.

lic" in European international affairs. Both appeals implied a subversion of previously accepted principles of authority. In the latter case, the idea of an international "public" emerged as a tribunal to which warring states referred their claims by means of printed propaganda.[18] The concept functioned, in effect, as an abstract authority invoked at a point when older principles of hierarchy and order in the international domain had lost their power to constrain political actors: the hierarchical universal order of Christendom had been dissolved into "Europe" — understood as a dynamic secular system of competing powers.[19]

In the case of the French monarchy under Louis XIV, however, there remained a fundamental conflict between the need to appeal its claims openly to an international public tribunal and the consequent risk of submitting its policies to the judgment of a domestic one. By the end of Louis XV's reign, the monarchy no longer seemed to have a choice in the matter. The logic of the new political situation required that the government address its claims to a domestic "public," deploying pamphlets and other devices of political contestation in internal affairs with as much energy as it had previously done in the international arena. As the essay by Jeremy D. Popkin in this volume suggests, this logic also required that the government tolerate (and attempt to use to its advantage) the circulation within French borders of relatively independent newspapers such as the *Gazette de Leyde*, which in turn advanced their own competing claims to define the nature and content of public opinion. But by accepting the logic of a politics of contestation in this way, the royal government unwittingly conspired with its opposition to foster the transfer of ultimate authority from the public person of the sovereign to the sovereign person of the public.

The English Model

As Jack R. Censer's article suggests, there was an example of the politics of contestation to be readily found across the Channel, one frequently invoked in France in the course of eighteenth-century po-

18. On this point, see the very suggestive analysis by Joseph Klaits, *Printed Propaganda Under Louis XIV: Absolute Monarchy and Public Opinion* (Princeton, 1976).

19. Denys Hay points out that the Treaty of Utrecht made the last (belated) reference to the "respublica christiana" to be found in a treaty between European powers. The moment coincided with the crystallization of the doctrine of the balance of power on the one hand, and with the identification of "Europe" as the object of schemes for perpetual peace on the other. See Denys Hay, *Europe: The Emergence of an Idea*, rev. ed. (Edinburgh, 1968), 118–19.

litical debates. But it was not an example that the French found altogether reassuring. Many, like the editors of the *Courrier d'Avignon*, found the English spectacle of party divisions and opposition politics both bizarre and profoundly threatening, even after the efforts made by Montesquieu to explain this phenomenon to his compatriots in *De l'esprit des lois*. Nor was Montesquieu himself perhaps as unambiguous in his evaluation of English politics as his current reputation as the founder of the modern liberal interpretation of the British constitution would suggest. His adumbration of a theory of the separation and balance of powers, understood as the essential condition of English liberty, did not entirely erase from his work the evidence of hesitations and ambivalences in the face of the English system of government. To many of his contemporaries, he still seemed to be describing an ambiguous, disturbing, and even dangerous phenomenon — a phenomenon to be understood and marveled at — rather than a model to be imitated.

In this respect, the second of Montesquieu's famous chapters discussing English politics is particularly revealing. In the first and most celebrated — chapter 6 of book 11, entitled "Of the English constitution" — he had outlined in relatively formal terms his theory of the separation of powers. In the second — chapter 27 of book 19, entitled "How the laws can contribute to the formation of the customs, the manners, and the character of a nation" — he turned to an analysis of the political practices and passions deriving from the nature of the English constitution — that is to say, to the character of English political culture more generally. This chapter opens with a theoretical explanation of the formation of political parties, followed by an extremely allusive interpretation of the Glorious Revolution of 1688. But the terms of this essay in political sociology are striking.

Montesquieu begins by pointing out that since there would be two prominent powers in the state he discussed in book 11, and since each of its citizens would be free to act independently according to his will, the majority of them would support one of these powers or the other.[20] Moreover, since the executive power had positions and employments at its disposal, people who hoped to obtain its patronage would gravitate toward it, while those who could hope for nothing from this source would attack it. This division between the "ins" and the "outs" would give rise to a constant play of political passions:

20. *De l'esprit des lois*, ed. J. Brèthe de la Gressaye, 4 vols. (Paris, 1950–61), 3:28.

All the passions being free there, hate, envy, jealousy, the desire to enrich and distinguish oneself would appear in all their extent; and if it were otherwise, the state would appear like a man stricken by illness, who would have no passions because he had no strength.

The hate that would exist between the two parties would last, because it would be always powerless.

The parties being composed of free men, if one of them became dominant, the effect of liberty would be that it would be brought down, while the citizens, as hands helping the body, would come to raise up the other.

Since each individual, always independent, would follow his caprices and his fantasies a great deal, there would be frequent changes of party; an individual would abandon the party in which all his friends would be left in order to join another in which he would find all his enemies; and often, in this nation, one would forget the laws of friendship and those of hate.

The monarch would be in the same situation as private persons; and, contrary to the ordinary maxims of prudence, he would often be obliged to give his confidence to those who would have offended him the most and to disgrace those who would have best served him, thereby doing by necessity what other princes do by choice.[21]

This analysis hardly seems to present to French readers a vision of a stable and orderly political process. Instead, Montesquieu portrays English public life as dominated by egoistic passions, played out in a world in which the relationships among political actors are constantly shifting according to the necessities — or the contingencies — of party conflicts. But hate, envy, jealousy, and so on, are not the only passions to appear in this strange political culture of the English. Montesquieu also finds the English moved by fear. This is not the heavy, silent fear of a people enslaved under the yoke of despotism. It is the unpredictable, anxious fear — Montesquieu uses the term "terrors" — of a people always "uneasy about its situation," a people that would believe itself constantly in danger, "even at times when it is most secure."

This would be all the more the case because those who would oppose the executive power most energetically, being unable to acknowledge the self-interested motives for their opposition, would increase the terrors of the people, which would never know exactly whether it was in danger or not. But that indeed would help enable it to avoid the true perils to which it could subsequently be exposed.[22]

Thus Montesquieu portrays the English as a free people, but a people thrown by its very liberty into a constant state of insecurity. It is true

21. Ibid.   22. Ibid., 3:29.

that the legislative body, more enlightened than the people whose confidence it has received, can calm these movements of popular agitation — this fact is, for Montesquieu, one of the great advantages of representative government over the direct democracy of the ancients, in which popular agitations were translated immediately into legislative effects.[23] But it is also true that the fear and insecurity he is describing seem to emerge as the virtual principle of English government (in Montesquieu's sense of that term — namely, the passion that makes a polity function).[24] Indeed, it is in the operation of this passion that Montesquieu appears to find his explanation of the Glorious Revolution.

Since this explanation contains a number of bizarre elements, it will be well to quote the relevant paragraphs in full:

> Thus, when the terrors imprinted [in the popular consciousness] had no certain object, they would produce only vain clamors and insults: and they would even have this good effect, that they would tighten all the springs of government and make all the citizens attentive. But if they occurred on the occasion of a reversal of the fundamental laws, they would be silent, deadly, atrocious, and produce catastrophes.
>
> Soon there would be a dreadful calm, during which everyone would unite against the power violating the laws.
>
> If, in the case where the anxieties have no certain object, some foreign power threatened the state and endangered its fortune or its glory, then the lesser interests would yield to the greater and everyone would unite in support of the executive power.
>
> But if the disputes were formed on the occasion of a violation of the fundamental laws and a foreign power appeared, there would be a revolution that would change neither the form of the government nor its constitution: for the revolutions shaped by liberty are only a confirmation of liberty.
>
> A free nation can have a liberator; a subject nation can only have another oppressor.[25]

It seems legitimate to find a reference to the events of 1688 in this discussion of the coincidence of a violation of the fundamental laws and the appearance of a foreign power. But there are, nevertheless, many rather odd aspects to the analysis that Montesquieu presents. How do we explain, for example, his introduction of quite particular

---

23. Ibid., 3:29 – 30.
24. Interestingly enough, Montesquieu never actually speaks of a "principle" of English government. On this point, see Thomas Pangle, *Montesquieu's Philosophy of Liberalism* (Chicago, 1973), 116.
25. *De l'esprit des lois*, 3:30.

facts — the appearance of "a foreign power," with its clear reference
to William of Orange, for example — without even identifying them?
How do we account for the fact that, here and throughout this chapter
of *De l'esprit des lois,* Montesquieu speaks of England without ever
explicitly mentioning the country by name (at the beginning of the
chapter, the nation considered is identified simply as the "free people"
about which the author has already spoken in book 11), even though
he introduces into his discussion the particulars of its history, its geography, its commerce, its internal and external politics? How do we
explain the fact that this entire chapter is written in the conditional
mood, even when it refers to well-established aspects of English society (we find, for example, such "conditionals" as "If this nation in-
habited an island . . ."; "If this nation were situated toward the
north . . ."; "If this nation established distant colonies . . .")?

In response to such questions, I would propose two possible hy-
potheses, which are not necessarily mutually exclusive. The first
points to Montesquieu's announced intention to be "more attentive to
the order of things than to things in themselves." [26] From this perspective, his use of the conditional mood allows him to analyze the essential functioning of English politics in a more abstract and theoretical
manner, as involving a series of logical consequences of certain given
conditions, and to introduce into a sort of mental experiment the
particularities of English history and geography. The result is an explanation of the phenomenon of English politics that is presented as
completely logical and necessary, once the details of the English situation are taken into account. While Montesquieu's profound impulse to
subordinate particular facts to the more general relations of a theoretical order of things is at work throughout *De l'esprit des lois,* however, it
is not always expressed in the conditional mood. The use of that mood
is quite rare, for example, in the early theoretical chapters of the book
explaining the typology of the three principal forms of government.
Why should it be employed so overwhelmingly in the particular discussion of England?

This question suggests a second hypothesis. Does the conditional
form of Montesquieu's analysis of English politics serve to underline
the profound strangeness of the political and social order he is trying to
understand and explain to his French audience? Among the English,

26. Ibid., 3:5.

as we have already seen, the passions are always at play and the laws of love and hate (to say nothing of the principle of honor) are constantly forgotten in the maneuvering among parties. This is a nation in which the partisan interests of the opposition nourish the terrors of the people, where the vain clamors that result from a kind of false political consciousness become the safeguard of liberty. This is a nation "always in the heat of excitement," which can therefore be "more easily led by its passions than its reason," a nation in which "it would be easy for those who govern to engage it in enterprises against its natural interests." [27] Yet it is also a nation in which "it could happen that it would undertake things beyond its natural strength, yet mobilize against its enemies immense fictional riches, which the confidence and the nature of its government would render real." [28] One of the effects of Montesquieu's reiterated use of the conditional mood in describing such a society is to foster an understanding of England as a singular, even fantastic phenomenon: a society in which the traditional boundaries between the true and the false, between stability and disorder, between the real and the possible, seem no longer to obtain. [29]

How then to explain such a phenomenon? To explain is to classify. But it is immediately evident that Montesquieu was unable to situate the English political system within the tripartite classification of the forms of government developed in the first books of *De l'esprit des lois*. It was clearly not a republic of the classical variety, for the individualistic, self-interested, unpredictable political behavior of the English was far from the civic virtue of the ideal republic. Neither was it a despotism, for there was a world of difference between the floating political terrors of a free people and the fear of a people subject to the arbitrary will of a despot. But neither was it a monarchy constituted by fundamental laws and sustained by the existence of intermediary bodies: the principle of honor was not to be found among the springs of English political action. Thus, the English political system existed outside the primordial classification initially announced by Montesquieu. It was "a nation in which the republic is hidden under the form of monarchy," [30] a kind of political mutation different from all other

27. Ibid., 3:30–31.   28. Ibid., 3:31.
29. This theme is suggested by J. G. A. Pocock, *The Machiavellian Moment* (Princeton, 1975), 490–91.
30. *De l'esprit des lois*, 1:133.

forms of government in that it had liberty itself as its object. From this point of view, then, Montesquieu's tendency to discuss the government of England simply as one of a "free people," without explicitly identifying the country by name, suggests an effort not simply to describe English politics but to conceptualize it in more abstract terms as a type — indeed, as an entirely new type — of polity.

It is therefore possible to discern in *De l'esprit des lois* the elements of a new classification of the forms of government, which emerges as the work develops.[31] In this classification, based on a new distinction between the ancient republics and modern commercial states, England becomes the very type of the modern state, free and individualistic, while the traditional French monarchy remains in the middle — the sentiment of honor being, in effect, the middle term between the civic virtue of the ancients and the egoistic individualism of the moderns. Thus a new classificatory schema — republic/monarchy/ England — is superimposed upon the old one — republic/monarchy/despotism — in the course of Montesquieu's argument. The first two terms are identical in both classifications; only the third term is transformed, as "despotism" gives way to "England." Is there any significance to be found in this relationship of substitutability? What is it that England may have in common with despotic regimes?

Montesquieu offers the elements of a fascinating response to this question in a well-known passage of his description of the nature of monarchy:

> There are people in some states of Europe who have thought to abolish all seigneurial jurisdictions. They have not understood that they are trying to do what the English parliament has done. Abolish in a monarchy the prerogatives of the seigneurs, of the clergy, of the nobility, and of the towns; you would soon have a popular state, or else a despotic state. . . .
>
> The English, to foster liberty, have eliminated all the intermediary powers that formed their monarchy. They have good reason to preserve this liberty; if they were ever to lose it, they would be one of the most enslaved peoples on earth.[32]

Marveling at the results of the English experiment with political liberty, Montesquieu seems, in some moods, to have regarded it as a risky

31. The elements of this new classification are suggested by Pangle, *Montesquieu's Philosophy of Liberalism*, and Mark Hulliung, *Montesquieu and the Old Regime* (Berkeley and Los Angeles, 1976).
32. *De l'esprit des lois*, 1:45.

experiment that has created a polity precariously close to despotism. It was not an experiment to be urged upon the French. This is perhaps the reason why he proceeds, in this discussion of the nature of monarchy, to offer an allusion to John Law, promoter in France of a financial system on the English model:

> Mr. Law, owing to his ignorance equally of the republican and the monarchical constitution, was one of the greatest promoters of despotism that Europe has ever seen. Besides the changes he made that were so abrupt, so extraordinary, so unprecedented, he wished to eliminate intermediary ranks and annihilate political bodies: he dissolved the monarchy by his chimerical reimbursements and seemed to want to buy back the constitution itself.[33]

What should we conclude from this argument? If I have insisted on some ambiguities and ambivalences in Montesquieu's thinking about English politics, I have not done so to deny his evident admiration for that "republic . . . hidden under the form of monarchy." But it is as well in this context to remember the strong sense of the term "admire," which implies wonder and amazement rather than mere approbation. Montesquieu presented his readers with a kind of political prodigy: a bizarre, disturbing, even dangerous phenomenon, not one that was necessarily to be imitated. As he concluded at the end of his chapter analyzing the English constitution, there was something unnervingly *extreme* about the English political experience.

> I do not mean by all this to diminish other governments or to say that this extreme political liberty must mortify those who enjoy only a moderate liberty. How could I say this, I who believe that the excess even of reason is not always desirable and that men almost always adapt better to the mean than to the extremes?[34]

"A Government Stormy and Bizarre"

Once we recognize Montesquieu's hesitations in the face of English politics, it becomes easier to understand how writers who wished to contest the model of the English constitution could turn his arguments against him. This was the strategy adopted in 1753 by one of his earliest critics, Véron de Forbonnais, in an essay entitled "Du gouvernement d'Angleterre, comparé par l'auteur de *l'Esprit des lois* au gouvernement de France." Véron de Forbonnais had relatively little to say about

33. Ibid., 1:47.   34. Ibid., 2:76.

Montesquieu's discussion of the balance of powers in book 11 of *De l'esprit des lois*, except to insist that he found only "principles of disunity in all this fine system." [35] It was rather the description of English politics in book 19 that attracted his attention. The play of passions depicted as evidence of political vitality in that analysis seemed to Véron de Forbonnais to be very far from the behavior normally expected in a healthy political regime:

> On the contrary, I would regard this state of agitation as that of a sick man, to whom a raging fever had given an unnatural force capable of killing him. . . .
> What? This nation that is so superior to all the others only ever acts by the agitation of the passions and is not capable of taking reason as its guide? Is this praise that the legislator wants to bestow upon it? [36]

Nor was Véron de Forbonnais convinced by Montesquieu's explanation that the "terrors" imprinted on English popular consciousness served to safeguard public liberty. In his view, such an explanation seemed to suggest that "the state of calm is for England the most dreadful state. Terror is the principle of movement in England." [37] Little wonder, then, that the English had been subjected to frequent and dangerous revolutions, which had brought them to the brink of destruction and cost them rivers of blood—"Was there ever a more chimerical good than a liberty that destroys me?" [38] According to Véron de Forbonnais, there was no alternative but to conclude from the analysis presented in *De l'esprit des lois* that England's vaunted liberty was illusory:

> It is free only in appearance because, if its happiness does not depend on a king, what is more frightening is that its happiness depends on the revolutions whose germ lives constantly within its bosom and permits no tranquillity to this state, because the most profound peace is followed in an instant by the most dangerous storm. [39]

Véron de Forbonnais was not alone in drawing such conclusions. Many were the works that denounced the instability of English government and the turbulence of its history. Numerous were the writers

---

35. In *Opuscules de M. F**** [Fréron], vol. 3., *Contenant un extrait chapitre par chapitre du livre de l'Esprit des lois, des observations sur quelques endroits particuliers de ce livre, une idée de toutes les critiques qui en ont été faites, avec quelques remarques de l'éditeur* (Amsterdam, 1753), 179.
36. Ibid., 179–81.   37. Ibid., 182.
38. Ibid., 185.   39. Ibid., 212–13.

who thundered against the example of this "government stormy and bizarre." Among the most zealous was the abbé Dubois de Launay, author of a *Coup d'oeil sur le gouvernement anglais* published in 1786, whose phrase this is.[40] Entering the lists against the "Anglomania" he saw subverting traditional values of order and authority, Dubois de Launay offered a whole repertoire of the vices of English government, the most fundamental of which was its constant instability. Not that this phenomenon was in his view at all surprising. Quite the contrary. "It would be astonishing," he insisted, "if a government established on so uncertain and shaky a basis were stable, constant, and uniform; it must necessarily totter and waver incessantly, bend before *every wind of doctrine,* and be as changeable as the empire of opinion."[41]

In Dubois de Launay's view, there were several reasons for the continual disorder found in English history and politics. The most important was the fatal ascendancy of the people within the English political system. *Tumultum ex tumultu, bellum ex bello ferunt:* brandishing a tag from Sallust to clinch his point, Dubois insisted that there was no system of government more stormy than the exercise of popular power.

It is impossible for the people, once it has made itself master, to put an end to one disorder except by another, to one revolt except by another even more deplorable than the first; with the result that, whenever this abuse prevails, the remedy for public misfortunes is still more disastrous than what it is meant to cure.[42]

But there was more to be found in England than dreamed of by the ancient political authorities. There, the age-old tendency of the people to remain in a permanent state of agitation was aggravated by such new developments as the liberty of the press and the system of political parties supported by it. "This liberty to grumble and complain about the established government is an inexhaustible source of trouble and revolutions," Dubois maintained. It led necessarily to "those sudden and unexpected movements, those violent commotions that disturb and sometimes overthrow states."

England has had this deplorable experience a hundred times. The history of English revolutions is almost the entire and complete history of the English. Why? Because in that country a combat reigns constantly between two parties,

40. *Coup d'oeil sur le gouvernement anglais* (n.p., 1786).
41. Ibid., 26.   42. Ibid., 132–33.

the party of the government and that of the *opposition*. . . . From these
continual debates are born the innumerable revolutions of which England has
been the theater, and which have made so much blood run.[43]

It goes virtually without saying that Dubois de Launay was an
enraged apologist for absolute monarchy, a form of government that
he defended in terms that appear to turn Hobbes back upon Rousseau.
"Only in monarchies is everyone truly free," he insisted. "The will of
all being submitted and united to the will of one, what each wills,
everyone wills; what everyone wills, each wills: and that is liberty.
Any other constitution will have the appearance of liberty, this one
alone has the reality."[44] But it was not necessary to be as conservative
as Dubois to find oneself uneasy in the face of the political contestations, the party conflicts, and the constant disorders of English government. The comprehensive studies of eighteenth-century French
attitudes toward the English constitution carried out by Gabriel Bonno
and Frances Acomb offer numerous examples of a similar unease,
even among the most enlightened thinkers.[45] Acomb finds two clear
strands within enlightened thinking critical of the English political
model. For republican writers inspired by Rousseau and frequently
sharing his distrust of representation, on the one hand, the existence
of party political conflicts in England demonstrated that liberty was
still far from fully established in that country. For the Physiocrats, on
the other hand, the same pattern of political contestation demonstrated how far the English were from the social tranquillity to be
assured by rational acceptance of the necessary and essential order of
society.[46] Currents of "Anglomania" notwithstanding, there was
clearly a strong — perhaps even a dominant — tendency within eighteenth-century French opinion to regard the English political model as
turbulent and dangerous. And the crisis of English government during
the 1760s and 1770s — from the Wilkes affair to the Gordon Riots —
offered abundant evidence to confirm such a view of English political
life.

43. Ibid., 168–70.   44. Ibid., 193.
45. Bonno, *La Constitution britannique devant l'opinion française de Montesquieu à
Bonaparte* (Paris, 1932); Acomb, *Anglophobia in France, 1763–1789* (Durham, N.C.,
1950). The most recent work on French attitudes toward England, although devoted
largely to "Anglomania," also points out the unease of French observers when faced
with the unruly English passion for liberty: see Josephine Grieder, *Anglomania in France,
1740–1789* (Geneva, 1985), 48–108.
46. Acomb, *Anglophobia in France*, especially 30–50.

It is not surprising, then, to find English politics figuring prominently under the entry "Anarchie" in the *Dictionnaire de jurisprudence* of Prost de Royer, published between 1781 and 1788, or to rediscover it in the article "Administration," under the rubric "Esprit de corps. Discorde. Opposition. Corruption. Influence. Probité. Justice." A moderate and enlightened spirit, a partisan of administrative reform and publicity in matters of administration, Prost de Royer followed English political events with great interest and spoke of them frequently. He had read *De l'esprit des lois*, Sir William Blackstone's *Commentaries*, and the influential *Constitution d'Angleterre* by Jean-Louis Delolme.[47] But despite the arguments of these works and his own admiration for the openness of English government, he found many unhealthy aspects of English politics. "This system of opposition is considered the shield of the English constitution," he maintained in his article "Administration." "But what is this violent remedy that acts only by disturbing the whole body, irritating the nerves, affecting the head, burning the entrails? Can this violent regime be durable?"[48] The same fear of the politics of constitutional contestation found its expression in the article "Anarchie":

What is, in effect, a government composed of three powers, which ceaselessly spy on one another, accuse one another, impinge upon one another, erode one another . . . ?

What is this *opposition* to the *influence* of the throne and to the activity and secret of administration . . . ?

What is this *coalition*, by turns extolled as virtuous and decried as shameful . . . ?

Either patriotism and virtue are the soul of this government, or they are not. In the first case, all these devices, all these words are dishonorable and useless. In the second case, they are still useless, and despite the efforts of genius, patriotism, and individual virtue, fundamental and constitutional *anarchy* will always reappear.[49]

The dictionary of Prost de Royer may seem a relatively obscure example of the characteristic uneasiness of the French in the face of the disorder of English political life.[50] But his work is revealing in yet

---

47. Prost de Royer's interest in England and knowledge of its public affairs is well illustrated in his article "Angleterre," *Dictionnaire de jurisprudence et des arrêts,* 5:1–56.
48. Ibid., 2:866.   49. Ibid., 4:763.
50. But see also the very lengthy article on England in J.-B.-R. Robinet, ed., *Dictionnaire universel des sciences morale, économique, politique, et diplomatique,* 30 vols. (London, 1777–83), 4:242–699; 5:1–205. The sketch of the history of England in that article

another respect. The discussion of English politics in his article "Anarchie" is followed immediately by a discussion of the problem of anarchy in a monarchical government such as France and, in particular,
of the conflicts between the parlements and the Crown that he describes as "l'anarchie judiciaire." In this context, he cites with approbation the discourse pronounced by Lamoignon de Malesherbes on 21
November 1774, at the time of the restoration of the parlements by
Louis XVI:

> Let us never forget that the gravest attack upon a nation is to sow the seed
> of intestine divisions . . . and that the greatest benefit of the monarch [who
> is] today so dear to his people is to have appeared as a peacemaker in the
> temple of justice. Let us crown the work that he has so gloriously begun, let us
> succeed in confounding the authors of public calamities by uprooting from
> our hearts all the seeds of discord and by ushering in — after the storms — the
> light of the purest, calmest, and most serene day.[51]

A fine hope indeed, although one not long to be realized! The
patterns of political and constitutional conflict that had culminated in
the Maupeou "revolution" of 1771 soon reasserted themselves to bring
about the new crisis that prepared the revolution of 1789. But by
assimilating party conflicts in England to practices of parlementary
opposition in France in this way, Prost de Royer was pointing to a
growing similarity between English and French politics at the end of
the Old Regime. It was a comparison favored increasingly by his
compatriots. In the 1750s, for example, the abbé Mably in his *Droits et
devoirs du citoyen* and the marquis d'Argenson in his journal had
detected a political wind blowing from across the Channel.[52] Their
perception was shared by Moreau, who found the growing political
challenge of the French magistrates even more threatening to the
exercise of monarchical authority than the power of Parliament in
England.[53] Such a view would have surprised an English visitor like

---

sets out to show how its government has taken form "amidst storms, factions, and
tumultuous movements that have never ceased to agitate it." Borrowing freely from
book 19 of *De l'esprit des lois*, it concludes that England is the "perpetual theater of
dissensions, intrigues, murmurings, discontent, and even tumultuous movements," as a
necessary consequence of a constitution that has liberty for its object (4:259–95). The
same theme is sounded in the article "Anglomania" (ibid., 5:250–54).

51. *Dictionnaire de jurisprudence et des arrêts,* 4:764.

52. See Baker, "On the Problem of the Ideological Origins of the French Revolution," 208, 213–14.

53. Ibid., 215.

Horace Walpole, who deprecated the efforts of his parlementary friends in the 1760s to represent themselves as the constitutional equivalent of members of Parliament.[54] But it was a comparison upon which ministerial propaganda was also to insist a decade later in the pamphlet war over the Maupeou coup.

Consider, for example, the argument of a pamphlet published in the form of a letter purportedly sent from London in May 1771, whose putative English author reproaches the French for the drift toward English practices he detects in their political culture:

> I revert to your facility in copying others' fashions; but permit me to tell you that you have pushed this talent to an unexpected point. It is true that this has happened by degrees, but they have been more rapid than one would have hoped for: I refer to the multiplicity of remonstrances of your different parlements or other courts, in opposition to what your king or his council have demanded. . . . We, your old neighbors and rivals, have long been acquainted with the birth, growth, successes, reverses, and pretensions of your parlements. But finally, I hear, you have in recent years formed a party of opposition, as we have done in England. . . . What! You wish also to liken yourselves to us in this respect and submit yourselves with your frivolous heads to all our political convulsions? Is it possible that you have so quickly forgotten the history of your former troubles, which have been described in every living language in order to leave to posterity a record of the evils that fanaticism, anarchy, disunity in government, and the influence of a few factious spirits caused in one of the finest parts of Europe?[55]

The rhetorical argument of this pamphlet may seem transparent in its efforts to mobilize against the parlements the profound French fear of civil strife inherited from the sixteenth century — a fear that had long sustained the appeal of absolute monarchy. But it was a shrewd move to link this fear to the example of English political instability by assimilating the magistrates' resistance to parliamentary opposition.[56]

54. *Memoirs of the Reign of King George the Third*, 2 vols. (London, 1845), 2:248.
55. *Extrait d'une lettre, en date de Londres, du 3 mai 1771* (n.p., n.d.), 4–5.
56. A similar argument was made in another pamphlet published in support of Maupeou, which invoked the spectacle of the Wilkes affair as symptomatic of the disorder that constantly threatened any state that abandoned the principles of absolute monarchy. "Take a look at England, partisans of mixed governments, and reflect thoroughly upon the present situation," this pamphlet enjoined: "You will see a Wilkes insolently mocking all the orders of the state, violating every law as he invokes liberty, opposing the taxes ordered for the defense of the nation, enlarging the number of seditious persons and public calumniators and absolving them by his personal authority, and balancing alone all the powers of the state combined." See *La Tête leur tourne* (n.p., n.d. [1771]), 17. Like other pamphlets from the Maupeou period, *La Tête leur tourne* reappeared (in several editions) during the constitutional struggles of 1787–88.

Indeed, the tendency to cast the magistrates in the role of a political opposition in the English manner — helped as it was by the willingness of a journal such as the *Gazette de Leyde* to report the magistrates' actions and deliberations in precisely this light — seems to have become increasingly explicit as the Revolution approached. By 1787, for example, reports from the British embassy in Paris could describe the antiministerial tactics within the Parlement of Paris quite simply as the work of "what they now style here, in the language of England, the side of opposition."[57]

In fact, the British diplomats (whose dispatches analyzed the development of the pre-revolutionary political crisis in France with considerable insight) frequently reflected on the nature of the changes in the political culture of the French that had "brought them nearer to the English than they had ever been before."[58] One of them, Daniel Hailes, ascribed this transformation in large part to French contact with revolutionary America. But he also argued for the impact of the foreign and particularly the British press in fostering public political interest. Reporting to his government from Paris in 1786, he concluded that "the almost unrestrained introduction of our daily publications (tolerated indeed by the Government from the conviction of the impossibility of preventing it) having attracted the attention of the people more towards the freedom and advantages of our constitution, has also infused into them a spirit of discussion of public matters which did not exist before."[59] In the light of such developments, the vehemence of Dubois de Launay's *Coup d'oeil sur le gouvernement anglais* is scarcely surprising. His denunciations of the dismal, destabilizing effects of public debate and party conflicts in England became the more immediate in their point as the French found their own public life transformed by similar processes of political contestation.

Nor is it surprising that, in the final confrontation between the parlements and the Crown in 1788, the specter of English anarchy again figured in prominsterial pamphleteers as a rhetorical weapon against parlementary claims. One such pamphlet derided the magis-

57. Oscar Browning, ed., *Despatches from Paris, 1784 – 1790* (London, 1909 – 10), 1:221.

58. Ibid., 1:148.

59. Ibid. Mercier had a similar observation to make regarding the reading of English newspapers: "The reading of English papers is as common in Paris as it was rare forty-five years ago. This must have influenced the ideas of the nation" (Louis-Sébastien Mercier, *Tableau de Paris: Nouvelle édition. . . . ,* 12 vols. [Amsterdam, 1782 – 88], 11:128).

trates for efforts to introduce the English constitution into France just as others had introduced English fashions. Such efforts, the pamphleteer argued, were misplaced — "one can certainly dress and get drunk like an Englishman from one moment to the next, but one cannot give the English national spirit to the French nation." [60] They were also dangerous. They conjured up images of the execution of Charles I — "the most execrable crime that could ever stain human memory" — and threatened France once again with a "horrible anarchy, [which] after having delivered over the citizens to all the cruelties of civil war, would inevitably bring about the ruin of the state." [61]

The English themes were played upon even more dramatically during the last months of the Old Regime by that master of the new political journalism — and most impassioned enemy of the parlements — Linguet. His vitriolic pamphlet, *La France plus qu'anglaise*, launched a powerful attack on the deliberations of the restored Parlement of Paris on 25 September 1788, which included the magistrates' celebrated declaration calling for the convocation of the Estates General according to the forms of 1614. The burden of Linguet's pamphlet was that parlementary resistance was propelling France well beyond anything the English had achieved in the domain of disorder.

In *hats*, in *frock-coats*, in *jockeys*, in *whiskies*, in seditious *gatherings* and turbulent and dangerous *rejoicings*, the French people has only been able to imitate the English, taking up their forms of behavior as it took up their dress. But in republican audacity — or rather, in anarchic license — the king's councillors among the Gauls have found means of far outdistancing the inhabitants of the banks of the Thames.[62]

In the wake of the May Edicts, Linguet insisted, resistance to government authority had reached a degree of license, fury, and publicity exceeding anything witnessed in England. The parlements' new demands for the punishment of the ministers Brienne and Lamoignon — which Linguet compared in detail with the trial procedures that brought the earl of Strafford to the scaffold and paved the way for the execution of his royal master — were simple declarations of revolt. If

60. *Songe d'un bon français, suivi de la lettre d'un anglais* (London, 1788), 37. The *lettre d'un anglais* is dated "15 July 1788."
61. Ibid., 29, 26.
62. [S.-N.-H. Linguet], *La France plus qu'anglaise, ou Comparaison entre la procédure entamé à Paris le 25 septembre 1788 contre les ministres du roi de France et le procès intenté à Londres en 1640, au comte de Strafford, principal ministre de Charles premier, roi d'Angleterre; avec des réflexions sur le danger imminent dont les entreprises de la robe menacent la nation, et les particuliers* (Brussels, 1788), 26.

they imitated English turbulence in their license, they lacked the English sense of proper procedure in such matters.

England is the example they constantly cite to us, the model they pretend to take. It is from this idol of Montesquieu's that his fellow magistrates want to receive the *antiministerial* sword—a blade stained with the blood of kings even more than with that of ministers. Yet what do we see in this *England* but the most solemn reproof of the actions and procedures of the parlements in *France?* There we find an almost superstitious respect for rules that are constantly being violated in *Paris* in the name of a desire to imitate *London.*[63]

Absurd and inconsistent in themselves, Linguet argued, the efforts of the parlementaires to transplant the English constitution to France were nevertheless profoundly dangerous.

But Linguet offered another, no less serious indictment of the political claims of the parlements in *La France plus qu'anglaise.* Not only were the magistrates threatening the state with the evils of anarchy and aristocratic despotism, but they were succeeding in "passing off their excesses as the result of *public opinion* and then wresting a solemn legitimation of them from the throne."[64] Addressing himself directly to Louis XVI, Linguet repudiated this appropriation of the public voice—which he himself had struggled so vigorously to articulate through the radical journalism of his *Annales politiques, civiles, et littéraires*—in the defense of aristocratic interests. "Your Majesty," he insisted ". . . should not allow himself to be alarmed or disheartened by this phantom of PUBLIC OPINION so artificially displayed on all the standards of the confederations that league together against his rights. No, Sire, the true *public opinion* is not against you, nor against your authority."[65] From the perspective of Linguet's pamphlet, then, the significance of the parlementary declaration of 25 September was clear. It presented the challenge of a yet more intense period of political contestation, characterized by an explicit competition to invoke the new authority of *public opinion* and to define and control its true expression. It is to the nature of the concept of "public opinion" that I now wish to turn.

"Public Opinion"

So far in this essay, I have sought to pursue two parallel themes. First, I have sketched the appearance within the context of the Old Regime of

63. Ibid., 82.   64. Ibid., 45–46.   65. Ibid., 12.

a politics of contestation, the terms of which compelled competing actors — whether they were engaged on behalf of the government or in opposition to it — to appeal beyond the traditional forms of absolutist politics to the tribunal of "the public." Sociologically, the nature of this entity remained ill defined — indeed, one can understand the conflicts of the Pre-Revolution as a series of struggles to fix the sociological referent of the concept in favor of one or another competing group. But politically, and more critically, the notion of the "public" came to function as the foundation for a new system of authority, the abstract source of legitimacy in a transformed political culture. As a result, French politics came increasingly to resemble English politics, with its open contestations and factional divisions played out in a constant competition to claim public support. With that development in mind, I have therefore suggested a second theme: the unease with which many French political writers regarded the passions and disorders, the perpetual conflicts and instabilities, that they found in the English political system. To the extent that English government exemplified the principles and practices of a politics of contestation, the attitudes of the French toward it suggest fundamental anxieties about a transformation that was introducing similar phenomena into their own political culture. The problem was to imagine a form of political practice that would acknowledge the new authority of "the public," on the one hand, while avoiding the conflicts and instabilities of a politics of contestation, on the other.

It is illuminating to address, from this point of view, the nature and meaning of the notion of "public opinion" itself. A comprehensive analysis of the significance of that concept in eighteenth-century French political culture remains to be written.[66] But it seems clear that

66. Habermas, *L'Espace public*, especially 99–112, offers the essential starting point for this question. The older works of Wilhelm Bauer, *Die öffentliche Meinung und ihre geschichtlichen Grundlagen* (Tübingen, 1914) and *Die öffentliche Meinung in der Weltgeschichte* (Potsdam, 1930), also remain informative. See also Paul A. Palmer, "The Concept of Public Opinion in Political Theory," in *Essays in History and Political Theory in Honor of Charles Howard McIlwain* (Cambridge, Mass., 1936), 230–57; Lucien Hölscher, "Öffentlichkeit," in Otto Brunner, Werner Conze, and Reinhart Koselleck, eds., *Geschichtliche Grundbegriffe. Historisches Lexikon zur politisch-sozialen Sprache in Deutschland*, 5 vols. to date (Stuttgart, 1978–), 4:413–67. For a recent discussion of the appearance of the concept in England, see J. A. W. Gunn, *Beyond Liberty and Property* (Kingston, Ont., 1983), chap. 7. Gunn is principally concerned to argue against the view that "public opinion" was a French invention and to show that the use of the term to describe the expression of the voice of the people in political matters first grew out of British political experience. Even allowing for the obvious differences in the institutional contexts of politics in the two countries, however, the contrast he draws between the French and the British histories of the concept may be somewhat overdrawn.

the meaning of the term underwent considerable elaboration between
its appearance in Rousseau's *First Discourse* in 1750[67] and the outbreak
of the French Revolution. For Rousseau, who used the term in a
number of his works, "public opinion" was the "opinion of others in
society" [68] — the collective expression of the moral and social values of
a people, the shared sentiments and convictions embodied in a nation's customs and manners and applied in its judgments of individual
actions. It was the source of reputation and esteem among men, the
judge of character and beauty, the customary sanction against immoral and improper actions. Its principal characteristic, in this sense,
was the complexity of its resistance to conscious attempts at change, a
point Rousseau liked to illustrate with reference to the history of
dueling in France. "Neither reason nor virtue nor the laws will subjugate public opinion, so long as one has not discovered the art of
changing it," he argued as he developed this theme in his *Lettre à M.
d'Alembert*.[69] "Public opinion" was therefore a social rather than a
political category in Rousseau's thinking, a challenge to the legislator's art rather than an expression of political will. Hence its appearance in *Du contrat social* in the chapter praising the Roman censorship
as a means of preserving a people's mores:

> As the declaration of the general will is made by law, so the declaration of
> the public judgment is made by censure; public opinion is the kind of law of
> which the Censor is the minister and which (like the prince) he merely applies
> to particular cases.
>
> Far from the tribunal of the censorship being the arbiter of the people's
> opinion, it is only the declaration; and as soon as it diverges from that opinion,
> its decisions are empty and without effect.[70]

67. Rousseau denounced "that crowd of obscure writers and idle men of letters who
devour the substance of the state to no benefit whatsoever" and accused them of
undermining faith and virtue. "They smile disdainfully at those old words 'patrie' and
'religion' and devote their talents and their philosophy to destroying and debasing all
that is sacred among men. Not that they hate either virtue or our dogmas; they are
enemies of public opinion, and banishing them among atheists would be enough to
bring them back to the foot of the altars." See Jean-Jacques Rousseau, *Oeuvres complètes*, ed. R. Gagnebin and M. Raymond, 4 vols. (Paris, 1959 – 69), 3:19. I owe this and a
number of the other references to *opinion publique* considered in the following paragraphs to research made possible by the textual database for American and French
Research on the Treasury of the French Language (ARTFL) at the University of Chicago.
68. Rousseau, *Lettre à M. d'Alembert sur les spectacles*, ed. M. Fuchs (Geneva, 1948),
89 – 90.
69. Ibid., 93. For Rousseau's discussion of dueling in relationship to "public opinion," see ibid., 90 – 99, and *Le Contrat social*, ed. Bertrand de Jouvenal (Geneva, 1947),
355.
70. *Le Contrat social*, 353 – 54.

This general social meaning of "public opinion" as a collective judgment in matters of morality, reputation, and taste seems to have been the most familiar one in French usage, particularly in the period from 1750 to 1780. Examples can be found in the works of such writers as Duclos, the marquis de Mirabeau, Helvétius, d'Alembert, Mercier de la Rivière, Mably, Beaumarchais, and Holbach.[71] From about 1770, however, the term begins also to take on connotations of the Enlightenment and to acquire a more explicitly political resonance. This shift is announced in the 1767 edition of the *Considérations sur les moeurs*, to which Duclos added a new paragraph elaborating upon his discussion of the role of men of letters. "Of all empires," he argued, "that of *gens d'esprit*, without being visible, is the most extensive. The powerful command, but the *gens d'esprit* govern, because in the long run they form public opinion, which sooner or later subjugates or overthrows every kind of despotism."[72] Raynal, in turn, made the political implications of such an argument more explicit in the *Histoire philosophique et politique des . . . deux Indes* (1770). "In a nation that thinks and talks," he insisted, "public opinion is the rule of government, and government must never act against it without giving public reasons nor thwart it without disabusing it."[73] A government in which neither "public opinion" nor the general will was consulted, he argued in condemning the unrepresentative character of the English House of Commons with respect to the colonies, would therefore be an instrument of slavery.[74]

But the idea of the emergence of enlightened public opinion as a political force was perhaps put most succinctly a few years later by that remarkably informative observer of French political culture at the end

71. See Charles Pinot Duclos, *Considérations sur les moeurs* (Amsterdam, 1751), 70 – 71, 122; Victor Riqueti, marquis de Mirabeau, *L'Ami des hommes*, 3 parts in 1 vol. (Avignon, 1756), part 1, pp. 52, 141; part 2, p. 24; part 3, p. 110; Claude-Adrien Helvétius, *De l'esprit* (Paris, 1758), 64, 69, 112; Jean d'Alembert, *Lettre à M. Rousseau*, in *Mélanges de littérature, d'histoire, et de philosophie*, 4 vols. (Amsterdam, 1759), 2:438; Pierre-Paul Mercier de la Rivière, *L'Ordre naturelle et essentielle des sociétés politiques*, in *Physiocrates*, ed. Eugène Daire (Paris, 1846), 635; Gabriel Bonnot de Mably, *Observations sur l'histoire de France*, in *Collection complète des oeuvres de l'abbé Mably*, 15 vols. (Paris, an III [1794 – 95]), 2:79; Pierre-Augustin Caron de Beaumarchais, *Addition au supplément du mémoire à consulter . . . servant de réponse à Mme Goezmann. . . .* (Paris, 1774), 41, *Quatrième Mémoire à consulter . . . contre M. Goezmann. . . .* (Paris, 1774), 4; Paul Thiry, baron d'Holbach, *La Morale universelle*, 3 vols. (Amsterdam, 1776), 1:126; 2:84, 87.
72. Duclos, *Considérations sur les moeurs*, 5th ed. ([Paris], 1767), 270 – 71.
73. Guillaume Thomas François Raynal, *Histoire philosophique et politique des . . . deux Indes*, 6 vols. (Amsterdam, 1770), 6:391 – 92.
74. Ibid., 6:415.

of the Old Regime, Louis-Sébastien Mercier. "In the last thirty years alone," he argued in the *Tableau de Paris* in 1782, "a great and important revolution has occurred in our ideas. Today, public opinion has a preponderant force in Europe that cannot be resisted. Thus in assessing the progress of enlightenment and the change it must bring about, we may hope that it will bring the greatest good to the world and that tyrants of all stripes will tremble before this universal cry that continuously rings out to fill and awaken Europe." [75] For Mercier, this revolution was the achievement of writers who had raised their voices against political vices and dangerous stupidities: "They have asserted the rights of reason, from the Menippean satire to the last political pamphlet; and recently, in very important crises, they have decided public opinion. On their account, it has the greatest influence on events. They seem at last to be forming the national spirit." [76]

Among the recent crises Mercier probably had in mind, the events of the Maupeou coup had been the most dramatic and the most powerful in fostering French political consciousness in the face of arbitrary government. Thus when Malesherbes insisted, in the celebrated *remontrances* written in 1775 on behalf of the magistrates of the restored Cour des aides, that all the agents of the sovereign power "must be subject to three sorts of restraints: the laws, recourse to higher authority, and public opinion," [77] the definition of public opinion he had in mind was not simply the generalized social practice of the nation's customs and values invoked by Rousseau. On the contrary, public opinion was to be the enlightened expression of active and open discussion of all political matters, the free exercise of the public voice regarding the daily conduct of affairs, the institutional remedy for the administrative secrecy and arbitrariness that was threatening France with despotism. This new role of the public in political matters had been made possible in a great nation, Malesherbes maintained, by the invention of printing and the growth of literacy.

The art of printing has thus given writing the same publicity that the spoken word possessed in the midst of the assemblies of the nation during the first age. But it has taken many centuries for the discovery of this art to have its full

---

75. Mercier, *Tableau de Paris*, 4:289.   76. Ibid., 8:109.
77. [Chrétien-Guillaume Lamoignon de Malesherbes], *Très Humbles et Très Respectueuses Remontrances que présentent au roi notre très honoré et souverain seigneur les gens tenants sa Cour des aides* (6 May 1775), in *Les "Remontrances" de Malesherbes, 1771–1775,* ed. Elisabeth Badinter (Paris, 1978), 204.

effect upon men. It has required that the entire nation gain the taste and habit of informing itself by reading. And it has required that enough men become skilled in the art of writing to lend their ministry to the entire public, taking the place of those gifted with natural eloquence who made themselves heard by our forefathers on the Champs de Mars or in the public judicial hearings.[78]

With the press as its forum, the printed word as its medium of persuasion, and writers as its ministers, the new tribunal of the public offered the possibility of achieving a functional modern equivalent of the primitive democracy of the Franks when they first appeared in Gaul. Reminding the young monarch of "the example of those early kings who did not feel their authority threatened by the liberty they gave their subjects to implore their justice in the presence of the assembled nation," Malesherbes invited Louis XVI to "imitate in this matter the conduct of Charlemagne . . . [and] reign at the head of a nation whose entire body will be your council."[79]

A similar vision of a king restored to communication with his people motivated the ideas for the reform of local government that Turgot developed in 1775 in the wake of the Maupeou coup. As described by Condorcet in his *Vie de M. Turgot* (1786), the hierarchy of local assemblies envisaged by the reforming minister were intended to substitute free, open, and rational discussion of administrative matters for "that public opinion [that is] a kind of obstacle common to all absolute governments in the conduct of affairs, the resistance of which is less constant but also less tranquil, often as powerful, sometimes harmful, and always dangerous." Once habits of rational participation in the conduct of local affairs had "subjugated public opinion" to the rule of reason, the conditions would be established for informed consent in an assembly at the national level.[80]

Although Turgot's ideas for public participation in government were never formally presented to Louis XVI during his ministry, we know that the monarch's later reactions to the published version of the *Mémoire sur les municipalités* were negative.[81] Nor was the king willing to accept the role of Charlemagne as Malesherbes held it out to him in the *remontrances* of the Cour des aides. Although the king ordered

78. Ibid., 273.   79. Ibid., 275.
80. A. Condorcet-O'Connor and F. Arago, eds., *Oeuvres de Condorcet*, 12 vols. (Paris, 1847–49), 5:123–24.
81. See J.-L. Soulavie, *Mémoires historiques et politiques du règne de Louis XVI*, 6 vols. (Paris, an X [1801]), 3:146–54.

these *remontrances* stricken from that court's registers, he could not long prevent their appearance in print before the tribunal that Malesherbes praised as "independent of all powers and respected by all powers . . . that tribunal of the public . . . the sovereign judge of all the judges of the earth."[82] There were to be many other appeals to that same tribunal in the years that followed, and from many different sides. It was the court of last resort—"that supreme judge to which the most absolute tribunals are subordinated, *public opinion*"—to which Linguet appealed from exile when he was disbarred from the practice of the law he had done so much to make the focus of public political attention.[83] It was the public consciousness that the younger Mirabeau insisted on his right to "arouse" in 1779 in condemning his father's arbitrary use of *lettres de cachet* to confine him in the prison of Vincennes.[84] It was the tribunal to which Necker addressed himself so loquaciously in the 1780s, explaining and defending his conduct of financial affairs,[85] and which his great rival Calonne invoked in condemning abuses before the notables in 1787.[86] As we have seen, the parlements proclaimed the force of "public opinion" in 1788, in justifying their resistance to ministerial authority; and Linguet acknowledged its power in denouncing the magistrates' claim to popular support.[87] A few months later, Sieyès could also be found appealing to the progress of "public opinion" in asserting the right of the Third Estate to constitute the nation and transform its constitution.[88]

Finally, even the dogged Moreau, defending the monarchical constitution to the last, attested to the new power of the concept of public opinion in the waning months of the Old Regime. He had long urged

82. Malesherbes, "Discours de réception à l'Académie française" (16 Feb. 1775), in *Oeuvres inédites de . . . Malesherbes*, ed. N. L. Pissot (Paris, 1808), 151. The *remontrances* of 6 May 1775 appeared in print in 1779 in [Dionis du Séjour], *Mémoires pour servir à l'histoire du droit public de la France en matière d'impôts. . . .* (Brussels, 1779).

83. S.-N.-H. Linguet, *Appel à la posterité, ou Recueil des mémoires et plaidoyers de M. Linguet pour lui-même, contre la communauté des avocats du Parlement de Paris* (n.p., 1779), 372; also cited in Darline Gay Levy, *The Ideas and Careers of Simon-Nicolas-Henri Linguet* (Urbana, Ill., 1980), 160.

84. Honoré Gabriel Riqueti, comte de Mirabeau, *Lettres originales de Mirabeau, écrites du donjon de Vincennes pendant les années 1777, 78, 79, et 80. . . .*, 4 vols. (Paris, 1792), 3:202.

85. See below, 240–45.

86. M. J. Mavidal and M. E. Laurent, eds., *Archives parlementaires de 1787 à 1860, première série (1787 à 1799)*, 47 vols. (Paris, 1867–96), 1:195.

87. See above, 229–30. Linguet's *La France plus qu'anglaise* cites parlementary declarations in which the term "public opinion" appears.

88. Emmanuel Sieyès, *Qu'est-ce que le tiers état?* ed. R. Zapperi (Geneva, 1970), 134, 144, 157, 187, 212.

the government to seize the ideological initiative in appealing to the public against the parlements. His *Exposition et défense de notre constitution monarchique française* was a now desperate effort to contest demands for revolutionary change being made in its name. "Allow me merely to observe," he argued, "that if the pamphlets are without number, their authors can still be counted, and neither their opinions nor mine will ever form what one means by the term 'public opinion'—unless one agrees that there can be an immense difference, in every sense, between public opinion and the unanimous wish of the nation." [89] In attempting to deny the authority of public opinion to demands for a new constitution, Moreau not only underlined the significance of the concept on the eve of the meeting of the Estates General. He was also obliged to uphold the legitimacy of a new political meaning of the term, defined as the unanimous will of the nation.

What, then, was the meaning and significance of the concept of public opinion on the eve of the French Revolution? How had it developed in the decades of increasingly intense political contestation that ushered out the Old Regime? For a preliminary answer to these questions, we cannot do better than to turn to the two most systematic and extended discussions of the idea to appear in France during this period. The first consists of the reflections on the subject offered by a political actor particularly well placed to understand the nature of French government at the end of the Old Regime: the minister Necker. The second is the lengthy essay on the relationship of enlightenment and public administration with which the editor Jacques Peuchet introduced the volumes of the *Encyclopédie méthodique* devoted to *police*. I shall consider them briefly in concluding this essay.

Between Liberty and Despotism

Necker's roller-coaster political career amply reveals the new dimensions of political contestation in French public life in the last years before the Revolution. The pamphlets circulated by his opponents toward the end of his first ministry subjected him to open and personal vilification of a kind more familiar to English ministers than to French; unprecedented public support, assiduously cultivated during the years out of power, forced his recall in 1788 to preside over a regenera-

89. Jacob-Nicolas Moreau, *Exposition et défense de notre constitution monarchique française*, 2 vols. (Paris, 1789), 1:xvii.

tion of French national life whose political dynamics he was quite unable to control; his dismissal in July 1789 sparked the popular insurrection that brought the monarchy to political defeat.[90] Necker's admiration for English government was well known; his reverence for "public opinion" no less explicit. Mme de Staël, reverting to the old topos, *vox populi, vox dei,* said of her father that public opinion "had something of the divine for him."[91] Whether or not this was the case, the controversial minister certainly made the appeal to public opinion a cardinal principle of his political practice. Necker's view of the problems facing French government was sketched out for the king in a memorandum on the creation of provincial assemblies written in 1778 and made public by his political enemies (to the minister's embarrassment) in 1781.[92] Convinced that monarchical government could not indefinitely tolerate the pattern of political contestations producing "all these continual shocks in which authority loses when it is not completely victorious,"[93] he argued for a systematic political strategy that would contain the power of the parlements to disturb the conduct of public affairs. Such a strategy, he insisted, must necessarily recognize that the parlements would remain a threat as long as they believed themselves "supported by public opinion." It was essential "either to deprive them of this support or to prepare for repeated conflicts that will trouble the tranquillity of Your Majesty's reign and eventually lead either to a degradation of authority or to extreme actions whose consequences cannot be precisely measured."[94]

But how was this campaign to wean the public from the parlements to be achieved? Necker proposed two modes of action. The first consisted of the creation of provincial assemblies with administrative responsibilities, institutions with which Necker began experimenting in Berry in 1778 and Haute Guyenne in 1779. Establishments of this

90. On Necker's political career and the importance of public opinion in relation to it, see the recent studies of Jean Egret, *Necker, ministre de Louis XVI (1776–1790)* (Paris, 1975); Robert D. Harris, *Necker: Reform Minister of the Old Regime* (Berkeley and Los Angeles, 1979). Necker's ideas are studied more generally in Henri Grange, *Les Idées de Necker* (Paris, 1974). His views on "public opinion" are also discussed in the works cited in note 66.

91. *Considérations sur les principaux événements de la Révolution française,* as quoted in Egret, *Necker,* 61.

92. Jacques Necker, "Mémoire au roi, sur l'établissement des administrations provinciales," in *Oeuvres complètes,* ed. A.-L. de Staël-Holstein, 15 vols. (Paris, 1820–21) (henceforth cited as *OC*), 3:333–67. On the circumstances of the publication of this memorandum, see Egret, *Necker,* 174.

93. *OC,* 3:347.   94. Ibid., 3:365.

kind, he argued, would eliminate the administrative abuses and fiscal evils that fed parlementary ambitions to intervene in political affairs. The second mode of action consisted of the introduction of publicity into all matters relating to government finances. As a banker, Necker was well aware of the importance of *la confiance publique* in financial affairs and understood the manner in which that confidence was maintained across the Channel by regular governmental accounting. By 1781 he had already moved the French government in this direction with the publication of the famous *Compte rendu*, envisaged as the first of a continuing series of published financial accounts.[95] The unprecedented success of the *Compte rendu* is well known — three thousand copies were said to be sold the first day of its publication, with perhaps as many as ten thousand a week in the period thereafter.[96] And while the veracity of the accounting Necker offered as controller general still remains a matter of debate, this should not blind us to the most revolutionary aspect of the publication of the *Compte rendu*, the fact that it opened the financial condition of the monarchy to public discussion.

The implications of Necker's decision for the political practice of the Old Regime were perhaps best described by the minister Vergennes in a celebrated letter written to Louis XVI in 1781. According to Vergennes, Necker's Anglomania had led him to forget the fundamental principle of monarchical government: "the monarch speaks, all others belong to the people and obey [le monarque parle, tout est peuple et tout obéit]." [97] Nothing was more dangerous for the political order of the Old Regime, then, than to attempt to introduce the English practice of publicity:

> The example of England, which publishes its accounts, is taken from a people that is restless, calculating, egoistic. Its application to France is an insult to the [French] national character, which is sentimental, trusting, and entirely devoted to its kings. Everything is lost in France, Sire, if Your Majesty permits his ministers to invoke the English system of administration, for which Your Majesty's predecessors have shown such frequent and justified aversion.[98]

As Vergennes rightly emphasized (without acknowledging how far his own political reliance upon the press to foster the French alliance

---

95. See "Compte rendu au roi, janvier 1781," ibid., 2:1–4; Egret, *Necker*, 170–71.
96. Egret, *Necker*, 171–72.
97. Soulavie, *Mémoires historiques*, 4:153; cited in Egret, *Necker*, 177–78.
98. Soulavie, *Mémoires historiques*, 4:158.

with the rebellious American colonies tended in the same direction),[99] Necker was teaching strange new doctrines and attributing a revolutionary significance to "the party that he calls 'public opinion.'"[100] Ascribing the disorders of the Wars of Religion, the Fronde, and the Regency to the baleful influence of foreigners, Vergennes insisted that Necker was, in his turn, endangering the French monarchy through his ignorance of its fundamental principles. "His *compte rendu* is, in the last result, a pure appeal to the people, the pernicious effects of which for the monarchy cannot yet be appreciated or foreseen."[101] But Necker, for his part, regarded the initiative taken in the publication of the *Compte rendu* as quite simply involving the recognition, now unavoidable, of the appearance of a new force in politics. He argued for the importance of this force at greater length in his *De l'administration des finances de la France*, the public defense of his ministerial conduct whose very appearance in 1784 offered yet another challenge to the secrecy of absolutist politics.[102] And in so doing, he offered a series of characterizations of "public opinion" that are of particular interest in relationship to the growth of political contestation in eighteenth-century France on the one hand and the fears of the politics of contestation exhibited in contemporaneous views of English government on the other.

These characterizations were taken up and amplified in a striking manner in the extended historical, philosophical, and sociological analysis of the nature and meaning of "public opinion" presented

---

99. On Vergennes's propaganda efforts on behalf of the American alliance, see Bernard Faÿ, *The Revolutionary Spirit in France and America*, trans. Ramon Guthrie (New York, 1927), especially 87–91, 141–45, 481–98. Vergennes's understanding of the need to control opinion seems to have been a relatively conservative one. "Opinion, it is said, is the queen of the world," he wrote in his first report to Louis XVI in 1774. "The government that can establish it to its own advantage doubles with the idea of its real strength the consideration and the respect that have been, and ever will be, the reward of a well-directed administration and the most certain guarantee of its tranquillity" (ibid., 50; source not given). But the pro-American propaganda he supported published excerpts from Thomas Paine's *Common Sense* and Richard Price's *Observations on Civil Liberty* (ibid., 89–90). The dangers inherent in this strategy were emphasized by one of the minister's writers, who questioned the prudence of putting "into the mouth of a King of France or his minister paradoxical assertions concerning *natural liberty, inalienable and inadmissable rights of the people and its inherent sovereignty,* which have not ceased to be repeated, commented, ransacked and compiled for two centuries, from François Hottoman's *Vindiciae contra tyrannos* to J. J. Rousseau's *Contrat social*" (ibid., 483).

100. Soulavie, *Mémoires historiques*, 4:159.

101. Ibid., 4:155.   102. *OC*, vols. 4–5.

by Jacques Peuchet in the *Encyclopédie méthodique* in 1789.[103] As a writer on *police*—the theory and practice of public administration—Peuchet offered a fascinating reworking of the principles of absolute government within the framework of a comprehensive discussion of the relationship between reason and authority in a progressively more enlightened society. His lengthy essay, informed by a broad familiarity with the classics of eighteenth-century political science and a keen interest in contemporary developments within French political life, is one of the most fascinating expressions of enlightened political culture to appear at the very end of the Old Regime.

Taken together, then, the views of the minister and the theorist elaborate in relatively systematic terms the meaning of the notion of "public opinion" as a central feature in the theory and practice of politics on the eve of the French Revolution. The nature and significance of the concept may best be suggested by a summary listing of the characteristics upon which their definitions converged.

1. "Public opinion," Necker argued, is the "spirit of society," the fruit of the continual communication among men.[104] Peuchet gave this theme a more extended treatment by placing his discussion of public opinion within the framework of a general account of the progress of European society—an account explicitly inspired by William Robertson's *History of the Reign of Charles V* (translated by J.-B.-A. Suard in 1771) and suggestive in many respects of Condorcet's later *Esquisse d'un tableau historique des progrès de l'esprit humain*. Social progress, he argued, had made the enlightened eighteenth century very different from the world of the ancients, among whom the phenomenon of public opinion was unknown. "Public opinion may thus be regarded as a social production of our century."[105]

2. As a social phenomenon and the expression of society itself, "public opinion" possesses none of the institutionalized power, none of the financial or military resources, of the state. It nevertheless represents a

---

103. "Discours préliminaire," in *Encyclopédie méthodique: Jurisprudence*, vol. 9, *Police et municipalités*, i–clx. This first of the two volumes on *police* edited by Peuchet for the *Encyclopédie méthodique* was published in Paris in 1789; a second appeared in 1791. I would like to thank Daniel Gordon for bringing Peuchet's discussion of "public opinion" to my attention.

104. *OC*, 4:47, 51.

105. Peuchet, "Discours préliminaire," x. For Peuchet's acknowledgment of his reliance on Robertson, whose work "has furnished the greater part of what we will say on the progress of civilization and of police in Europe," see ibid., xi.

force far greater than any formal agency of political constraint. In Necker's words, it is "an invisible power that, without treasury, guard, or army, gives its laws to the city, the court, and even the palaces of kings." [106] It is "a tribunal before which all men who attract attention are obliged to appear: there, public opinion, as if from the height of a throne, awards prizes and honors, makes and unmakes reputations." [107] The same emphasis on "public opinion" as an enlightened court of last resort appears in Peuchet's definition of the term: "this word designates in a general manner the sum of all social knowledge [*lumières sociales*], or rather the result of this knowledge, considered as grounds for the judgments made by a nation on the matters submitted to its tribunal. Its influence is today the most powerful motive for praiseworthy actions." [108]

3. "Public opinion" is therefore a court. As such, its authority is universal; its sway extends to all estates and conditions of men. In insisting on this point, in fact, Peuchet found that he could do no better than to quote directly from Necker's *De l'administration des finances*. "It reigns over all minds, and princes themselves respect it whenever they are not carried away by excessive passions: some willingly take it into account, moved by their ambition for public favor; and others, less docile, are still unwittingly subject to it as a result of the influence of those around them." [109]

4. "Public opinion" is peaceful. It is incompatible with divisions and factions. Consequently, it is the characteristic expression of the politically tranquil eighteenth century. "This authority of opinion was unknown," Necker argued, "so long as internal troubles exhausted all sentiments, occupied all thoughts. Spirits divided by factions according to which one could only love or hate were incapable of uniting under the more tranquil banners of esteem and public opinion." [110] Elaborating upon the same theme in slightly different terms, Peuchet represented the growth of "public opinion" as a cause, rather than simply a consequence, of eighteenth-century political stability: "It has extended the sphere of useful and beneficent principles, repressed a host of abuses, declared an implacable war against all the systems of persecution and intolerance; finally, it has become our firmest support for order, the guide and the guardian of *police* and of manners." [111]

---

106. *OC*, 4:50.   107. Ibid., 4:47.
108. Peuchet, "Discours préliminaire," ix.   109. Ibid., quoting *OC*, 4:49.
110. *OC*, 4:47–48.   111. Peuchet, "Discours préliminaire," ix.

5. As a basis for social order, "public opinion" is stable and durable. There is nothing ephemeral in its operation. "Very slow to take form," as Peuchet insists, it alone "can oppose a dike to the torrent of disorders." [112] Long synonymous with fickleness, flux, and subjectivity, the very notion of "opinion" has now been stabilized by its conjunction with the term "public"— thereby taking on the universality and objectivity of *la chose publique* in absolutist discourse. Necker made this point emphatically: "It is necessary to avoid confusing public opinion, as I have described it here, with those ephemeral movements that often pertain only to certain societies and certain circumstances. It is not before such judgments that the man capable of conducting a great administration should prostrate himself. On the contrary, it is necessary to know how to disdain them, in order to remain faithful to that public opinion whose characteristics are all authoritative [*imposants*] and which reason, time, and the universality of sentiments alone have the right to consecrate." [113]

6. The universality and objectivity of "public opinion" are constituted by reason. Its force therefore derives from "the progress of enlightenment," which Necker invoked and Peuchet analyzed at considerable length. This is why "there will never be a powerful safeguard against errors and false systems so long as public opinion is feeble in its judgments, uncertain in its knowledge, and distracted in its attention." [114] For Necker, it followed from the power of language in human affairs that the monarch was under an obligation to enlighten the public by explaining his actions and giving the preambles to his laws "that imprint of truth that is so easy to recognize." [115] Peuchet drew a more radical conclusion. He claimed that true legislative authority had already passed from the monarch to the enlightened elite, whose public function it was to lead the nation toward greater knowledge

112. Ibid., lxxx–lxxxi.
113. *OC*, 4:56. This passage reappears in the article on public opinion in the section of the *Encyclopédie méthodique* devoted to "Finances," an article that is basically a compilation of excerpts from Necker's discussion of the subject. See *Encyclopédie méthodique: Finances*, 3 vols. (Paris, 1784–87), 3:262–64. It is interesting in this context to discover that the article on opinion (which in the original version of the *Encyclopédie* had provided a good statement of the traditional usage of the term to connote flux, subjectivity, and uncertainty — as opposed to enduring rational knowledge) seems to have disappeared entirely from the *Encyclopédie méthodique*. There is no such entry in the volumes *Logique, métaphysique, morale* or *Philosophie*. Thus, "opinion" seems to have migrated from the philosophical to the political sections of the *Encyclopédie méthodique*, becoming stabilized in the process by its new conjunction with the term "public."
114. *OC*, 5:613.   115. Ibid., 4:59.

and rationality. "Public opinion has its source in the opinion of the enlightened, whence it gains partisans and becomes the general conviction [*le voeu général*]," he argued. "The most important revolutions have been accomplished by public writings, by more or less dogmatic works. Writers have become the true legislators of peoples. . . . They have laid hold of public opinion, making it the universal instrument and determining cause of all the movements that occur in the state of peoples." [116]

In Peuchet's view, moreover, the emergence of the periodical press was a particularly important aspect of the process by which enlightened writers had displaced the public authority of rulers. Journals and newspapers, "these means of universal communication," had become "the nourishment, the support, and the weapon of philosophy." Through their agency, "an entire sect, an entire nation, the whole of Europe, is called to pronounce judgment upon a host of objects regarding which, previously, only despotism or the interest of particular individuals had the right to make themselves heard. From this gathering of ideas, from this concentration of enlightenment, a new power has formed that, in the hands of public opinion, governs the world and gives laws to the civilized nations." [117]

7. The power of publicity in political affairs was particularly visible among the English, whose practices in this respect both Necker and Peuchet admired. But they also agreed that "the authority exercised in France by public opinion" [118] was a specially important phenomenon. "This power of public opinion is infinitely more feeble in other countries and under different forms of government," Necker argued. Among enslaved peoples, everything depends upon the will of the monarch. Republican regimes, on the contrary, "know only popular support or the ascendancy of eloquence in the national assemblies: moreover liberty, which forms the essence of such governments, inspires in men more confidence in their own judgments, and one could even say that, jealous of every kind of empire, they cherish their own opinions to the point of independence and take a secret pleasure in diverging from the opinions of others." [119] In explaining why "public opinion" must be a particularly important phenomenon in France, these considerations suggest a broader conclusion. They imply, in

---

116. Peuchet, "Discours préliminaire," x, li.   117. Ibid., lxxxvi.
118. *OC*, 4:50.   119. Ibid., 4:49–50.

effect, that "public opinion" expresses the political sociability of a nation that is neither enslaved nor truly free.

Necker invited this conclusion somewhat obliquely by insisting on the remarkable effects of this "spirit of society" when it "reigns in all its force in the midst of a sensitive people, which loves equally to judge and be judged, which is neither distracted by political interests nor enfeebled by despotism nor dominated by too seething passions." [120] But the point was made quite explicit by Peuchet. "Public opinion," he insisted, "differs from both the spirit of obedience that must reign in a despotic state and the popular opinions that prevail in republican deliberations. It is composed of a mass of ideas that human experience and the progress of enlightenment have successively introduced into a state whose government does not permit expression of the energetic character of national liberty, but where the security of the citizens is respected. . . . It is the weapon that an enlightened people collectively opposes to the precipitous operations of an ambitious minister or a misguided administration. Its slow action would be little suited to a free people, and slaves would not have the force to direct it against the undertakings of an irascible and powerful master." [121]

Taken together, then, the characteristics imputed to "public opinion" by Necker and Peuchet present an image of a political system in remarkable contrast not only to the traditional politics of French absolutism but to the politics of contestation often exemplified in contemporary French discussion by the English model. "The ascendancy of public opinion, more than any other consideration, often opposes obstacles in France to the abuse of authority," Necker argued. "It is uniquely this opinion and the esteem in which it is held that preserves a sort of influence for the nation by giving it the power to reward and punish by praise or disdain." [122] "Public opinion" therefore functions, in effect, as a mean between despotism and extreme liberty. It serves as a barrier against arbitrary will and the abuse of power; yet it implies none of the divisions, factions, passions, or political conflicts of a completely free government — phenomena that presented so alarming a spectacle to many French observers looking across the Channel. "Public opinion," in other words, implies acceptance of an open, public politics. But, at the same time, it suggests a politics without

120. Ibid., 4:50–51.   121. Peuchet, "Discours préliminaire," ix–x.
122. *OC*, 4:52–53.

passions, a politics without factions, a politics without conflicts, a politics without fear. One could even say that it represents a politics without politics.

Rather than suggesting a politics of contestation, the concept of "public opinion" therefore constitutes an image of a politics of rational consensus, untroubled by the passions of willful human action. In this context, once again, Montesquieu's reflections on the nature of English political life seem suggestive. "In a free nation," he argued, "it is very often a matter of indifference whether individuals reason well or badly; it is enough that they reason: from this ensues liberty, which guarantees the effects of this reasoning. Similarly, in a despotic government, it is equally pernicious to reason well or badly; that one reasons is enough for the principle of the government to be shaken."[123] According to this logic, the difference between reasoning well and reasoning badly matters neither to those who are free nor to those who are enslaved. But to those who are neither enslaved nor fully free, the difference must matter a great deal. The explications of the notion of "public opinion" offered by Necker and Peuchet suggest that the concept took form precisely in this intermediate space between liberty and despotism. It offered an abstract court of appeal to a monarchy anxious to put an end to several decades of political contestation. And it held out the ideal of a tranquil expression of public reason to a people who, in wishing for responsible government, remained nonetheless horrified by the spectacle (and haunted by the memory) of the play of divisive political passions.

123. Montesquieu, *De l'esprit des lois*, 3:38.

Notes on Contributors

Keith Michael Baker is a professor of history at the University of Chicago. Included among his publications are *Condorcet: From Natural Philosophy to Social Mathematics* (1975) and *Condorcet: Selected Writings* (1976). He has also authored several articles on French political theory. He is presently one of the editors of the *Journal of Modern History*.

Jack R. Censer is an associate professor of history at George Mason University in Fairfax, Virginia. Originally interested in the revolutionary press, he has authored articles and a book, *Prelude to Power: The Parisian Radical Press, 1789–1791* (1976), on that subject. More recently, he has published articles on the Old Regime press.

Nina Rattner Gelbart, assistant professor of history, coordinates a European Culture core program at Occidental College in Los Angeles. Educated at Harvard University and the University of Chicago, she has written articles on the history of science, utopian thought in the Enlightenment, and the pre-revolutionary French press. She is the author of *Feminine and Opposition Journalism in Old Regime France: "Le Journal des Dames"* (1987), and is currently working on a new project dealing with the medical journalism of eighteenth-century France.

Carroll Joynes is an assistant professor of history at the New School for Social Research in New York and has also taught at the University of Chicago and the Ecole des hautes études en sciences sociales. His current research focuses on the problem of the ideological origins of the French Revolution. He is writing a book on Jansenism and parlementary constitutionalism and their role in the development of public opposition to the monarchy in the last decades of the Old Regime.

Jeremy D. Popkin, associate professor of history at the University of Kentucky, is the author of *The Right-Wing Press in France, 1792–1800* (1980). He has also written on journalism in Old Regime Europe and is currently writing a history of the *Gazette de Leyde, 1770–1800*.

Index

Designer: Betty Gee
Compositor: Progressive Typographers
Text: 10/13 Palatino
Display: Palatino
Printer: Braun-Brumfield
Binder: Braun-Brumfield